The Complete Stein Poems

Hardcopy

edited by Nick Montfort and Mary Flanagan

Output: An Anthology of Computer-Generated Text, 1953–2023, edited by Lillian-Yvonne Bertram and Nick Montfort

The Complete Stein Poems, 1998–2003, Jackson Mac Low, edited by Michael O'Driscoll

The Complete Stein Poems

1998–2003

Jackson Mac Low

Edited with an Introduction and Notes by Michael O'Driscoll

Foreword by Anne Tardos

The MIT Press
Cambridge, Massachusetts
London, England

The MIT Press
Massachusetts Institute of Technology
77 Massachusetts Avenue, Cambridge, MA 02139
mitpress.mit.edu

The open access edition of this book was made possible by generous funding and support from MIT Press Direct to Open.

The MIT Press would like to thank the anonymous peer reviewers who provided comments on drafts of this book. The generous work of academic experts is essential for establishing the authority and quality of our publications. We acknowledge with gratitude the contributions of these otherwise uncredited readers.

This book was set in ITC Stone Serif Std and ITC Stone Sans Std by New Best-set Typesetters Ltd. Printed and bound in the United States of America.

Library of Congress Cataloging-in-Publication Data is available.

ISBN: 978-0-262-55286-8

10 9 8 7 6 5 4 3 2 1

EU Authorised Representative: Easy Access System Europe, Mustamäe tee 50, 10621 Tallinn, Estonia | Email: gpsr.requests@easproject.com

Contents

Series Foreword

Hardcopy features computational artworks that manifest themselves in print. Works in the series engage with and arise from computation in culturally important ways. The series is a space for (among other things) books that are computer-generated by artists and poets, whether they include text, image, or both; print works based around glitched media formats; ones that feature type-in programs with sample output; and ones arising from online interaction with automated agents.

The publications presented in Hardcopy are themselves the primary artworks. A Hardcopy book is a literary art project, not a work of literary studies, for example. Rather than being catalogs for shows, publications in the series are more aligned with the traditions of artist's books, bookworks, and publishing as an artistic practice. By presenting innovative and compelling projects, we aim to reveal the diversity of the computational arts—found in algorithmic and software art, electronic literature, digital gaming, the demoscene, livecoding, generative systems—while also showing connections between historical, current, and emerging practices. Hardcopy publications live alongside other remarkable books within easy reach of readers, available for browsing, study, and sharing in new and familiar contexts.

Hardcopy does not aim to simply place computational artwork on a shelf or coffee table, however. The series shows that traditions of innovative artistic and literary work in print form—in the book arts, in innovative publishing done on many different scales—are in conversation with the computational arts, and that these threads of artistic practice enliven each other.

—Nick Montfort and Mary Flanagan

Foreword

Anne Tardos

Jackson and I first became friends in 1979. I remember him coming to my loft carrying a stack of his books. I understood that to be his way of introducing himself. I was flattered and moved by this gesture. At first, his poetry seemed strange in so many ways. His invention and use of new poetic forms and structures was foreign to me. Initially, I couldn't understand what he was doing or how he was doing it. When I read the poems simply as poetry, I sensed their beauty and elegance. Each poem lovelier than the last. Jackson was a poet of unusual intelligence and intuition. For our first date, we met in the street in front of my building. I found him sitting cross-legged on the bare sidewalk, writing in his notebook. In our years together, I scarcely remember occasions when he was not writing . . . on the road, at concerts, poetry readings, in the cab taking us to the airport, and on planes.

In 1998, Jackson began to write the Stein poems, his most voluminous work. They are a "formally and procedurally inclusive sequence of poems" using Gertrude Stein's writings as source material.[1] At around the same time, he also wrote his seminal essay on art, "Poetry and Pleasure." The essay's focus is on the importance of pleasure in making artworks and the pleasure in experiencing them. "Poetry and Pleasure" is perhaps the most comprehensive account of Mac Low's work methods, his philosophy, his politics, his view of art's role in society, and his lifelong devotion to Buddhism. In *Thing of Beauty*, I placed this paper in lieu of an author's introduction.[2]

To my knowledge, the Stein poems were the first and maybe the only work he composed directly on the computer without any preliminary handwritten drafts. He loved the technology that allowed him to create the Stein poems. He downloaded the entire

1 From Michael O'Driscoll, introduction to Jackson Mac Low, *The Complete Light Poems*, ed. Anne Tardos and Michael O'Driscoll (Victoria, TX: Chax Press, 2015), 15–21.

2 Jackson Mac Low, "Poetry and Pleasure," in *Thing of Beauty: New and Selected Works*, ed. Anne Tardos (Berkeley: U California P, 2008), xxvii–xxxvi.

volume of *Tender Buttons*, and directly applied his various procedures, some of them automated. He wrote "Stein 18—Duo Version" as a performance score for the two of us. It was his way of including me in his Stein world. We often used to perform together, his work and mine, during our years and travels together. Back at home, he would later enter and edit his poems on his computer.

As he wrote the Stein poems over the years, he sent out individual poems to several journals for publication, as was his custom. The poems have become well known. His desire to have them collected in a book went without saying, but he had not yet taken any steps in that direction. At that time, he had no way of knowing that I would set myself the task of publishing posthumous works, such as *Thing of Beauty*, *The Forties*, and the *Complete Light Poems*.

Two months before his death, we spent some time in Bob Creeley's house in Maine. Jackson was not feeling well at all during his last weeks. Still, we took walks in the woods, and then back at the house, sitting outside in Adirondack chairs, he wrote simple, modest poems describing his surroundings. After Creeley read these, he wrote to me that "somehow his writing always is so close, as here, I feel the whole fact of the house and its ambiance as in reading anything he wrote. I felt him there writing it and enjoying it."

I have often thought how curiously related Stein and Mac Low were in their respective tone and revolutionary spirit. Stein. Why Stein? Was it because her writing was already decontextualized? Or the simplicity of her language? His lifelong admiration for her? Whatever the reasons, I think of the Stein poems as his crowning achievement.

Professor Michael O'Driscoll, who expertly edited this volume, also coedited with me a few years earlier *The Complete Light Poems* by Mac Low. That project too required extensive research. For this book, I stayed mostly in the background, helping when help was needed. O'Driscoll found many different versions of Jackson's Stein poems on my hard drive and in the Mac Low archives at UC San Diego. It took him several years to sort out the final and correct versions. I am glad I maintained Jackson's hard drive over the years by continually backing up the data, updating the files to adapt to changing operating systems and new computers. O'Driscoll's yearslong study and profound knowledge of and devotion to Mac Low's works is exceptional. I am grateful to him for taking on this enormous task that is *The Complete Stein Poems*.

"This shining makes revision of a string more strange": An Introduction to Jackson Mac Low's *The Complete Stein Poems*

Michael O'Driscoll

Late at night on April 27, 1998, celebrated poet, performer, and artist Jackson Mac Low composed the first of his Stein poems. Plucking from his book shelves an old high school volume of math tables, he opened the textbook randomly to a set of logarithms of sines and, pointing to the top left log sine's mantissa, singled out the number 241. Turning, then, to his copy of Ulla E. Dydo's *A Stein Reader*, Mac Low opened the volume and selected the ten paragraphs on page 241, including the last line of the preceding page, as the source text for his planned poem. Having, next, meticulously transcribed those same paragraphs—derived from Gertrude Stein's 1933 publication *A Long Gay Book*—into his computer as a .txt file, Mac Low then directed Charles O. Hartman's DIASTEX5.C program to both that source text file and a separate seed text file (which he'd identified as the first of the ten paragraphs). Run from a floppy disk on Mac Low's computer, Hartman's program was designed to emulate a manual procedure of a "Diastic Reading-Through Text-Selection Method" that Mac Low himself had invented in 1963 in order to generate poetic material determined by algorithmic rules. This latest version of the program, created in 1994 at Mac Low's request, was a fifth generation of the original 1989 DIASTEXT code, now revised to handle larger inputs. The algorithm, following Mac Low's procedure, sequentially drew words from the source text that correspond to the placement of letters in the seed text. The placement of letters in the first word of the seed, "l-i-t-t-l-e" in this case, resulted in the first line of the output: "Little lIngering faTher litTle reguLar simplE." Having completed a full cycle of testing the source text against the seed text, the program terminated its output at thirty-five lines. Saving the results to his hard drive, now in the wee hours of the morning of April 28, Mac Low would go on to massage the raw output the following day, excising and altering redundant words, introducing capitals, periods, and line spaces to give the poem its desired form, titling the result by drawing from the initial and concluding words of the poem, and recording the whole process and the interventions he'd made into a summary "makingways" note along with the location and date that concludes the poem.

Modestly titled "Little Beginning (Stein 1)," this inaugural effort was to become the first of 161 iterations of one of Mac Low's most ambitious engagements with deterministic procedural composition. Indeed, the Stein poems stand alongside his other monumental achievements, such as *Stanzas for Iris Lezak* (written in 1960 and published in 1972), his *Asymmetries 1–260* (written in 1960 and published in 1980), and the *Light Poems* (written from 1962 to 1988 and published in complete form posthumously in 2015). In drawing liberally from various methods developed across a lifetime of work, the series serves as a culminating engagement with deterministic compositional methods that—whether produced through manual operations or computer code—were foundationally, brilliantly, algorithmic by design. By May 11, two weeks later, he had produced the first ten in the series—or at least the computer-generated texts (what Mac Low called his "raw outputs") that would become the foundation for each of the resulting poems. By the end of that summer, he had the makings of forty-one Stein poems, or some 152 pages of material. Never one to do things in a minimal fashion, however, Mac Low continued typing, processing, formatting, and editing, and one year later, in May 1999, he had produced seventy-six Stein poems comprising almost three hundred pages. Two years into the process, he generated Stein 122, topping the four-hundred-page mark. And, in late December 2000, Mac Low printed the last raw output of his Stein poems, now totaling, after two and a half years of dedicated and seemingly tireless labor, 161 poems in almost five hundred pages.

I begin with the bare facts of effort, process, time, and scale here in order to emphasize the extraordinary commitment that this, Mac Low's last great poetic creation, represents. The manuscript materials—raw outputs, multiple versions of digital files for each poem, hard copy variants with manuscript corrections and notes, performance scripts, publication copies, email correspondence, lecture notes—that detail the working records of the Stein poems comprise many, many thousands of pages. What, one might well ask, would drive this fervent, protracted—and perhaps sometimes tedious—production of creative text? As Mac Low himself notes in "A Talk about My Writingways"—a previously unpublished lecture delivered in Tucson on January 28, 2001, and included in this volume—the poet had, from February 1989 through April 1998, almost entirely abandoned the use of deterministic procedural methods in the composition of his works.[1] Poetic series such as his *Twenties: 100 Poems* (published

1 For additional insights on this lecture, see "Making Poetry 'Otherwise,'" published in *Jacket* 34 (October 2007), a transcript of the dialogue that followed the unrecorded presentation of the Tucson lecture. In a letter to Dan Featherstone, dated March 3, 2001, and retained on his hard drive, Mac Low writes: "I'm very sorry you didn't preserve the tape of my main lecture. The discussion makes little sense without that. While giving the talk I continually departed from the printed-out

a "broken showing of an orderly courteous likeness," Mac Low's revisions take the raw output and make of it a self-reflective meditation on his relationship to Stein's text, to the DIASTEX5 output, and to the work of revision itself:

> If a frightful bag were misplaced in time, plenty of places might be utterly
> broken.
> He authorized those shows.
>
> Her orderly likeness was singularly courteous.
> This shining makes revision of a string more strange.
> There it's more of the same.
> His little sentence yesterday was largely due to terror of authority.
> It was curious how the safety of those four little tomatoes was so easily
> established.
> Four curious tomatoes were safe.
> On the whole, a breakfast of little potatoes cannot easily be established.
> The center of his tongue was singular.
> Her scissors persuaded them of this.

This passage suggests, to me at least, an argument for Mac Low's authoritative practices in the moment. Having often authorized "frightful bags" in all their wonderful, disruptive potential, he nonetheless respects Stein's "orderly likeness" that was "singularly courteous." One thinks here of Stein's rather proper, even prim, vocal delivery of her own revolutionary poems. Stein's "shining," that is, her distinctive vocabulary and unique compositional style, "makes revision of a string more strange" (in the best possible way) as Mac Low engages with the raw outputs. The speaker, seeming to reconcile for the moment with the "terror of authority," notes that establishing stable referents in the Stein poems—safe tomatoes, as it were—is easier than anticipated. Mac Low too has a distinctive voice in these poems—"The center of his tongue was singular"—and it was Stein's own compositions, "her scissors," and his intimate relationship with that corpus, that makes this even possible.

Importantly, Stein 104 also provides a ready example of some of Mac Low's other typical practices, often rule-bound practices, in revising the raw outputs of DIASTEX5. Most obvious is his division of the output into eight stanzas that follow the sequence of prime numbers from two to nineteen. More common, however, was Mac Low's use of the Lucas sequence to structure his stanzas: using line counts of 1, 3, 4, 7, 11, 18, 29, 47, and so on. In "A Talk about My Writingways," Mac Low himself offers a fulsome account of his relationship to the Lucas sequence:

> After the first number, each subsequent number is the sum of the two before it. This sequence was developed by the French mathematician Edouard Lucas. After 1871, when he was released

> from the French army, in which he'd served as an artillery officer in the Franco-Prussian War, by the defeat of the French army, he became a professor of mathematics in Paris. He investigated the well-known Fibonacci sequence and developed the Lucas sequence (which bears a mathematical relation to the Fibonacci sequence) to test the primality of Mersenne prime numbers. He published the Lucas sequence and his test for Mersenne primes in 1880.
>
> I found the Lucas sequence somewhere many years ago, probably in an issue of *Scientific American*, and I jotted it down on a little piece of blue paper that I then misplaced. I found this piece of paper again in 1989 and have used the Lucas sequence off and on since then to determine the divisions of poems and musical works. Poor Lucas died at the age of 49, in 1891, as a result of a freak accident at a banquet, when a plate was dropped and a piece of it flew up and cut his cheek. He died of erysipelas a few days later.

What I find particularly compelling about this account is Mac Low's narrative entanglement of precise genius and "freak accident"—despite one's penchant for the most severe calculations, the world's contingencies will nonetheless impose themselves, sometimes to fatal effect. Mac Low's own losing and finding of his note on the Lucas sequence—and its subsequent employment in the creation of these poems—is part of that same dynamic between contingency and authority. This is, indeed, the tension that animates these poems.

And that tension is very much a part of Mac Low's interactions with the raw outputs of Hartman's DIASTEX5. In many ways, scale is at the heart of Hartman's final version of the DIASTEXT series. Hartman's notes on the program (available in UCSD Special Collections) indicate that Mac Low specifically asked for "greater input-file capacity," and Hartman details his deliberations on how to achieve this—whether through a huge memory model, a buffering memory system that considers successive portions of the source text, or reading directly from the disk file. While he opted for the latter, slower, solution, Hartman estimates that a fast machine (he points to the Intel 486 with the 66 MHz chip released in August 1992) could process all of Bob Dylan's lyrics (about half a megabyte) in thirty seconds. Interestingly, Mac Low's input files for the Stein poems never required more than about 32 KB, and all of *Tender Buttons* requires about 43 KB of storage, so he certainly underutilized the capacity of the program. However, the request for a program that could handle bigger input files suggests the level of his ambition for the project and the degree of contingency with which he imagined contending.

As mentioned, Hartman's initial production of the DIASTEXT program was motivated by his encounter with Mac Low's 1986 volume *The Virginia Woolf Poems*. In producing that volume, Mac Low employed the diastic method manually with minimal editing of the outputs. In reading Mac Low's endnotes to the collection, Hartman recognized the diastic method's potential as an algorithmic process that produced evocative textual outputs, and so he designed and forwarded his emulating program to Mac

Low for his consideration. For Hartman, the distinction between the random, the arbitrary, and the contingent is key here, and his understanding of their interanimations puts a finer point on Mac Low's production of the Stein poems. Hartman concludes the analytic portion of his *Virtual Muse: Experiments in Computer Poetry* by considering the operations of two of his programs:

> One effect of computer poetry experiments is usually to release language from contingency. The randomness of Prose, the arbitrariness of Diastext are contingency breakers. Of course, the meaning of a bit of language depends heavily on the contingencies that have shaped it. If we get rid of contingency entirely, replacing it with purely random or arbitrary linguistic acts, we get genuine gibberish. The point, rather, is to introduce calculated bits of mechanized anarchy into the language, put the results back into the contingent world where language lives, and see how the dust settles.[20]

Contingency, in this conceptualization, is quite specifically the indeterminate space of encounter between human and machine—the threshold, as it were, of human expression, and the very edge of calculation. Mac Low's engagements with contingency, then, balance precariously on this precipice, held tentatively by the stabilizing force of syntax.

Mac Low's typical, although not universal, response to the outputs was to alter the text with, as he puts it in the Tucson lecture, "plenty of wiggle room." As he indicates in that text and in the above note to Stein 104, those revisions could include word order and shifts in person, case, number, tense, and mood, but also the addition of helping words such as articles, conjunctions, prepositions, and pronouns. Mac Low also introduces capitalization and end punctuation as required. Such changes result, most often, but again not always, in seemingly normative sentence structures that convey the promise of meaning, and those sentences, more often than not, give structure to the verse lines. The syntactically normative sentence thereby becomes the basic unit of meaning in the Stein poems, even when the resulting contents challenge the reader to participate more actively in the production of meaning. Such might be the case of one of my personal favorites in the series, Stein 9, "Begin a Piece Of the Whole":

> If every preceder bites a piece the whole piece still is eaten.
> Happy peculiar people may refuse refining any time.
> Refusing certain regular materials they're choosing necessity.
> Every piece of a whole precedes all pieces.

Here, we readers learn, nibbling away at the pieces leads to the consumption of the whole, refusing and choosing is instrumental to the process making meanings, and

20 Hartman, *Virtual Muse*, 109.

the end result, whether refined into a coherent whole or not, presumes its constitutive elements.

Importantly, Mac Low's production of the Stein poems was deliberately multifarious. In addition to applying his own editorial decisions to the outputs of DIASTEX5, he would occasionally allow chance operations to determine margin size or the justification—left, right, or centered on the page—of blocks of text. Chance operations also played an occasional role in the identification of source texts in the *Stein Reader*, or the order of the source text's paragraphs and sentences; in such cases, Mac Low drew from his well-worn copy of the Rand Corporation's table *A Million Random Digits and 100,000 Normal Deviates*. He also practiced what I would describe as a "cumulative" processing of the poems, using earlier generated poems as further source texts in a kind of recessive devolution of the raw poetic material. For example, Stein 69 is derived from the use of Stein 65 as source text and five lines from Stein's "Pink Melon Joy" as seed text. Stein 65 itself was derived from Stein's "More Grammar for a Sentence" as source text. What one sees across the series is a continual invention and complication of method that results in poetic outputs and authorized poems that are varied and dynamic in relation to each other and in their relation to the Stein originals.

That invention also included, as in the example of Stein 65 and elsewhere, the use of a second computer program called Travesty. Travesty is a program developed by Joseph O'Rourke, a professor of computational science and mathematics, along with the illustrious scholar of Ezra Pound's poetry, Hugh Kenner, himself a regular contributor to *BYTE* magazine. Mac Low first deployed the Travesty program in Stein 31, "When He Did He Thought This Was Not Living A . . . ," and describes it in the accompanying writingways note:

> TRAVESTY is a program written in about 1980 by Hugh Kenner and Joseph O'Rourke, who published an early version in *BYTE* magazine in 1981. It draws word groups from source texts by a process that depends upon letter-sequence frequencies in English. It can produce nine "orders" of "travesties" running from order 3 (the least like normative discourse) to order 9 (the most like normative discourse). The user of TRAVESTY can specify the order of the Travesty to be produced as well as the number of characters in it.

Mac Low deployed Travesty in eight of the poems in the Stein series, with varying orders of normative discourse. Stein 43, "It Remember Splendid and Religou," for example, introduces an order-4 travesty into his procedural process, and the results are distinctive. Interestingly, Mac Low restores syntactical order to Travesty's raw results in his editing process, but retains the disruptive neologisms of the program's output, maintaining, again, the sentence as the primary unit of meaning, regardless of the linguistic content.

Much of what I've been able to describe about the production of the Stein poems here is available to us as readers because of Mac Low's scrupulous preservation of the details of his process. The "makingways" notes (Mac Low's own coinage) that conclude each of the poems provide a record throughout the collection that tells each poem's story and offer evidence of Mac Low's relationship to the materials at hand. Importantly, the makingways notes are integral to the poems—they are not subsidiary texts—and each note makes an essential and unique contribution to the sense of the text it describes. The makingways themselves evolve over time. Mac Low would often cut and paste the core elements of the notes from one to the next (we know this because of repeated typographic errors in the originals), but then he revised each note to address the specificity of its poem. At times, Mac Low would also radically alter the form of the makingways notes. We see, for example, a dramatic shift in their presentation with Stein 87, in which the more narrative form of its predecessors is broken down into what reads more like metadata field entries detailing "method," "source," "seed," and "editing" in a more economical fashion. Stein 97 introduces a new and intriguing element: Mac Low declares, in square brackets and italics, and punctuated by a happy-face emoji, "*[Precedent for the endnotes*: La Vita Nuova ☺*]*." This small joke makes a big claim. *La Vita Nuova* is Dante's 1294 compendium of prose and verse that tells of his enduring love of Beatrice. The volume is a famous example of the *prosimetrum* form, containing autobiographical accounts interspersed with sonnets, ballads, and canzoni. Each poem, and this is the connection Mac Low is drawing, is followed by a short description of its form and an explication of its contents. Mac Low here situates the Stein poems in a venerable tradition indeed.

The editorial interventions captured in the makingways notes extended Mac Low's time devoted to the Stein poems well beyond the production of the raw outputs. While the last raw output was created around Christmas 2000, the last editorial date on the poems (noted not in his digital files but on a hard copy located in the UCSD Special Collections and Archives) is March 10, 2003: Stein 111, "Pointing / All Glazed Elephant Seasoning," would be the only poem Mac Low would revise in the final year of his attentions to the Stein poems, and the last full year of his life. The bulk of the final revisions took place in late April and early May 2002. By the end of June 2002, Mac Low had organized the full series into a digital folder titled "stein series all." Importantly, the last two poems in the series, Stein 160 and 161, were numbered and included by Mac Low out of sequence, having been initially produced on January 1, 2000, and introduced into the series in celebration of the new year and the new millennium. Both are dedicated to poet and performance artist Anne Tardos, Mac Low's life and creative partner, who preserved the digital and print materials that are the records of these poems, and who has thereby made possible their publication.

Coda

On July 27, 1946, Gertrude Stein passed away following surgery for stomach cancer at the American Hospital in Neuilly-sur-Seine, France. One day following, a twenty-three-year-old Jackson Mac Low, some 3,600 miles and a generation or two away, wrote "An Elegy for Gertrude Stein." Never to be published, the poem, in nine sections over an equal number of typescript pages, laments the loss of Stein with passionate regret. "Gertrude Stein is dead," Mac Low writes, "The singer of the repetitive cadences / is dead. The seas & rivers of France and America mourn their sister. / She is dead, the singer of repetition—is dead." Inspired by a *New York Herald Tribune* article of that morning, Mac Low celebrates Stein as a champion of "the smallest words, the slightest words," whose tireless "repeating and qualifying, qualifying & repeating" was a matter of infinite patience:

> Never a break in the effort of continual qualification, in
> the continual repetition:——not <u>quite</u> that, <u>this</u> yes this yes this,
> not <u>quite</u> that this. yes this. not quite that, this. this. this.
> yes <u>this</u>. this.

That pattern of repeated indication, assessment, adjustment—"not <u>quite</u> that, <u>this</u>"—might well serve as the syntax of the Stein poems as a serial form.[21] Stein is, Mac Low tells us, "the mother of modern American writing" whose "words got under our skin." In form and diction, the elegy conveys a sympathetic sensibility that tells us much about why Stein would figure so prominently in Mac Low's final, great work:

> All of us who have loved her smallest slighted words, her
> mother's patience——she it was who paused at the smallest adverbs:
> when, where; at the smallest adjectives & pronouns: what, that, who;
> at the prepositions;—it was she who remembered the conjunctions &
> the articles; with a mother's patience pausing beside the words
> they had hurried by for hundreds of years——all of us who love
> her motherly pauses weep, <u>weep</u>, in the sunday sunshine weeping
> salty tears.

This early poem in Mac Low's oeuvre is evidence of an already established sensibility that is not just in keeping with Stein's own stylistic tendencies, but that also clearly

---

21 In consideration of the performance of Mac Low's simultaneities, Hélène Aji writes, "What generates the idea of 'simultaneities' in Mac Low's poetics is the potential for iteration that his work entails. Iteration, but not without structural variations—in a sense very akin to Gertrude Stein's practice of repetition." "Impossible Reversibilities: Jackson Mac Low," *The Sound of Poetry, The Poetry of Sound*, ed. Marjorie Perloff and Craig Dworkin (Chicago: U Chicago P, 2009), 149–65.

aspires to a poetic ethos of meticulous, painstaking care. Stein's creative work was not just any source for Mac Low's poetic productions; Stein was his ultimate model of patient, detailed, and sustained attention to ways of making in language. And here, at the end of his life, after almost sixty years of emulating that caring, creative disposition, Jackson Mac Low, interacting with writing technologies that Gertrude Stein could never have possibly imagined, performed the most remarkable homage imaginable.

= = = = =

This is my opportunity to thank Anne Tardos for her tremendous support, encouragement, and advice during the yearslong adventure of editing Jackson Mac Low's Stein poems. This task has been an enormous privilege and pleasure, and I'm so grateful for Anne's invitation to take it on. Anne should be thanked and recognized by all for her enduring commitment to the stewardship of Jackson Mac Low's writing and other creative works and her demonstrated dedication to ensuring that the best of his unpublished creative work find its way to admiring audiences. Anne should also be celebrated for being herself a brilliant poet and performance artist, who continues to create and share her work with the world even while attending to the details of Mac Low's legacy. I would also like to thank the staff at UC San Diego's Mandeville Special Collections Library for their support and assistance in preparing these materials, and the Faculty of Arts at the University of Alberta for its support of my research and teaching.

My greatest thanks goes, as always, to my partner in life, and love, and learning, the brilliant and beautiful Professor Cecily Devereux. Her support and generosity make everything possible, and her impeccable scholarship on the journeys of bold women at the edge of empire is my inspiration to always go further and do better. This book is dedicated to my father, Kenneth F. O'Driscoll, a polymer chemist, and my mother, Patricia B. O'Driscoll, a painter, who demonstrated to our family the nurturing and vital entanglement of science and art.

A Talk about My Writingways

University of Arizona, Tucson
28 January 2001

by Jackson Mac Low

From 1937 to 1954 I wrote many poems. Most of them were written in ways generally accepted then—the usual ways—and they often said things about specific subjects or to specific people. However, at times, I wrote in ways I've learned to call "liminal," briefly, working from the threshold between the consciousness and the so-called unconscious. (I'll come back to this later.)

At first I wrote what is still, I think, called "free verse" (though Eliot and others have insisted that no type of verse is "free"—I think they've meant "devoid of discipline") but in 1939 and after, I taught myself to write metrical verse, rhymed and unrhymed. After that I wrote poetry alternately in metrical and free verse as well as in prose—what David Antin has called "a kind of concrete poetry with justified margins."[1] I've also written several kinds of visual and sound poetry as well as verbal and/or musical performance works, plays, radioworks, essays, and talks. (Some of the essays and talks, including this one, deal with descriptive poetics.)

I wrote free and metrical verse alternately until 1954, and I sometimes still do so, but late in 1954 I began devising and employing "systematic" methods, in composing both verbal works and also music and performance works. The first such methods I invented and used were ones that involved various kinds of chance operations.

Artists employing chance operations are usually not concerned with interesting or specific results, but rather with making works that are (to the extent possible) free of individual taste, memory, psychology, and traditions of artistic and literary value judgments.

My motivation for writing verbal works and composing music in these ways generally more "impersonal" than those usually followed came from an interpretation of Zen Buddhism that led me and other artists (writers, composers, and visual artists

1 [Ed. Note: David Antin, *Radical Coherency* (Chicago: U Chicago P, 2012), 234.]

active from the early 1950s through the 60s, and later) to try to make artworks that were "minimally egoic." We tried to make artworks with as little intervention as possible from the individual ego. We considered the ego a formation that stood in the way of one's perceiving "reality as such" ("suchness" is a translation of a widely employed Sanskrit Buddhist term for this). The use of chance operations seemed at the time a good way to minimize egoic motivations. The definition of the term "ego" implicit here is that of Zen Buddhism, not that of Freudian psychology. It includes all the Freudian "institutions of the psyche"—id, ego, and superego—all "layers of the mind," conscious, liminal, and unconscious. To use a Zen Buddhist term, we were attempting to write and to make other kinds of audible and visible artworks "from the No-Mind."

It was only later, after years of studying and irregularly practicing Buddhism, as well as years of utilizing such artmaking methods, that I realized that using those methods is as egoic as other ways of making artworks—that, in short, there are no shortcuts to "enlightenment."

Moreover, while Buddhism enjoins us to lessen the hegemony of the ego in its most widely accepted sense—the dominance of what one experiences as her individual will—it more importantly calls us to realize that the self is ultimately illusory. As the eighteenth-century Scottish philosopher David Hume observed, we never experience the self but only perceptions. "When I enter most intimately into what I call myself, I always stumble on some particular perception or other," he wrote. "I never can catch myself at any time without a perception, and never can observe anything but the perception."[2] But an understanding of the self—even though the term is ultimately meaningless—is only attained by working *through* what each of us thinks of as "my self," not by attempting to evade or abolish it.

However, by the time I realized that the artmaking methods that I'd mistakenly thought were "nonegoic" are not, I had come to value them for their own sake. As often happens, what were conceived and devised as means toward a highly elevated end came to be valued, if not as ends in themselves, as means toward less exalted ends: I liked the kinds of poems and other verbal works and the music that I could make with those methods. So, I continued to employ them (though not exclusively) and came eventually to combine them with other artmakingways. Buddhism had led me to them but no longer provided me with justifications or motivations for utilizing them.

But I've gotten ahead of my story. I employed chance operations predominantly—as well as "translation methods" whereby one "translates" the notation of musical works

---

2 I owe this quotation from Hume to the art critic Arthur C. Danto's recent review of an exhibit of works by the conceptual artist Sol LeWitt (*The Nation*, 2/5/01, p. 34).

"into" words and vice versa—from December 1954 until May 1960, when I began devising the two main groups of methods that I've since come to call "deterministic."[3]

(Actually, my translation methods were already deterministic. I've used them in making poetry and music every so often since January 1955. At that time, I "translated" the pitches of a motet with two simultaneously sung texts by the fourteenth-century French composer Guillaume de Machau[l]t into words from a nineteenth-century children's book on "natural history." The words drawn from the book correspond, by a strict system, to the pitches of the motet. When making music by "translation," one uses a similarly strict system to translate the successive letters of words of a selected text, and other features of the text, into pitches. I mistakenly thought until recently that translation was a kind of chance operations, because I could not predict their outcome.)

Each of my principal deterministic methods utilizes two texts, "a source text" and a "seed text," to produce their "raw output." (I mean by this the unmodified output of the method.)

In the 1960s, when I first devised and utilized deterministic methods, I thought that the methods that I now realize are deterministic were kinds of chance operations. It was only in the early 90s that I realized that such methods are basically different from chance operations. The principal difference is that if one employs a deterministic text-selection method *correctly*, using the same source text and seed text *and making no mistakes*, the method's output will always be exactly the same. Chance operations produce a different output each time they are utilized. Deterministic methods do not involve what could rightly be called "chance," or as many artists have termed it, "objective hazard."[4]

However, neither chance operations nor deterministic methods are "truly nonegoic." Even when an author (to narrow this to verbal art) does not consciously choose either the chance-operational or deterministic methods used or the sources of their verbal materials or the verbal elements used in them (e.g., the source texts and seed texts utilized in deterministic methods), some layers of the author's mind are inevitably involved in their selection, if only at a distance. And this is also true of the ways in which the verbal materials are placed in the works made by these methods.

---

3 The term "deterministic" was suggested to me in the early 1990s by my son, the astrophysicist Mordecai-Mark Mac Low, during one of his visits to New York from Heidelberg, where he was then doing his research. (He's now an assistant curator in astrophysics at the American Museum of Natural History's new planetarium, where he does research in star formation.)

4 This is a term often used by Dadaists, Surrealists, and other artists (visual, verbal, sonic, and conceptual) from sometime in the teens of the last century till, perhaps, the late 40s.

I rarely employed chance operations alone after April 1960, except as auxiliary methods. Deterministic methods don't involve chance even though authors or composers using them cannot predict their outputs. Although I now realize that neither chance operations nor deterministic methods used in artmaking are nonegoic, the illusion that they *were* helped motivate and justify my utilizing those methods.

My first deterministic text-selection method was "acrostic reading-through text selection," which was the principal method I used when making poems and other verbal works from May 1960 to January 1963. In using such methods, one reads through a "source text" to find, successively, words and/or other verbal units—word fragments, phrases, other sentence fragments, or even whole sentences—that have the successive letters of the words of a "seed text" as their first letters. What kind or kinds of verbal units are selected are determined by deliberate choices or by chance operations or other "impersonal" methods at the beginning of each poem's composition. I often used as the seed text the title of the source text and/or of the poem that was being written.) Here's a simple example of acrostic text selection: one may spell "cats" acrostically by finding, as one reads through the poem's source text, the words "Castrated Animals Tire Soon."

I wrote many poems and other verbal works by means of acrostic text selection. Among them are the poems in *Stanzas for Iris Lezak* (New York: Something Else Press, 1972) and my non-stanzaic "Numbered Asymmetries." Most of the latter were written in 1960–61, though I continued to write some Asymmetries later without numbering them. *Asymmetries 1–260* (New York: Printed Editions, 1980) comprises a little over half of the 500 Numbered Asymmetries. However, *21 Matched Asymmetries* (London: Aloes Books, 1978) comprises three groups of Asymmetries written in 1967 by a "*diastic* reading-through text-selection method" (described below).

Although I rarely used chance operations alone to make poems—except rarely as auxiliary methods—after April 1960, I did so a few times, notably, when I composed the *125 Postcard Poems* in September 1992.[5] It was in early January 1963 that I first devised and employed the deterministic methods that I call "diastic reading-through text-selection methods." As with acrostic methods, a seed text is used by the author

5 Each of these very short poems was composed by chance operations with a view to copying it onto a "funny dog" postcard—a colored picture of dogs doing such things as playing poker. Each postcard was supposed to be placed in one of the boxes that were part of a Cologne gallery owner's "Fluxus Virus" festival (mostly located in a parking garage on Cologne's pedestrian mall). They were designed to take the place of catalogs. Unfortunately, they [the boxes] were executed quite sloppily, so that my funny-dog postcards with short poems on their address sides were left out of many of the boxes.

to select the words (or other linguistic units) that are brought from a source text into the method's "raw [unmodified] output." However, in diastic methods, the seed text is "spelled *through*" in words (or other linguistic units) that the author or her computer comes across as she or it reads through the source text. These words, or other linguistic units *have the letters of the seed text in the positions that they occupy in the seed text.* That is why I called this method "diastic," on an imperfect analogy with "acrostic," when I devised the method in 1963. The Greek *dia* means "through" while the Greek *akros* means "at an extreme," in this case, at the beginning or ending of a verse line or other unit. The Greek *stichos* means, roughly, "verse line." Here's an example of diastic: the word "word" may be "spelled through" in the sentence "White gOats agReeably heeD."[6]

I've often written with the help of diastic reading-through text-selection methods from 1963 until now. However, as you'll hear, I've not done so exclusively, especially after 1980, and between February 1989 and April 1998 I used no systematic methods, except when writing the "Postcard Poems" in 1992. (When I returned to such methods in April 1998, my ways of using them were quite different than before.)

Some of my diastic methods have drawn other linguistic units than whole single words. For example, my book *The Pronouns* was made by a diastic method that drew "ing" phrases from an index-card pack in which each card was inscribed with one to five such phrases. (This card pack was made in 1961 for the dancer Simone Forti to use as a source of materials from which to improvise dances or other performances. Forti and other dancers have made improvisations from the phrases on these cards.) The poems in *The Pronouns* were written by a modified-diastic method through which each "ing" phrase selected by it was incorporated, along with adverbs of time, into sentences. Each of the forty poems in *The Pronouns* comprises a connected group of instructions for dancers or other performance artists. They have been performed in many ways.

In addition, I wrote *Words nd Ends from Ez* by reading through Ezra Pound's *Cantos* and finding words and ends of words (ranging from all except the first letter of a word

---

6 Since 1989, I've drawn only single words from the source text into the "raw output" of my diastic method, because I've usually employed one of the diastic computer programs written for me by Prof. Charles 0. Hartman, a poet and critic who is a professor at Connecticut College, New London. Hartman's programs automate the reading through and finding work of a diastic program, but they only find single words in the source text. When I did diastic text selection—and from 1960 through 1963, acrostic text selection—"by hand," I often used these text selection methods to find not only single words, but often also phrases, words from an arbitrary point in a source sentence to its end, whole sentences, or words and "ends" of words (letter strings and/or single letters ranging from all the letters of words except the first to only the last letter).

to only its last letter) by means of a diastic method in which the name "Ezra Pound" was the seed text.

From 1981 to 1989 I alternated between employing those deterministic methods and a free kind of verbal composition that I came to realize (with the help of the Canadian musicologist Austin Clarkson) entails what he calls (following certain neo-psychoanalytic theorists) "liminal decisions." The latter are thought to take place at the threshold between consciousness and the layer of the mind in which unconscious—or not quite conscious—ideation takes place. Most of the verbal works I wrote in the 80s were written either by diastic methods or ones involving "liminal" decisions.

In 1989–90 I wrote *Twenties: 100 Poems* (New York: Roof Books, 1991). The 100 poems in this book were made by "gathering" words, phrases, etc., from my inner and outer environments, that is, from words, phrases, and sometimes sentences that I thought of or that I saw or heard while I was writing the poems' first drafts, which I subsequently revised a bit. These words, etc., were drawn into a simple but "fuzzy" verse form: each poem comprises five unrhymed quatrains composed of lines of varying lengths.

Then, from November 1990 through early 1995, I wrote the first drafts of my "154 Forties" by "gathering" into the poems words, phrases, and sometimes whole sentences that I saw, heard, or thought of while writing those beginning drafts.[7] Such "gathering" of verbal materials during the writing of both *Twenties* and "154 Forties" entailed, more often than not, "liminal decisions." I used no "method" in making these poems except to employ the same forty-line "fuzzy verse form" for each poem: eight five-line stanzas comprising three rather long lines, followed by one *very* long line and then a short line.

Twenty of the Forties poems were published as a chapbook entitled *20 Forties* (Tenerife, Canary Islands, Spain: Zasterle Press, 1999). Zasterle books are published by Manuel Brito Marrero who directs the press. The poems in this book come from various parts of the "154 Forties." Since no chance operations or deterministic methods were employed in writing these poems, I selected the 20 Forties poems from the 154-poem series by means of random-digit chance operations.

I revised and corrected the Forties poems from 1990 through 2000.

However, in April 1998, I began a new series, called "Stein," which was finished (except for some revisions) on Christmas Day 2000. It comprises 161 poems, most of

7 [Ed. Note: Mac Low's *154 Forties* was posthumously edited and published by Anne Tardos (Denver: Counterpath Press, 2012).]

them two to four pages long, but some longer (and one very much longer). All the "Stein" poems include words (or rather, root morphemes, in the case of lexical words—nouns, verbs, adjectives, and adverbs) and "helping words" (a term I'll soon explain) from works by Gertrude Stein.

The first step in making a Steinpoem was to select a source text and seed text to run through DIASTEX5, the latest update of C. O. Hartman's 1994 update of his program automating one of my diastic text-selection methods. Sometimes I chose—at other times I employed chance operations to select—one or the other or both of these texts. As I said earlier, I call the product of this automated method its "raw output."

To make the final poems, I revised the raw output of the diastic method to a greater or lesser extent, following certain rules allowing plenty of wiggle room. The revisions included changes of word order affixes (primarily suffixes), inflections, and other changes that resulted in changes of person, case, number, tense, mood, etc. In addition, I often changed, deleted, or added new "helping words." These include both function words (including articles, conjunctions, prepositions, relatives, auxiliary verbs, and certain pronouns, etc.) as well as all other pronouns and all the forms of "to be." Making these changes in the raw output allowed the author to produce normal sentences, if desired, or to make other kinds of word strings, normative or not, in the course of composing one of the poems.

Most, but by no means all, of the Steinpoems comprise sequences of verse lines that are sentences, and each sequence of verse lines is divided into a series of strophes. The numbers of verse lines in successive strophes most often (but again, not always) correspond to a mathematical number sequence.

The number sequence that I have employed most often was the Lucas sequence: 1, 3, 4, 7, 11, 18, 29, 47, 76, 123, etc. After the first number, each subsequent number is the sum of the two before it. This sequence was developed by the French mathematician Edouard Lucas. After 1871, when he was released from the French army, in which he'd served as an artillery officer in the Franco-Prussian War, by the defeat of the French army, he became a professor of mathematics in Paris. He investigated the well-known Fibonacci sequence and developed the Lucas sequence (which bears a mathematical relation to the Fibonacci sequence) to test the primality of Mersenne prime numbers. He published the Lucas sequence and his test for Mersenne primes in 1880.

I found the Lucas sequence somewhere many years ago, probably in an issue of *Scientific American*, and I jotted it down on a little piece of blue paper that I then misplaced. I found this piece of paper again in 1989 and have used the Lucas sequence off and on since then to determine the divisions of poems and musical works. Poor Lucas died at the age of 49, in 1891, as a result of a freak accident at a banquet, when a plate was dropped and a piece of it flew up and cut his cheek. He died of erysipelas a few days later. His methods of testing primality (involving the sequence bearing his name) are still used, as refined in 1930 by two American mathematicians named Lehmer, to test the primality of large numbers.

Other number sequences I've employed to determine numbers of verse lines in successive strophes of Steinpoems include the sequence of prime numbers (2, 3, 5, 7, 11, 13, 17, 23, etc.) and that of the integers (1, 2, 3, 4, 5, 6, 7, 8, 9, 10, 11, etc.). However, in making some Steinpoems, I've allowed the divisions of the lines in the raw outputs of the diastic method to determine the placement of strophe breaks, and at times I've determined those strophe breaks deliberately or "intuitively," i.e., liminally.

The way I wrote making the Steinpoems permitted me to use all of my writingways, or just a few of them, as I preferred. It also allowed me to intervene in the making-process more flexibly than when I only selected source and seed texts (personally or methodically) and ran them through the diastic word-selection process without altering its output in any significant way.

Though the whole makingprocess starts out with someone else's work and a deterministic method (which may be preceded by auxiliary chance operations), this combination of writingways allows me "to engage with contingency" rather than simply "to accept the results of contingency"—as I did before and during the 80s at those times when I composed verbal and musical works by means of chance operations and/or deterministic methods.

Performers of my musical and verbal performance works are enabled to engage with contingency by the partially indeterminate nature of most of my scores. Only specific parameters of these works, such as the successive pitches of music, are determined by those scores. Others are determined by choices of the performers, which are often made improvisatorially during performances.

In summarizing what I've said about my writingways, I must emphasize that I've often composed poems, music, etc., without employing any systematic methods. I did this from 1937 to late 1954 and intermittently afterwards, when I often worked with systematic methods. In the 80s I usually alternated between methodical and liminal writing, and from late February 1989 to April 1998 I usually wrote by gathering verbal materials from my inner and outer environments into fuzzy verse forms by mostly liminal choices whose results I intermittently revised—both deliberately and liminally—over several years before I considered the poems complete. From spring 1998 until Christmas 2000, I wrote the "Stein" series, by means of the combination of writingways that I've outlined, while intermittently continuing to revise the "154 Forties."

In 2001 I have continued making poems by means of combinations of makingways similar to those through which I wrote "Stein," but I've started off from sources and seed by authors other than Gertrude Stein. Among them are a poem by John Keats and a book of poetry written collaboratively by Rosmarie and Keith Waldrop. However, I may well start making poems in entirely different ways in this new year that begins a new century, and millennium.

Jackson Mac Low

New York: early December 2000–24 January 2001

List of Abbreviations

The titles of source, seed, and other texts used by Mac Low in composing the "writing-ways" notes appended to each poem have been abbreviated after their first use. Each first instance of a title is identified in whole. Subsequent iterations are noted by abbreviation. Titles appearing only once are not abbreviated.

ASR = Gertrude Stein. *A Stein Reader*. Edited by Ulla E. Dydo. Evanston: Northwestern UP, 1993.

AMRD = Rand Corporation. *A Million Random Digits and 100,000 Normal Deviates*. Glencoe, IL: Free Press, 1955.

CC = "Capital Capitals." *ASR*, 415–26.

CE = "Composition as Explanation." *ASR*, 493–503.

LGB = "A Long Gay Book." *ASR*, 151–253.

MoA = "Making of Americans." *ASR*, 17–99.

OOD = "Orta or One Dancing." *ASR*, 120–36.

PMJ = "Pink Melon Joy." *ASR*, 280–305.

SiM = "Stanzas in Meditation." *ASR*, 568–87.

TB = Gertrude Stein. *Tender Buttons*. New York: Claire Marie, 1914. Bartleby.com, 1999. www.bartleby.com/140/.

TW = "Two Women." *ASR*, 104–19.

Little Beginning

(Stein 1)

Little lingering father little regular simple.

Little long length there louder happening deepening.

Beginning and little way singing neat cooked.

Difference certain length time light much lighting.

Description certain choosing is the piece.

Pleasant the deranged rhubarb pudding permitted stay.

Sit sing laugh soiling not lingering sing.

Singing difference conclude long so to mention.

Length is stay sit sing laugh soiling beginning.

Singing and any and which the way singing has higher.

Is material long very fried the pears when abuse.

And say filled makes afternoon with children there.

It is.

That the preceder whole that room whole lingering pleasant pressure.

The whispering necessity pressure whispering conclude.

Of the bread there little pieces often better peculiar.

Any people and this the beer time and the light words.

The soiling preceder which comes so simple necessity.

Necessity there the way there way say stay sit sing.

Laugh soiling beginning singing was description.

We that still figs whispering blanket regular conviction.

Whispering whispering and surely cooked there.

Then that bread all pears when thickness people dearest.

It is no conviction.

Biting sample longer refusal seat beginning regular surely.

Pleasant pressure is every there and every the.

Seat the preceder and more lighting and not so and not.

More not more green no deranged pears better no to not.

All in any makes here time noise well that does that.

Light likely.

Biting seat.

Little little.

Little little long length there louder happening deepening.

Beginning.

Derived from a page (and preceding line) of Gertrude Stein's "A Long Gay Book" (*A Stein Reader*, edited by Ulla E. Dydo, last line of 240 through 241—determined by a logarithm table) via Charles O. Hartman's program DIASTEX5, his latest automation of one of my diastic procedures developed in 1963, using the 1st paragraph of the source as seed, and subsequent editing: some excisions of words, changes of word order within lines; and changes and additions of capitals, periods, and spaces.

New York: 27–28 April 1998; 23 March, 29 April 2002

Pleasant Regular Neat and Gave That Much More

(Stein 2)

Pleasant regular neat.

Peas and and did green fried the same often pleasant permitted.

Meaning this and an and sing much more gave.

Little surely cooked.

So food talking there filled this the beer doors noise with way.

Best and dearest likely refusing half there larger.

Difference merriment difference a simple difference.

Did time happy peculiar people stay have time happening.

Completer refined difference simple did cause material.

True figs better this shows that best day leave best.

Piece description material description necessity.

Description description description.

So conclude that there when there will be clear love sing piece.

Sample pressure concluded mentioned there the meaning.

That is of them the open merriment noise it is four completer.

The whole food there the there there is is not no have.

Time light much there larger pleasant blanket neat.

No description there and not often such mentioned.

Thickness talking day leaves fire pleasant green deranged.

Potatoes deranged and red there the bread and no pears.

Such time shows necessity's dearest description happening.

The whole way there will show the abuse not permitted.

Peculiar description here makes happening dearest.

The necessity is true the green there is the matter.

There bread is mentioned say not more is clear there.

Peculiar materials leave particular people peculiar.

This pressure comes and an and gave the green peas description.

Figs stayed and gave that much more.

Derived from Stein's LGB (*ASR* 240–41) via DIASTEX5, using the 2nd paragraph of the source text as seed, and subsequent editing: some excisions of words and changes of word order and suffixes within lines and additions of capital letters, periods, and spaces. Finally, the lines were grouped into strophes of which the numbers of lines/sentences correspond to the Lucas-number sequence 1, 3, 4, 7, 11, followed by two one-line codas.

New York: 28 April 1998; 22 May 1999

Little Lingering Pudding

(Stein 3)

Little lingering father little regular simple.

Little leg figs of afternoon.

Marking much.

Little happy pudding lantern mutton always dear as all potatoes.

Say its soiling follows.

And the little necessity causes pressure.

No little potatoes mentioned.

Lengthy light not pleasant clearly thickens potatoes.

Does little staying louder make excess.

The green preceder gave pressure that came.

Little potatoes be certainly little.

All time clears excess samples nicely singing no more beginning.

This whole pear shows the time there.

Happy light of afternoon does likely days.

Biting seat.

Little regular sheets cause rhubarb certainly louder rhubarb.

All is refined and refusing sings it all.

Which whole.

The true little green there matters little as each is certainly best.

There most days time to time the best pieces sit discussing time.

Same pieces discuss a little better matter there louder.

Little refined piece with that not completer piece.

Place every whole preceder of mutton and if pudding.

Not mentioning thickness is not more talking.

Red for staying refined refusing and learning.

Little father's regular simple little place.

Discuss the matter of little fish growing best with fire.

Children saying things nicely the maker is that it is there.

Excess pressure deranged the completer beginning.

Peculiar people often fried little pieces better.

There necessity still places pieces with pieces.

There clearly the better breadth is one pleasantly fried.

Where children hear excess is they sample that.

Much lighting of the place and celery is happy.

Every happening happy and eaten.

Nothing is not cooked.

Little time no fishing for pears.

Pears that pleasant permitted making that meaning there.

Every beginning was growing more obliging.

Little green figs this fish here nothing necessary.

Have love have seat much fish say necessity as way.

All that talking there makes all that time there.

Where it is best dearest and not longer.

Whisper so the cooked pears show.

All say this is best and that way shows when filled.

This the beer.

Bake it well is conviction's best most deepening word.

Certainly mentioned that rhubarb and this beer.

Will that there noise and use it there.

There then there the noise is louder

Say that the little come more than color.

They.

The whole way there to there.

Little celery bread no pears to abuse obliged four houses.

A pleasant time discussing celery there the rhubarb.

That same time is used there.

It is there then that merriment means noise.

That very light blanket makes the hymn completer.

Mention all this as certainly the best.

Singing that potato is permitting more conviction.

Most certainly mentioning love permitted meanings best.

All any and the.

There the house is more comely.

Still eating all this lengthened day so sing.

There is lengthy laughter lighting this talky place.

Nothing deranged all thickened blankets' thickness.

Pleasant all that there.

Leave peculiar singing laughter length is breadth growing light.

Pleasant fried breadth breadth talking all the way.

Every pleasant blanket is marking a smiling soiling opening.

Pleasantly deranged necessity chooses pleasant wishes.

There is father's way and then that.

No thing not showing length enough is often eaten.

Time's little place is not permitting louder noise.

Well more room breadth permitted completer singing.

There the meaning is mentioned.

Leave afternoon merriment open.

Marking the show the doors' noise is placed well away.

Dearest sample that piece more.

Little particular singing material.

The sitting time makes every place particular.

It is there that dearest singing is more than best.

There nothing clearly sings celery bread.

Leave sitting with little cloths dearest choose beginnings of light.

Surely noting much.

Little as all mutton pudding.

Derived from Stein's LGB (*ASR* 240–41) via DIASTEX5, using the 3rd paragraph of the source as seed, and subsequent editing: some excisions of words, changes of word order and suffixes within lines, and additions of capital letters, periods, and spaces.

New York: 29–31 April 1998; 29 April 2002

Little Open Place

(Stein 4)

Little regular neat.

Well leave leave them the open place refusing nicely.

Little materials light peculiar happy people here who little choose
hearing deepening words made whole.

That whole little half gave more coming than the larger pressure.

Have time of an afternoon and say days' dearest may likely refuse
learning.

Leave leave them the very open room and sing it as one blanket.

Such time's better and in and here have love have this.

Likely well do those four sing the opening of that thing.

Use open fire to cook with there the whole following afternoon.

The four likely gave the whole thing more pressure.

The mentioned pears were very green like matter showing more.

Children's merriment happening and merriment.

Not an afternoon describing apples and nothing more.

Whispering afternoons.

Little leg pears.

Leave leave them well nicely refusing the open place.

Derived from Stein's LGB (*ASR* 240–41) via DIASTEX5, using the 4th paragraph of the source as seed, and subsequent editing: including some excisions of words and changes of word order, tenses, and suffixes within lines, and additions of capital letters, periods, and spaces. (Each of two pairs of output lines was combined as a single sentence.)

New York: 1 May 1998; 3 May 1999

Father Soils

(Stein 5)

Father cooked more mutton puddin' but no bread or nuttin'.

Such smiling noise convicts an apple of deep soiling.

If these pears are bread does the day stay.

Choosing choosing there shows rhubarb happily eaten.

Every happy happening-cloth comes cooked in that very blanket.

Staying makes hearing the deepening word.

An' likely.

Biting learning deranged the there there.

The little time of opening deepens convictions difference soils.

Mention food's necessity so pieces of figs say make our day.

The afternoon show's noise is a louder thing.

This loud pressure cooker shows there's little to give abuse to.

Apple children may say wordy nuttin' cookin' mutton.

Smiling bread pudding convicted such apples of noise.

Deepening soils.

Derived from Stein's LGB (*ASR* 240–41) via DIASTEX5, using the 5th paragraph of the source as seed, and subsequent editing of the output, including some excisions of words and changes of word order, spelling, tense, and suffixes within lines, and additions of capital letters, periods, spaces, and a few function words.

New York: 1–8 May 1998; 23 February 2002

The Big Stay Away

(Stein 6)

The big way there like green rhubarb mattered little last time.

Such a little place and they stay away.

All the cooks chose to come and that means any obliged.

The the.

All the happy apples there place every open excess differently.

Sample pears' thick pieces there all day.

The singer there opens with not much of this thing.

Surely it is difference and long concluded.

Still better times will not abuse all peculiar ways.

Here there're nice little ways.

Children color light convictions.

Make hymns to.

Pleasant celery shows this thickness better'n pears or rhubarb.

This makes merriment that stays the opening doors.

That.

This that is there is all that is there.

All they hear there's all that's there.

An and and a the.

There the house is more than those that come there more.

All begin things when obliged.

Little concluders show choosing the celery means refusing learning.

The that.

The whole way is little and celery's place is in bread.

And certain pears're best.

Come sit and leave the light so celery chooses lighting's color.

The bigger wish is making that little there completer.

Last time there rhubarb mattered like the little green way.

Such a little place to stay all and any stay away.

Derived from Stein's LGB (*ASR* 240–41) via DIASTEX5, using the 6th paragraph of the source as seed, and subsequent editing: excisions of words; changes of word order, tense, and suffixes within lines; and additions of capitals, periods, spaces, and a few structure words.

New York: 4–7 May 1998

Very Pleasant Soiling

(Stein 7)

Very pleasant celery and rhubarb there discuss the pear.

Better pears endear completer convictions.

Soiling follows better frying's thick and smiling merriment.

On a happy day the thing that's there is there.

They may say that anywhere.

They differentiate.

No material eaten all day is still nothing at all.

When they're louder no more they choose the dearest apples.

They may say that they make way.

Very happily pears are there.

Asking when that is staying there is best when pears stay with it there.

Choose the dearest there where it is not.

Larger happy people are leaving half their afternoons to happenings.

Which beginnings deepen the little.

They cooked.

So conclude.

Leave merry conviction whispering into completer conviction.

If difference is conviction then happiness is description.

There thick happenings deepen beginnings.

Staying the very same each way is abuse.

Merriment's dearest noises stay there all the day and leave.

They complete conviction.

That follows soiling.

21 verse-line sentences derived from Stein's LGB (*ASR* 240–41). [Ed. Note: Two of the lines were later divided to make 23 verse-line sentences in the final version of the poem.] I found "241" by opening a math-table book I used in high school to a table of logarithms of sines of numbers and pointing to the top-left log sin's mantissa. I sent the source text and a seed text (par. 7 of the source text) through DIASTEX5. I revised the program's output by deleting or inserting a few function words; changing some word orders, tenses, and suffixes within lines; and replacing lowercase initial letters of sentences with capitals. I inserted a period at the end of each verse-line sentence and placed one- or two-line spaces between the verse-lines according to line-groupings in the output.

New York: 6–9 May 1998; 15–16 January 2001

Big Bites

(Stein 8)

Big singers are asking half the regulars there to begin completing their
hymns higher.

If every this is cooked whole choose the very long and louder.

Laughter's much completer than learning in every four places.

Half the rhubarb shows the way there showing likely greens.

Abuse will clearly never refine love's completing happening time.

Blankets completely conclude.

Every excess is a much more pleasant necessity than red refined rhubarb is.

Learning bites.

Conclude that little place is there.

Little is still little little pieces make afternoons nice.

To come best there dearest begin refined.

Half the the there bites.

Derived from Stein's LGB (*ASR* 240–41) via DIASTEX5, using the 8th paragraph of the source as seed, and subsequent editing: excisions of words, changes of word order, tense, and suffixes within lines, and additions of capital letters, periods, spaces, and a few structure words. Some successive output lines are combined.

New York: 10 May 1998; 23 March, 30 April 2002

Begin a Piece Of the Whole

(Stein 9)

Begin big singing not asking.

If every preceder bites a piece the whole piece still is eaten.

Happy peculiar people may refuse refining any time.

Refusing certain regular materials they're choosing necessity.

Every piece of a whole precedes all pieces.

Little lengths of eaten rhubarb ask for dearest light and cloth.

That hearer began refusing learning a little lighting.

Refined matter there comes singing of long red pears.

Refuse refusal pleasant refusal and sing.

Enough thick talking sing of whole puddings.

At the beginning every little seat is there.

Then materialize no more days as there are no more.

No fish will follow preceders all follow pressure.

Which preceder filled with merriment cooked the beginning.

Ask the little father to begin.

Every preceder bites a piece of the whole.

16 verse-line sentences derived from Stein's LGB (*ASR* 240–41). I sent the source text and a seed text (par. 9 of the source text) through DIASTEX5. I revised the program's output by inserting or deleting a few function words; changing some word orders, tenses, and suffixes within lines; and replacing lowercase initial letters of sentences with capitals. I inserted a period at the end of each verse-line sentence and placed one-, two-, or four-line spaces between the verse-lines in accordance with line-groupings in the output.

New York: 10–11 May 1998; 15–16 January 2001

The Whole Matter Is Better Half-Filled There than Here

(Stein 10)

The whole matter is there so the whole is cooked to pudding.

There each uses such of this that's best there.

Here all have filled every half there is.

If cooked long the very material pears are fried.

Here love's louder when abused.

Where's a likely sample dearest there that there is this.

Does this grow there.

Baking gave more than the pressure which cooked the whole there.

All light beer begins here when there's still enough.

That lingering beginning soiled a refined happening.

The deepening word there is soiling the whole preceder.

Singing songs is surely necessary more than fishing for pears.

This shows the there there is all had there better half-filled there than here.

Derived from Stein's LGB (*ASR* 240–41) via DIASTEX5, using the 10th paragraph of the source as seed, and subsequent editing: excisions of words, changes of word order, tense, and suffixes within lines, and additions of capital letters, periods, spaces, and a few structure words. Two successive output lines are combined.

New York: 11 May 1998

And Sing More Very Loudly

(Stein 11)

for Anne Tardos

And sing more than Father and more food's mutton and always.

Mentioning more to say more louder follow necessity.

Always and long like the eaten very loudly follow necessity.

Derived from Stein's LGB (*ASR* 240–41) by running the passage through DIASTEX5, using the name "Anne Tardos" as the seed text, and by minimal subsequent editing: changes of word order, tense, and suffixes within lines; and addition of capitals, periods, spaces, and one final "'s."

New York: 11 May 1998; 17 January, 27–28 May 1999

Use and Choose

(Stein 12)

for Ulla E. Dydo

Use

all
all breadth
enough
days

hymn and choose.

Derived from Stein's LGB (*ASR* 240–41) via DIASTEX5, using the name "Ulla E. Dydo" as seed, and by minimal subsequent editing: addition of a capital letter, a period, an "s" and line breaks.

New York: 11 May 1998

Green Completers So

(Stein 13)

for Gertrude Stein

Green peas surely that description concludes obliged completers.

So it's the asking that begins giving by beginning more
    little descriptions.

Conclude obliged completers so.

Derived from Stein's LGB (*ASR* 240–41) via DIASTEX5, using the name "Gertrude Stein" as seed, and by minimal subsequent editing: addition of capital letters and periods and a few structure words and suffixes, and thus a few tense changes.

New York: 11–12 May 1998

Meaning Was Certainly Always This Him

(Stein 14)

meaning was certainly certainly anything

it and a meaning him

meaning was certainly very certainly always meaning was were

They certainly always meaning was working
They certainly

meaning was certainly certainly anything

meaning was certainly certainly anything

that the one they living been

meaning was certainly very certainly always meaning was were

They certainly always meaning was working
They certainly

meaning was certainly certainly anything

and one and repellent very out struggling clear meaning interesting
it this working meaning needing as one and real meaning
out

meaning was certainly very certainly always meaning was were

They certainly always meaning was working
They certainly

meaning was certainly certainly anything

meaning was certainly certainly anything

meaning was certainly very certainly always
This whom were some himself and it had was solid

meaning was certainly certainly anything

and one and then that were something himself and it had was solid

meaning was certainly very certainly always meaning was were

They certainly always meaning was working
They certainly

meaning was certainly certainly anything

meaning was certainly very certainly always it repellent very
repellent ever himself always repellent something
complicated was certainly following would meaning
was working
They certainly always interesting repellent very

meaning was certainly certainly anything

and one and was were and bringing then perplexing clear pretty
always almost completely

meaning was certainly very certainly always meaning was were

They certainly always meaning was working
They certainly

meaning was certainly certainly anything

meaning was certainly very certainly always needing to so be

meaning was certainly certainly anything

and one and never not something been

meaning was certainly very certainly always meaning was were

They certainly always meaning was working

meaning was certainly certainly anything

meaning was certainly having disturbing always meaning was
were having disturbing always meaning was were having

meaning was certainly very certainly always
This some so be one always and had
This working something meaning ever meaning was working they
certainly always there something something never
been always one had
This something solid perplexing clear meaning was working

They certainly always there something something never been
always one had
This something solid perplexing clear meaning was working

They certainly

and one and and one and a
One and and one had all one had and
One and and one and and one and always one had always one had always
one and as one and and one and and one and as one and always
one did always one and and one and an and and and one had
all one had and
One and and one and and one and always one had always one had always
one and as one and and one and and one and as one and always
one did always one

meaning was

meaning was certainly certainly anything

meaning was certainly having disturbing always meaning was
were having disturbing always meaning was were having

meaning was certainly very certainly always meaning was were

They certainly always meaning was working

They certainly

meaning was

and one and and one and a
One and and one had all one had and
One and and one and and one and always one had always one had always
one and as one and and one and and one and as one and always
one did always one and and one and an and and and one had
all one had and
One and and one and and one and always one had always one had always
one and as one and and one and and one and as one and always
one did always one

meaning was certainly very meaning was working

They meaning was working they meaning was certainly very meaning
was working
They meaning was working

meaning was certainly certainly anything

meaning was certainly very certainly always it and

meaning was certainly certainly anything

meaning was certainly very certainly always

meaning was certainly certainly anything

that the one they disconcerting complicated needing to out
be needing following having himself

meaning was certainly very certainly always
This him

Derived from Gertrude Stein's "Picasso" (*ASR* 142–43). The source site was determined by 142, a permutation of 241, a number drawn from a logarithm table. All of "Picasso" was run through DIASTEX5—Charles O. Hartman's latest program automating one of my diastic text-selection procedures developed in 1963—44 times, using as successive seeds the successive typographical lines of the last part of the 4th section of Stein's play *A List* (*ASR* 412–13 [1 page + 6 lines]). The seed site was determined by 412, another permutation of 241. The 44 outputs were not edited (except that "a and" was changed to "an and"), but the placement of each was determined by a die-throw in a method that excluded identical successive placements. Extensions of the source and seed sites beyond the determined pages were matters of choice.

New York: 16–30 May 1998

And One That Clear

(Stein 15)

for Anne Tardos, Ulla E. Dydo, and Gertrude Stein

and one

going were working that clear

The 3 lines of this poem were determined by running Stein's "Picasso" (*ASR* 142–43) through DIASTEX5, using in turn the names Anne Tardos, Ulla E. Dydo, and Gertrude Stein as seeds. In the case of each seed name, I accepted the program's being stopped by a "mismatch" (not finding one or more letters of a seed text in positions corresponding to those they occupy in the seed word). In the case of "Ulla E. Dydo," there were no "matches" whatsoever, so there is a silent line in the middle of the poem. The placement of the 3 lines and the five-line space, indicating that the 2nd line is silent, were chosen.

New York: 30 May 1998

One Completely

(Stein 16)

one
one
one who.

This who them son
not came something
was her
her come
come be her that.

<|>

She not something
something was beginning
were others children
been married that

<|>

one
one
one who.

This who them son
not came something
was her
her come
come be her that.

<|>

She not something
something existing
fourth believing
something finishing
having fading
fading be meaning.

She thing children
not completely living
living having one
quite not one
of having living
some could were
were quite.

<|>

one
one
one who.

This who them son
not came something
was her
her come
come be her that.

<|>

one
one
one who.

This who them
son not came
something was her

her come
come be her that.

<|>

This the being.

This one
one
one who dancing
has who going.

Very.

<|>

This the being.

This one
one
one who
dancing has one in one
was that who
who dancing was
was not.

Very.

<|>

This the being.

This one
one
one always all always
always marry

always has
was ending.

She not something
something existing
fourth believing something
finishing being meaning
being then being
completely could come
fading
asking
asking one
quite not one of that
that existing.

This one
one
one
the that
existing ones one
and then with was

was
was four
were.

<|>

This the being.

This one one
one who dancing
has one in one
was that who
who dancing was was not.

Very.

<|>

This the being.

This one
one
one who dancing
has changing be.

Very that.

<|>

This the being.

This one
one
one
who dancing has
one in one
has having living beginning
living ending
an all always
always marry
always.

She not something
something existing
fourth believing something
finishing being
meaning being
then being completely
could come fading
asking

asking one
quite not one
of having living
some she
not commencing
were fourth
together believing something
finishing having fading living
living having living completely going
coming completely
completely interesting
forgetting completely
completely
completely a remembering
he that could
meaning be meaning
meaning meaning
meaning knowing that.

She still existing one
enough then was
was
was of
and
one was then knowing them
son not came
something was her
her come forgetting son.

All children completely.

Poem derived from a source passage in Stein's "Orta or One Dancing," Stein's portrait of Isadora Duncan: the last three lines of *ASR* 123, 124–25, and the first two lines of 126. The number 124 was drawn by opening a logarithm table I used in high school and blindly pointing to a number. I chose to include the rest of the source text. This passage from OOD was run twelve times through DIASTEX5. I used as successive seed texts the twelve paragraphs of Stein's play "Picasso" (*ASR* 142–43), beginning page determined by permuting 241 to 142. I chose to use all of the "Picasso" paragraphs as seeds. Each paragraph produced one group of strophes, groups being separated by "<|>." Editing of the program's output was minimal: choices of word order in lines and of line breaks, insertion of periods and strophe breaks before given capital letters, and of periods after strophe groups and before strophe-group breaks between them.

New York: 22–26 May 1998; endnote revised 10 February 2002

Always One's Others'

(Stein 17)

for Anne Tardos, Ulla E. Dydo, and Gertrude Stein

Always one's finishing
something that's having.

Very needing supporting
always
a one many were
then was married.

Needing supporting

going 's being.

Very
that's
others'.

Derived from Stein's OOD (*ASR* 123–26), run 3 times through DIASTEX5, using as successive seeds the names Anne Tardos, Ulla E. Dydo, and Gertrude Stein. The first name produced the words before the large space, the 2nd, the space, and the 3rd the words after the space. Editing was minimal: line breaks, insertion of periods, strophe breaks before given capitals, a few new capitals, *s*'s and apostrophes. Placement of lines was determined by a die throw except for that of the parts of the sentence broken by silences.

New York: 2 June 1998

Time That Something Something

(Stein 18)

Time.

That
        being

This,

One and one is is,

        The.

There everybody's one
and sees
being seen being,
been using,
                did,
was.

Anne's successful,
        hearing hearing,
feeling they.

They said
                those of and
are is,
                is to thing one
of and.

They're that thing,
        friendly,
                been quickly laughing,
                        laughing sounding is
        and

Being regularly,

Talking seeing expressing,
                                discovering something,
                something
        happening.

It and did was long successful hearing,
hearing feeling he was,
        have again coming,
saying meant he that meant meaning
        walking,
                talking,
                        talking that

This existing one,
        one preparing is,
                is one and everything badly.

He all motion,
noise,
wherever something,
something happening,

It and

That,

That being being quickly laughing,
laughing sounding talking
showing imitating existing one,
and then

If is one one,
one to the thing,
then quickly laughing laughing,
sounding is and disappearing,
waiting,
continuing,
discovering lacking motion,
staying
had saying,
living
coming often
having might,
he that thing convincing
convincing hearing they what?

This thís.

One and one is is,
one one's seeing be were,
all asking leave received,
expecting something,
expecting is and difficult easy
kindly which,
walking talking,
talking happening easily,

Waving saying saying saying meeting,
being leaving being staying
beginning hearing they what?

This this.

One,
and one is,
is one,
one seeing dead,
came,
gone successful hearing,
hearing feeling they.

They said those of
and are
is,
is one anything,
when thing then
then that anything one enjoying one that they being
says one
and they is is open,
and when be be
quickly being thing is
and

Being regularly,
quietly,
been going one,
one,
one was then who is,
is,
did was long successful hearing hearing feeling
they.

They said those of and are
is,

is one anything they be,
be said when
thing one,
one one tell then doing
says one and they is,
is open
and when be be quickly being thing
is
and

Being regularly quietly been going one,
one,
one to the thing,

This

One and one,
is ís then there,
everybody one
and seen
being seen being,
been.

Using did,
was

Anne successful?

Hearing,
hearing feeling,
they,

They said,
those of and are is,
is to things one,

one of,
                    and they that thing
          friendly,
been quickly laughing,
                                        laughing sounding
                                is
          and

Being
                    regularly

Talking,
                    seeing,
                                        expressing,
discovering something something.

Derived from Stein's LGB (*ASR* 214–18) by running it through DIASTEX5. This diastic program, like its non-digital predecessor, functions via an algorithm that draws words from a source text by "spelling out" a "seed text" with words having the seed's letters in places corresponding to those they occupy in the source text. (Diastic methods are "nonintentional" but "deterministic" rather than "chance-operational" since whenever they are utilized correctly with the same source and seed texts, they will always produce the same outputs, whereas the outputs of chance operations will always be different from one another. The seed in this case was the first paragraph of a passage from OOD (beginning on 123 and ending on 124). The numbers 214 and 124 were found by permuting 241, a number determined by opening at random a book of math tables that I used in high school and adopting the three-digit number in the upper left corner of the logarithm table on the left-hand page. Intuitive choice extended the source passage from the top of 214 to the bottom of 218. Editing was limited to insertions of intuitively determined line and strophe breaks, punctuation marks, indentations, and a few apostrophe-*s*'s. Rules adopted for this poem placed single-line spaces before capitals within strophes, end marks at the ends of strophes, and two-line spaces after periods. The program's output was unchanged as to words (except those with added apostrophe-*s*'s), word order, and capitalization (except for the first "T").

New York: 2–7 June 1998; endnote revised 15 January 2002

Time Be We Going Then

(Stein 19)

Time,

That being

This

One

and one

is,

is
one.

One seeing came,

then dead being,

being offering,
standing,
standing to,
they,
things,
prospering.

One óne.

Every in is óf

and are what they who he easily answering be,

be been.

Been what.

That enough any all saw began every expressing.

He was,

was
been.

Wé been then.

One enough one be we going,
then being.

Living did have having,

having coming is one being.

Get

things.

Things enough talked when that.

What one.

And been that.

What being.

This.

One and one was saying was one,
and one questions

purpose,

being

continuing where liked,
like having finished again eating is,

and badly.

He's noise

then going

That thé that thát one,

one then the thing,

said,

This

One,

and one is is,

one one's seeing feels.

Finding

Anne again,

Henns thought

directing,
directing expecting long tired have.

Again coming saying it,

and be be said when things then,
then that anything one enjoying one that they being
says one and they is,
is they,
they that that óf in the tó,
them quickly this one and every happening

easily answering,

badly,

He pleased been to that.

What.

That one and then that thát said

This.

One,
and one is,
is one,
one seeing he was living,
living having arranged

being seen one's been.

If

Anne to they,

them,
back,
wearing urging,

urging intended hearing,

expecting repeating,
repeating being left,
they,

things,

to what hearing.

What one.

One one that thát said amusing.

One in one has,

can,

has been,

be,

everything doing going,

sounding,

waiting.

Being going,
one óne be we going,

then being

That.

That staying went one and been that.

What being.

This.

One,

and one is,

is question,

purpose being continuing where finish did.

Donger,
asked,
refused enough answering happening,
answering
badly.

He,

noise,

then going long time living,

coming often having,
is any

being being going then enough to what.

That.

That one.

And been that what being.

This.

One and one is ís.

One one's seeing came then dead being béing
offering stánding,
stánding to thém,

things

prospering.

One one every in is of,

and are what they who he easily answering be,

be been.

Been what.

That enough any all saw began every

expressing.

He was,

was been.

We been then one,
enough one be we going then.

Derived from Stein's LGB (*ASR* 214–18) by running it through DIASTEX5 using as seed the second paragraph of a passage from OOD, the first paragraph beginning and ending on

ASR 124. Editing was limited to insertions of intuitively determined line, strophe, sentence, and phrase breaks; punctuation marks; left or right justification or centering (which were literally aleatory: decided by die-throws); capitalization in addition to that in the unedited output (which was always accepted); and insertions of a few apostrophe-s's and other suffixes and occasional acute accents clarifying grammatical stresses. Rules adopted for this poem placed line breaks after commas, single-line spaces before capitals within strophes, periods at the ends of strophes, and two-line spaces after periods. The program's output was unchanged as to words (except those with added suffixes) and word-order.

New York: 7–9 June 1998

Time to Be We

(Stein 20)

Time:

That being:

This.

One

and one

is ís:

one óne seeing what then's

enough.

Hearing,

saying,

was,

being seen.

One's been one and

she's bought remembered things.

Standing,
George did back gone successful hearings,
hearing feeling them.

They said those of ánd are hearing
waiting visited,
being hearing.

One when óf
and théy
be being begun again,
again méant
something,
something something ís.

Any,
being decided,
who stand enough of—
in the being,
very quickly being,
thing—
doing walking,
continue quickly walking,

Talking turning truly what existing chosen ones,
and then he,
said,
misunderstood,
being he knew turned going would.

Things,
seeing things,
one,

Enough being
leaving,
quite being enough,
long did living ask,
asking,
asking if,

In beginning remembering being
doing being,
one and one'd been
determined.

Doing doing béing,
doing was going successfully.

Hearing hearing feeling,
they,

Théy said those of ánd are hearing waiting visited,
being hearing one when's easily ánything,
and again coming saying it,
and being being said when things—
one . . .
one . . .

one—
’re going sounding waiting,

Being going,
What to bé we did
was
long,
successful
hearing hearing feeling.

They—

They said those of ánd
are.

Ís is friendly,
disturbing,
gone again,
pleasing something,
something, something,
something
liked,
like having finished again eating is
—and badly.

He's noise.

Then going one . . .
one . . .
one . . .
dóes say long,
successful
hearing.

Hearing feeling,
they–

Théy–
said those of ánd are ís.

Is one ánything.

They're what they enough have.

Has disturbing been telling one then one's interesting.

Then be telling,
doing,
then being.

Donger saw finishing,
which's walking,
talking,
talking that they–

This existing one–
one
preparing–

He–
was . . .
was . . .
's been;
we been then one.

Enough one be we,
we might asking ask.

Beginning something,
something admitting,

If any being be thís being,
being one–

one–

one–

beings were beings then being.

Did.

Was.

Anne successfully hearing hearing feeling them,

They said those of ánd are hearing waiting visiting
being.

Hearing,
one,
when gone,
cóming,
said,

when things one óne's being
be dóing,
then being's liked—
like having finished—
again—
eating ís.

And—
badly—

He's nóise.

Then going one . . .
one . . .
one . . .
be we going then.

Being did—
was—
long.

Successfully
hearing–
hearing feeling–
they–

They said–
those of ánd are hearing waiting visiting being–
hearing

One.

When easy,
anything–
and
again coming saying it,
and
béing
being said–
when things're one–
one óne's,
going,
sounding,
waiting.

Being góing:
Thát's to be we.

Derived from Stein's LGB (*ASR* 214–18) by running it through DIASTEX5, using as seed the third paragraph of a passage from OOD, the second paragraph beginning and ending on *ASR* 124. Editing was limited to insertions of intuitively or deliberately determined line, sentence (= strophe), and phrase breaks; punctuation marks; capital letters additional to those in the unedited output (which were always accepted); insertions of suffixes, genitive endings, contracted forms of "to be," and acute accents clarifying grammatical and rhetorical stresses. Indentations were determined by random digits from the RAND table *A Million Random Digits and 100,000 Normal Deviates* (Glencoe, IL: The Free Press, 1955). Rules adopted for this poem placed line breaks after commas (other line breaks being optional), single-line spaces before capitals within strophes, periods at the ends of sentences/strophes, and varying numbers of vertical spaces between the latter, each decided by a die-throw. The root morphemes and word order of the program's output were unchanged.

New York: 10–11 June 1998

Time Pleases Understanding

(Stein 21)

Time That *Being*!—*This* One! And one is—*is* one?—one seeing *not*. *Some* not. Came *what?* What *then? Being* offering *standing*—standing to those things prospering. One—one?—every *in* is *of* and are commencing something, commencing again, coming saying that *not* being's being *one*. *One!* One comes to coming purposes, likely pleased, *understood*, sometimes pleasantly, pleasantly being told. Tell *again* there! *Discover* something—something *happening!* It and That, *That* being *being* quickly laughing, laughing, sounding, talking, showing, imitating, existing. *One!* And then? If it's *one* one, one *being*, we might *ask*—ask to *begin* something, something admitting—if any being be *this* being being one *one*, one *coming* some—some living.

Living, having, they're gone—being seen being—*been*. Polly, again suffering, *received*, expecting something, expecting . . . [that waiting!] . . . existing. Of *and* they . . .—It is gone! Come! [Said when things one—one's *being's* being, doing *then* being or *enjoying* then being . . .] He's well, asking there, discovering something, something happening: It. And might he? That thing's convincing, convincing hearing.—They what? This. This. One—and one *is*, is *one*—one's seeing gone, would be being using offering [and to what things?]—standing, quickly laughing, laughing . . .

Sounding is, and *Being*, regularly Talking, seeing, expressing, discovering something, something . . . happening—It! And might he—that thing convincing, convince hearing . . . ? They. . . . . *what?* This. This One—and one *is*—is *gone!* Would being've been using offering and be needing . . . ? Helbing, again suffering, received expecting. *Something* expecting is, and they—things, *things*, THINGS—quickly laugh. Laughing sounding is and happens easily. Waving, saying, saying, saying, meeting being, leaving being, staying, beginning hearing—they *what?* This *this*. One and one *is*—is *gone*—would've [being] been using offering. And if Anne be needing Helbing—again suffering received expecting, *something* expecting to. . . . ?

That waiting, existing *of* [and *they*]—it is gone! Come! [Said when things—one *one*, it and *being* being telling exciting *theres*—discovers something—something happening:—*It* and *That*—That *being* being quickly laughs láughing-sounds, talking showing imitating existing ones—and then? . . .] *If* is *going*, long being, being enough one—and then *what* things? Things quickly laughing, laughing sounding *Is* and *Being*.

Regularly, Talking sees expressing *discovering* something, something happening. It and happenings happen, have having. Having coming, might he that thing convince, convincing hearing? [They what? This? This One?] And . . . and . . . one *is*.

Is *gone?* Would being've been using *offering?*—and to *what?* Things? *Prospering* Ones? Ones every *in* is of? And are friendly disturbings *gone* again? Please, Something, *something something sómething,* if knowing that *that* thing's meaning's quickly laughing!—laughing's sounding *is* and *Being*—regularly. Talking's seeing.

Expressing discovers something. Something's happening. *Happenings* happen—*have*—*having* having come. Might he that thing convince? Convincing hearing is annoying. Doing was gone. Successful hearing's hearing *feeling,* they—*They*—said.

Those of *and* are *is*. Is friendly disturbing *gone* again? *Pleasing* something? Something (something [something]), if known, may be determined. And said meaning's enough. One and they (they [they]), being quickly sounding, exist. Existing is known. Been. Him all noticing quite received, *expecting* something. Expecting *is* and *might be* again. Being difficult commenced hearing what the *friendly* said one *one's* been. It is forgotten—disappointing—gone!

Again pleasing something, something (something [something]), if known may be determined *well.* Asking's there discovering. Something—something's—*happening.* It and That's *That being,* quickly laughing, laughing, sounding, talking *showing,* imitating an *existing* one, and then, if it's feeling, finding Anne again. Henns thought, directing directly expecting in one's being *hearing,* will visits commencing *discovering* something, something *happening.* It and happenings *happen.* Have. *Having* having come, might *he?* That thing's convincing. Convincing hearing, they what? This. *This?* One and one *is.* Is feeling finding Anne again? Henns thought *directions* directed expecting in one being. Hearing will visit *commencers.* Discover something!

Something's happening. That. That *being.* This One. And one *is.* Is feeling *finding?* Anne again, Henns thought, directly directing *expecting* in one. They that said, when quickly laughing, laughing's sounding's *is* and *being,* regularly talked—seeing *expressings*—discovering something's *something* happening. *That.* That being's *This* one. And one's *is* is feeling finding Anne again. Henns's thought directed direct *expecting.* In one being, hearing will visit commencings. Discovering something, something *happens.* That—That being This—One and one is *is-es* one *one* sees *not.*

[Some *not!*] Came *what?* What *then?* Beings offering *standing?* Standing–to *them's*–things, *prospering* ones, ones every *in* is *of*. And are commencings something commencing again? Come! Say that *not!* Be! Be One!–One coming to *come*.

Purpose likely pleases understanding.

Derived from LGB (*ASR* 214–18) by running it through DIASTEX5, using as seed the fourth paragraph of a passage from OOD, the third paragraph beginning and ending on *ASR* 124. Editing included insertions of intuitively or deliberately determined sentence and phrase breaks; punctuation marks; capitals additional to those in the unedited output (which were always accepted); insertions of suffixes, genitive endings, contracted forms of "to be," and a few auxiliary verbs, italic and enlarged and reduced typefaces signifying degrees of grammatical and rhetorical stress and its opposite, and the dividing of the edited output into prose paragraphs. Numbers of lines in paragraphs were determined by random digits from *AMRD*. Numbers of empty lines between paragraphs were determined aleatorily, that is, by die throws. The root morphemes and word order of the program's output were left unchanged.

New York: 11–19 June 1998; 23 February, 12 March, 29 May, 19 December 1999; 16 February 2000

Then What Thing Might Be?

(Stein 22)

Then what thing is noise? One and one is one
pleased. Walking that knows is what that opens.
Anything that open wills that enough.
Donger said, isn't successful hearing
hearing feeling? It is what their brother
is: one intended to be needing to
be wearing things, standing and using. She
did not. Offering being's been enough.
There to hear what they said, being's being
what was enough, was Clellan one being
leaving? Quite. Then they went enough. One and
all they noticed one noise. Discovering
answering imitating answering
is—might be—intermittently funny.

One says walking's continuing meaning.
To that being, meaning's one being seen.
It begins repeating being one thing.
Sender said, when one thing is intended,
needing is again wearing suffering.
Helbing, wherever someone's preparing
something, is truly one that's existing.
Quickly turning each intended sounding,
he might be that sounding asking hearing.
Having hearing, that sounding, when Antliss
intended being prospering, as if
standing needed wearing things on one's back,
offered using, she being all-seeing
wherever anything's being prepared.

What's continuing there? What might funny
walking be meaning? Enjoying meaning?
If anyone says something exciting,
is it pleasing an existing one and
is one asking of that existing one
that they be married? When he continued,
what would he be needing getting? Standing?
Things? Quickly, efficiently, existing?
Being regularly existing is
wanting something, receiving, suffering,
pulling again, doing what's upsetting,
one being asked and then being gotten,
wherever something funny's happening.

One might be meaning walking continues
meaning one is what one is hearing said.
What they're doing is preparing something.
Who is what one would be? One being seen?
If what one intends needing is lacking,
what might they be doing? Talking? Waving?
Anne turned back to show other proud meanings.
This thing is enough. Decide and stand there!
Ask them to tell one something exciting!
Receiving suffering is upsetting.
What things are staying? That. It's amusing.
Everyone is going, being other.
Enough of going there and asking this!
This thing's meaning is agreeable enough.

Donger walked there. Being there is asking
suffering to exist. Do it quickly.
Existing efficiently might be that
way of having what's intended happen.
When Antliss heard that being prospering,
he needed to wear things on his back as
if she had been an all-seeing being

and he were standing there offering them
unintentionally to that being,
Clellan noticed the noise, discovering
meaning intermittently, repeating
successfully what feelings he heard meant.
Anne was turning feeling into sounding
truly existing as what that might be.

Five freely written unrhymed syllabic sonnets composed of words obtained by reversing the order of 43 paragraphs of Stein's LGB (*ASR* 214–18) and running them through DIASTEX5, using as seed a paragraph of Stein's OOD (*ASR* 124, par. 4). Words in each sonnet usually came from the same area of the output.

New York: 23 June–1 July 1998; 17–24 January, 28 December 1999

Seat That One End

(Stein 23)

Seat that one that one was not to.

Antliss was not feeling feelings holding feeling.

Pulling the gone being gets one badly.

He's saying that all there wherever something's beginning
might be staying, turning, continually showing one
if copying be needed,
standing things being everything.

Who expects unamused children to be quiet?

Saying what she was offering certainly was not easy.

He when told of amusing feelings
said the feelings truly existed.

What's waiting going to do?

Beginning has not been said to be staying.

When hearing that saying being said, Father turned the thing back.

They did not refuse one. They said it was difficult to commence.

Hearing *being* being said often meant just doing too much saying.

Clellan had not then been told of that amusing feeling.

Hearing what that feeling might be, the thing he lacked was staying.

If this is very exciting, this about laughing, *anything* is.

Sender had not intended laughing at something he was expecting.

Something he had not seen had been saddening.

Nothing that might be staying looked amusing.

Everything children expect is copying.

Something continuing turning is offering quiet sounding.

Certainly something commencing meant something amusing.

At the same time Donger and Clellan had often been
showing something, telling something, doing something,
and being something enough for very many—many walking, going and
coming, very many living and asking what this thing was
that they had been hearing, told, and shown.

If some had been talking again, asking something, saying what having
enough of that thing was, showing that imitating need not be
working, they might have said what any one seeing that
may have said if he had been asked.

Then he said that he meant one thing, that walking has meaning, walking
being doing something quite exciting and expected.

What is Clellan describing? Something existing? Something exciting?

Something very many existing ones have been imitating?

Very many had said that walking meant leaving being.

Having enough is having what one may be needing.

They are all proud and pleased.

One if one be coming is staying.

When they are talking they sit showing things.

Every one had come wearing many things.

As one again sees everybody offering to stay and talk,
she might not be pleasing any one sitting there
or standing.

Walking is exciting.

They have taken things that they lacked
and have then seen that they were not very pleased.

What is walking said to be meaning?

The thing he is laughing about is a thing that they've
been laughing about.

It is being kept open when one is leaving.

Walking is existing doing exciting meaningful difficult things.

If every one has been saying what they meant children to be hearing,
they have been saying what they commenced hearing when they
were beginning to be hearing things being explained.

He is walking and continuing to be seeing what is amusing.

Answering one saying what was being explained
certainly offered quiet amusement.

Some one saying what he meant
might be staying wherever he had no need get standing.

When need she say easy things? Not quite then.

She need not show them everything they expected.

Having what she needed
that one called every meaningful saying
a copy of something another one had said.

He said that what turned things very unquiet
was one's getting a hearing but not the other ones.

Staying in that turning thing they were sounding again
as if being in that thing is a sound thing
and going is not.

Then that being saying that is staying there and saying that.

the end

Fifty strophes. Each strophe includes one to three freely composed sentences comprising words—sometimes modified by insertion or deletion of affixes—obtained by randomizing the order of 43 paragraphs of Stein's LGB (*ASR* 214–18) by chance operations involving truly random digits and ascending numeric sorting, and then running them through DIASTEX5, using as seed a paragraph of Stein's OOD (*ASR* 124, par. 5). Words in each strophe usually came from roughly the same area of the output, which was mined for words and root morphemes until nothing was left except a few crumbs.

New York: 1–6 July 1998; 4 May 1999

Stay There That One Sing

(Stein 24)

Stay there where what has been was what one was urging. Tell that then when every three whom he was quietly seeing are doing very often what has been taken to have meant doing that that they might like enjoying. He arranged intermittently that others would like doing that later because it would be leaving them laughing.

Donger said something that one of them was repeating and urging Henns to be repeating. Asking and answering being saddening, who was left turning quietly when that being was disappearing? Might living enough have finished Father's asking what he was seeing and saying what he had been looking for? Living not having been repeating like turning motions, was living like having enough and then saying one has had enough? Seeing meaning coming and going, Donger expected to hear some one not standing there to tell what it might have been. She says the things she has been doing and being were expressing truly what she liked doing and being. Hearing this thought pleased not. Expressing the feeling made what they might have said they could have been doing or being quite common. Not wearing things could been have been made something they would have been saying something about. Given that looking, seeing, and finding could be answering much talk, she intended to be looking and answering.

Not expecting motion, Anne was repeatedly turning. Antliss having been looking and looking made answering truly complete. Finding that seeing did not give every answer, Antliss intended to hear a certain meaning. Then they married. Being regularly married, they could then be talking about being ones existing and living. Staying when meeting, they made talking saying something.

The very thing they were asking one another was expressing what they were saying to one another again and again. Some one was asking another one what she liked. Everything she had been urging Antliss to complete he had intermittently arranged.

They have been walking very much later because that was enough. See what they would stand! Antliss continued standing whatever another visited upon him. One was not being easy. Staying there was being the very thing one liked being. Coming they call one another, one answering the other like one being having to leave another. Has one seen the other one having something that was not enough? Then what one was regularly asking for something that was not enough?

They have not, some of them, that one thing, that one sing.

Five paragraphs, each made up of one to ten freely composed sentences comprising words—sometimes modified by insertion and/or deletion of affixes—obtained by randomizing the order of 43 paragraphs of Stein's LGB (*ASR* 214–18) by chance operations involving "truly random" digits from *AMRD* and descending numeric sorting, and running them through DIASTEX5, using as seed text a paragraph of Stein's OOD (*ASR* 125, par. 1). Words in each paragraph came from various areas of the output. The number of sentences in each paragraph was determined by a random digit. Structure words not found in the output were only inserted when all attempts to find suitable ones in the output proved unsuccessful. The poem ended when mining the output for words and root morphemes had left nothing but an "an."

New York: 5–6 July 1998; 22 May 1999; 23 March 2002

Something She Had

Was Dancing

(Stein 25)

Something she had was liked.
Was one not having charming friends again?
Did each of them want them to have things told again,
hearing that this will stand?

Some one asked Donger something.
Anything pleasing?
Tell one.

If all who could feel that feeling tired,
could answering then be commencing to feel something like that again?
Could all there then feel that being coming?
All.

Sender intended describing the happening for them quickly.
They were saying that one was then going.
He hoped that their purpose was friendly and pleasant

Commencing again, he questioned everything.
Their answers being amusing and convincing,
they were appreciated everywhere.
Often forgetting to finish every thought,
they said things some misunderstood.

This exciting feeling left what they were saying convincing.
Who feeling being waiting would imitate being living?
No baby would.

Laughing, Antliss went directly to the astonishing children,
for he had heard that they came there needing some purpose.
Saying little and having little and being little,
they would all repeat what any older one said.
Could they be lacking something?

That little one wanted to be one living and enjoying sounding.
What being prospering would not?
Having been continuing successful answering of what was said,
that one was asking something.

Who was opening the way?
Donger went that way.
Was this one very tired later?

Doing that and hearing this,
are we going to be meeting and determining that we are going to open all
meetings to every one living where we are meeting?
Doing that will be a veryagreeable thing.
One of them was very tired later.

Where was that one going?
To some meeting.
Can that be all?

If one of them had been prospering,
can the one who was there have told many children?
We knew one that did.
Was that one pleased?

Donger misunderstood something.
What was that thing?
Describing that would be describing some disturbing feelings.

Asked what stands without feeling and without remembering much living,
Donger might have said one feeling disappointment.
Can living give one something truly satisfying?
Talking did when eating certainly did not.

Later when Sender was tired of living,
he asked Donger what funny astonishing sayings he would be hearing.
What happened was a little disappointing.
Everything was taken.

Something did not feel disturbing enough.
The thing was very interesting if not astonishing,
Children tired of expecting interesting happenings
urged George not to ask that living give them.

Some did remember some very interesting things.
They intended remembering them when they were feeling they might be dying,
when disappearing was what they needed.
What would be doing convincing then?

Anne was enjoying being there very much.
Having gone there again,
that one then told waiting children everybody's pleasing feelings.
Some hearers left

Make Henns leave.
He being packed,
couldn't one make some chosen one
commence answering ten things commonly asked?
No.

Did living please all told feeling was not enough?
The saying goes that seeing would mean hearing.
That's not the saying.

Quickly urging the living to talk,
arrange that thing when all are saying feelings and some leave.
Would this answer?
Very likely.

When the thought was heard all liked it.
When was that?
Then.

Have they been perplexing things?
What things?
The ones they all heard.

Donger remembered something.
This thought.
All finish living.

When one heard feelings being sounded,
was there anything being asked there?
Not easy for one to say.
Then would one leave?

What would one have done?
Waving.
Can it be arranged?

Everybody talked .
Saying what?
Would sounding sound convincing?

Talking would not give much sound feeling.
Could one there feel it?
Indeed.

If one knew what they could stand,
what would he have intended?
Their prospering long after?
Quite.

There being feelings,
which feelings would one be feeling if some one came and asked one to leave?
Urgent ones.
Ones coming to a living being.

After asking me to talk to Andy,
Inger came back eating.
Andy said Inger would have been coming to stand in that thing and be seen.
Intending to look at Inger,
Andy discovered coming bought by asking.

Did Andy give Inger his discovery?
He did say he'd been preparing to ask Ed.
Did asking Ed end Andy's living and saying?

Andy and Inger were living.
Andy and Inger were saying all to one and all.
All Andy and Inger were doing was dancing.

Each strophe comprises three freely composed sentences made up of words—sometimes modified by insertion and/or deletion of affixes, etc.—obtained by randomizing the on-screen lines of a previous randomization of the order of 43 paragraphs of Stein's LGB (*ASR* 214–18) by chance operations involving truly random numbers from *AMRD* and ascending numeric sorting, and running the randomized lines through DIASTEX5 using as seed text a paragraph of Stein's OOD (*ASR* 125, par. 2). Words in each sentence came from various areas of the output. Structure words not found in the output were only inserted when all attempts to find suitable ones in the output proved unsuccessful. The last three strophes ("The Story of Andy and Inger") combine discreetly modified suffixes and conjunctions with the last remaining lexical words and remaining and inserted structure words. The poem ended when mining the output for words had left nothing but a few suffixes and conjunctions.

New York: 8–10 July 1998; 16 January 1999

It Is a Difficult Thing Continuing

(Stein 26)

It is a difficult thing to commence answering something and them.

Anne did not come back again and she was not suffering.

Donger said that what that one had been doing and saying and repeating had been annoying.

They all liked asking that any one who decides what is decided decides.

He determined to ask something that he had just asked.

Another came and one left and another left and everybody did.

This can be common.

This can be convincing.

This can be perplexing.

It is not disturbing that three who have come do not to tell it again and one can tell it again and one can be interesting then.

Henns had a brother.

The brother was prospering.

He was directing everything.

He and she have asked a question and gone.

It is not interesting when some one who is long and being long and doing
what he did not intend to do is not staying.

It is easy to begin again if repeating is anything.

He had been misunderstood and he said that he would repeat what some
who were not dead had not said.

That was what he had been saying.

It is easy enough not to be enjoying.

If it is not pleasing is it continuing?

Twenty freely composed sentences made up of words, phrases, and clauses obtained by "mining" a previous randomization of the on-screen lines of a randomization of the order of 43 paragraphs of Stein's LGB (*ASR* 214–18). Both randomizations utilized truly random numbers from *AMRD*. The number of sentences in the poem was determined by a random number. Words, etc., in each sentence came from various areas of the line-randomization. Structure words not found in the output were only inserted when all attempts to find suitable ones in the output proved unsuccessful.

New York: 14–16 July 1998

Enough of Them Who Walk Come Again

(Stein 27)

Enough of them who walk
walk quickly
and so there are very many.

If in having told a thing one has been appreciated
then one can want two who have come and gone to have had that feeling.
If all did what they turned to do they would all stay wherever they went.

Each one is saying when it is to be decided
that that which is to be decided is to be decided.
It is disappointing
that some one is not saying one has forgotten something.
Clellan not staying was something.

Clellan staying was something.
It is not very disappointing that it would be finished
in the way it came to be finished.
All who have a way of not completing, and any one having a way of
not completing is any one, all are having a way of not completing some time.
Each one is saying everything that each one is saying.

That did happen. That did not happen. It is kindly to be friendly.
It is pleasant to be repeating what every one could be hearing.
What he said meant something.

It is charming that some one says Antliss was not successful.
Antliss expected to be returning having been answering.
Antliss was not successful in urging every one
to be the one hearing. It was a happy way
the way he stayed all day any day.

It is agreeable to be hearing that
and he said what they are repeating.
Some one who is waiting is going to ask if he will be visited.

They all stand
and they all open what has been open. It is exciting to be tired
and to sit and tell all about everything. Then he said
that he had not been understood
and that he would not ask anything. He did this thing
and might have asked what they heard
and he did not
because he was not asking anything again. He said
that he had gone and that he had seen what is lacking
and that he would be seeing
all that there is to be seen. All who are tired
and are hearing what they are hearing
are expecting to know
that when he asked if something was something
he did know
that an answer that came
might come again
and he did say
that any answer that came
might come again. He would come again.

Seven strophes comprising twenty-eight freely composed sentences made up of words, phrases, and clauses obtained by "mining" a previous randomization of the order of the on-screen lines of a randomization of the order of 43 paragraphs of Stein's LGB (*ASR* 214–18). Both randomizations utilized truly random numbers from *AMRD*. Words, etc., in the sentences came from various areas of the line-randomization. The number of sentences in the whole poem was determined by a random number. The number series 1, 2, 3, 4, 5, 6, 7 determined the number of sentences in successive strophes, and a die toss determined each strophe's placement on the page. Structure words not found in the source text were only inserted when all attempts to find suitable ones in the output proved unsuccessful.

New York: 14–16 July 1998; 23 February, 12 March, 19 December 1999

When He Came Again
He Would Say
What He Had Just Been
Wearing

(Stein 28)

When he came again he would say something badly chosen.
He
was
holding
all
he
was
expecting
to
be
able
to
hold
of
everything.
He was one discovering that he would not ask again.

Donger saw where it stays and if it stays where it says is it what it has been? He was directing and he was accidentally dying and he said that if it meant something he was successful.

Henns
did
not
come
back.

If it was a long time being living coming and leaving
It might be the thing that they all would not hear.

All
that
there
was
if
some
said
what
they
said
was
what
they
all
did
if
he
married
again
and
he
need
not
have
done
it.

He did not keep everything
and some did not hear everything
and some did not see everything then.

Do
so
as
quickly
as
some
one

else
would
do
something
that
one
had
come
to
do.

They did what they did and said that he had not seen what he had seen.
If it is not existing is it continuing?

If
it
is
what
it
is
then
it
is
easy
enough
to
stay.

He was pleased to hear that we ate all we ate.
He did not take what he had intended to take.

He
was
pleased
to
hear
that
what
he
said

had
that
meaning.
It
is
saddening
that
someone
had
put
something
back
and
had
gone
then
and
had
come
to
leave
nothing
that
he
had
given
every
one.

Something
is
something.
It was all very well for him to have asked
what he had been remembering
and not to have been admitting
anything that one was working on
and that then something certainly had happened

and someone was working.
In the beginning one saying something
and doing something
was likely working
and certainly knew
that something had happened
when anything had happened
and that we had left
what we had left.
Anne Helbing is standing.
Then
certainly
something
has
happened.
Henns
had
a
father
and
a
brother.
Anne Helbing in standing was wearing what had come.
His
father
was
prospering.
Anne Helbing had them on and she was standing.
If he was asked he said perhaps it is perhaps it isn't.
Anne was standing and sitting.
Is it or isn't it pleasing not to be enjoying them?
Anne
Helbing
was
wearing
the

things
she
had
just
been
wearing
and
he
said
that
if
he
had
been
asked
he
would
have
had
to
tell
each
one
what
he
had
told
one
whom
the
things
she
had
just
been
wearing

had
belonged
to.

If he and she had just been wearing something
he was pleased to hear this and she was too.

He
came
to
get
what
he
asked
for
and he
did
not.
He
came
to
get
what
he
had
just
been
wearing.

Thirty-three freely composed sentences made up of words, phrases, and clauses obtained by "mining" a previous randomization of the on-screen lines of a randomization of the order of 43 paragraphs of Stein's LGB (*ASR* 214–18). Both randomizations utilized truly random numbers from *AMRD*. Words, etc., in the sentences came from various areas of the line-randomization. The number of sentences in the whole poem was determined by a random number. The placement and orientation of each sentence were determined by a die toss.

New York: 17–18 July 1998

When Is Enough?

(Stein 29)

When we had not said all that we had been feeling he told each one what each one wanted to know and where to get any answer later.

If the one saying all was then saying all would they then say when they would come? If any one can determine what they are saying what are they saying? Who asked him who he was?

The thing that he came to get is not amusing.
They were feeling what they were feeling.
Saying what

he asked he
was pleased
to hear that
we asked
what we
asked.
Antliss was
not living.

One asked and he did not commence answering. One heard and another one heard and he did not. Donger said that he saw what he said meant something. He was prospering when he received what he received and when he did he began being living. Any one can be one. If some one came and another one came when did some one come to be dead? Some one said there would be enough if every one was being one admitting something and saying what he was hearing.

He was doing what he was doing and he was determining what he was saying. Not every one who was saying all would then say enough. If every one was being convincing what were they all saying to one another? One said and some saw what they had been admitting. Any one is one being and any one is one being convincing. If it is not pleasing to be enjoying what are they doing? They are determining that if it came again an answer would come and if it came it might not come again. Pulling and going is regularly sounding and answering is intermittently funny. Donger asked if he could go where that easy thing is existing. This is not certain. He was pleased to hear that we knew something.

That is open. He had looked at what they had looked at and continued seeing what he was seeing. Determining what he was doing he did not have very many children. Running and disappearing and gesticulating he was hearing what he was hearing. We were enjoying what was not being convincing. Some who were not successful would be continuing feeling pleasing. That one was older. One has pleasantly explained everything. What they are pleased to hear is that we knew what he knew. One's purpose in enjoying being pleasing then and saying something and doing something is to be efficiently existing and saying what is truly efficiently existing. He did not need answering enough to be repeating what he could ask. Being older was doing that thing remembering that he was not asking to have any more children. He remembered enough. Certainly if there is any one feeling what every one is feeling one could say that they had heard all that they heard. One is said not to expect that it is an easy thing not to hear what they are hearing. Not to repeat what they can not complete George did not come back when he had not had all that he would have. It is astonishing that some one was not expecting something that he is hearing. What would he ask if he knew what he knew?

Doing was not repeating. All that has been told is exciting. Being and saying what he liked Donger knew about it and he did all he would do when he saw all there was to see in looking for everything and finding everything. Urging all he could urge in explaining the way he was he was waiting for something astonishing. Being was being long enough. All who have left have not come again. Henns was prospering that is to say that he had a wife and a baby. Donger knew enough to remember that. The brother continued not being annoying. Some are not asking what they might be asking. Admitting that talking and not turning and quietly answering and not seeing is disturbing they do not like to be tired and not to be expecting any one to be coming. Polly was not using all she had bought. If he said that he knew what he would not hear to make any one remember all of the thing that was seen when some did not see what they saw is it pleasing that some one has heard something? All that he kept when he thought this was not all he had was not all he had. Is some one copying something? Coming again they are saying it is something he is hearing and then explaining. They will ask if his waving and showing what he is imitating is what he likes to do. They all ask and they all do not refuse to open all Polly is offering. If every one is saying one laughing might be meaning that they were feeling that some one was a being living and waiting what had he arranged to feel? All and every one is saying enough. He had been sick. That we are coming is not very likely. Clellan did not stay. Ask what he had asked when he came. They were dead. Polly did not remember everything. Every one is saying what happened. He was not asking and he did not need to remember when he was where he was and he did not continue when he did what he did. To have seen what they have seen is enough.

Seventy-three freely composed sentences made up of words, phrases, and clauses obtained by "mining" a previous randomization of the on-screen lines of a randomization of the order of 43 paragraphs of Stein's LGB (*ASR* 214–18). Both randomizations utilized truly random numbers from *AMRD*. The sentences are divided into seven paragraphs. The numbers of sentences in the successive paragraphs follow the Lucas sequence 1, 3, 4, 7, 11, 18, 29. The margins of the paragraphs were determined by chance operations involving random numbers. Words, etc., in the sentences came from various areas of the line-randomization.

New York: 17–19 July 1998

Some Did Not See Who Had Come

(Stein 30)

Some did not see everything. Clellan stayed and hoped to ask what she would give to anyone laughing. A little one was preparing to give what she had stayed and hoped to ask whether she should give to Clellan. He found a thing that one could enjoy. He is a little one expressing very much. If they heard that said they would not repeat it. There would be enough. Sender did not stay long when they had seen enough. That is the other way. That is the same way. Everyone who has come is not pleasing.

Quickly walking and sufficiently eating they all did leave all they had. He talked when he talked very much and it was not satisfying. They are seeing all that is being said about what another did and one heard. Sender came and he said that Anne told someone what she had had them on and was sitting. Some are dead. Having been feeling that one was living one saw what another saw. Any one going away would notice something.

If he had gone everywhere he could go he would not be needing to be wearing what some said he was wearing. He who made a motion to call someone made a noise. Everyone talking did not intend to finish everything. Sometimes remembering a thing is not very interesting and then it is exciting.

There what is truly expressing what anyone is sounds a little like what another has heard. Walking and talking is existing. What they said can be quite exciting.

Those who were not dead pleased everyone who'd come.

Twenty-six freely composed sentences made up of words, phrases, and clauses obtained by "mining" a previous randomization of the on-screen lines of a randomization of the order of 43 paragraphs of Stein's LGB (*ASR* 214–18). Both randomizations utilized truly random numbers from *AMRD*. The sequence of sentences is divided into five paragraphs. The numbers of sentences in the paragraphs follow the reverse Lucas-number sequence 11, 7, 4, 3, 1. The margins of the paragraphs were determined by chance operations involving random digits. Words, etc., in the sentences came from various areas of the line-randomization.

New York: 19 July 1998; 24 February, 19–23 March 2002

When He Did
He Thought
This Was Not Living A . . .

(Stein 31)

When he did.

When he had asked what they all liked Donger
saw where he could enjoy it. He was a little like what
each one was who was successful
and would not ask for an answer again. One heard
and hoped to ask
what she would be finished with the way it came
          and was going away
and when she would notice something.

Some did not.
He came to get what they were all standing for
and did that the same way.
Then every one was sounding like a little one preparing.
Do so quickly walking
and doing what they all would do if he would be visited.

They were
feeling. Saying what he knew? Doing
what some one says he is doing
perhaps it is not disturbing
when some one who is long says enough.
If everything that each one who is long is not seeing

is not being seen
is it continuing?
He came
and one can want two who have a way
    of not coming again. It is easy enough
to be wearing what they saw. Is it pleasing?

Quickly as one who was being pleasing he had
    asked when he was successful
    what he would be repeating.
All that he had had been annoying.
What are they then determining?
Henns did not intend to finish everything.
If it is what is deciding it decides.
He determined to ask with his waving
    whether he could go and would be hearing
    any one remembering that they had been
    answering something
    and certainly knew that answering
    is to be returning
    having been told a thing one had said
    and what one had had on when sitting.
All that we had had been misunderstood
    and they turned to ask
    what he was hoping to see
    in looking for something
    that had been annoying.
Sometimes we remembered the way
    he was wearing it
    and how someone had been feeling.
Saying what that one is hearing
    to be efficiently existing
    he did what they are saying is exciting
    when it is decided and is to be enjoyed

    when they are hearing
    and answering something.
Was it pleasant to be dead?
Some one was being convincing.

Did we knew that he would come?
Is any one feeling something?
Coming and saying something we are coming.
    Polly did not.
He came to get what had not satisfied.
They did what they had come to do.
Enough of the things she had seen. All who were tired
    and someone else
had come again.

He was pleased to hear that one who was tired
    hoped to ask something. Clellan
did not come again.
It is an easy thing if it means something
and Anne told some who did not see it anywhere
    it stays where he is directing everything.
After she'd been urging all the ones she'd just been
    wearing out and disappointing
that someone should make a motion to call someone
someone made a motion to call some one
copying something again and saying that she could say
    something certain.
Henns was prospering.
It was all very well for him to have been answering
    enough to be decided decided decided decided.
It is exciting to know where each one is feeling pleasing. Quickly
walking and not seeing
what had he arranged to feel?
All and everybody did.

Having left and having asked
he would be asked.

Antliss
expecting to give what another gave came
and going away would notice something.
What would they be saying everything?
Clellan staying when he had gone
it was then an easy thing
being a living one laughing.
A little like what the other one is doing
    when what he has is a father prospering.
Any one came to get what he liked to do.
They were feeling.
Saying what they said when they heard that meaning
that one wanted to know if they had decided
that that which was to be decided was to be decided. He determined
to ask what some one could want
and two who had been asked said he would not be
    convincing when another left and then everybody
    did. This can be quite exciting.
Being certainly had happened
and was it not to be decided that what he came to get
was not all he could enjoy?
Is he a little like what he would have been hearing
    had he not seen everywhere what it is to be
    repeating what they were doing not to have any
    more children?
Running certainly had happened
and he said that Anne had told what each one was
    feeling.
If he and she were not being too convincing
what was he?
She was not successful in urging that everything that
    had certainly happened had happened

and that they were hearing the meaning they
  were hearing. He was prospering
when he said what they said they heard him say when
  they were hearing it.
What he knew.
One's purpose being enjoying
they do not all refuse to open all that Polly is offering.
If he had been showing what he had just understood
and he did not.
Donger said that it meant something.
Coming and not turning having been feeling as he did he was asked
if he if he was successful
would do something to give every one
what he had given one.
Sometimes remember what we had left
if there is any one left remembering that.
He was not completing
all that any one was having
and he did not. Donger knew enough
to remember what was being said
and that one would come to get what she would be
  continuing to feel that any one might answer for
  later.
If that one says
Antliss
was not asking.
Admitting and saying that all of that thing is existing
some had not said that all he was
was not all he had belonged to.
If he and she refuse to open all that Polly was not
  remembering and doing
what are they saying that he is hearing?
Not to repeat what some one saw and what he is
  hearing
quietly answer whoever will come.
If any one is said

not to keep everything.
Not every one that they had heard answering
and leaving
is pleasing.

Quickly
some one had been remembering
that what he had come to get
was certainly not what he had had on
and saying what we would not have asked.
Another did not come again.
Donger said that he was feeling that some one who was
  not dead had not been saying that.
Then he had certainly heard
and hoped to ask if she had a way
of not completing something
and if he had not been saying what he had
that would have told one that he knew something.
This can be coming
and it is not disturbing that one could go where he
  could go
and they would all stay wherever they were feeling one
  laughing.
Or else a little one would come again.
Pulling and waiting for something too
he had been asked who he was. It is astonishing.
Being what he did
did he begin being a living one admitting something
  was badly chosen? He had looked at what was
  being said about every one. Sometimes
remember that.
The brothers' way. That did happen. That did happen. It is an easy
thing that is not very likely working.
In the beginning one saw what they had seen
  enough of. Sender

was not being convincing and what he could go to
          he would not have had happen.
Was he pleasantly explaining something that he was?
The thing that he liked asking
that easy thing
was not to be finished by anything.
He was directing everything. Clellan
was not turning and doing anything
and if he meant something to commence
he was not doing very much. If they heard.
One is saying that
to ask what she had just been wearing
and what we knew and what he had seen
and what it then was and is very much
or perhaps it isn't.
Anne Helbing is someone who is
someone
and doing what she likes to do.
They all ask whether he is waving and some one
          is putting something there something
that they then say they have when they have it.
He talked when he did not hear anything. He
was prospering.
It is disappointing that each one is feeling what one was
          asked and not turning
having been told that a thing is existing.
He was pleased
by everything. Clellan staying.
Not to repeat what he had bought.
If he was showing what we had left.
Anne Helbing
is existing.
That he was prospering
was what he was not expecting to know
and he was not expecting to know that we were coming   again
and that another one can be coming. Polly did not keep everything.

Urging all they would turn to do they went.
Each one is one being
and finding every one by whom the thing is remembered
all of them are saying it.
It is not very likely working. In the beginning
one saying what he saw and all that they had heard
did not commence to answer that.
The brother was prospering doing what he liked to do.
They were feeling what they were feeling.
If it is perhaps it isn't.
Anne Helbing was living. Antliss
was not suffering.
Any one may be one being convincing.
That we had been sick.

That did not. He came to get an answer
and doing something then
some one said what was there.
Was it a difficult thing that they had looked at
    and were continuing to?
He came and it meant something astonishing.
If being was not to be using all there was
then was it to be enjoying being pleasing?
Anne Helbing was some one he liked to do.
They all do not repeat that they had been asked
    where he had gone
and everywhere he was
he was hearing and expecting anything
and talking
and certain. He was prospering.
If he was not using all that had just been understood
and sitting and telling all that every one was hearing
and expecting
did we know what he had not said? That did happen.
That did happen. It is easy enough.

He had left them
for they were dead.
Polly was not asking
and then
it was an easy disappointing thing that he had seen.
If it is perhaps it isn't. If Anne Helbing
in standing
was wearing what had been appreciated
then it was not very likely.
Clellan would not have been be needing to have asked.
Another left
and every one had to have been admitting what one
          coming and going away would have.
It is not very likely. Clellan
not completing something
was going to ask whether something had happened
but has not said so. That was not asking.
Admitting something
they said that with all they had
they had not been staying
and another came again with an answer
and was not asked again.
It is astonishing that they might come back
and he thought that if this was not using all
then something was.
Every one can determine to ask if he married again
and an answer that came might be about the things she
          had just been wearing.
He was one discovering that they had heard that what
          he would not be being was long enough.
If every one is saying enough. He certainly knew
that some one had come and had not heard everything
and might have a way of not coming again. Donger asked what they
were pleased to hear and we asked if he
          was not suffering. Anne did not happen to come
and when he asked if she had married again

they were all open about it and then
it was the other one who was prospering.

It was being annoying.
They were dead.
Polly does not stay long when it is not pleasing.
Quickly walking he did not need to be friendly.
It is not very interesting
anything.
Every one was being and gone. It is easy enough to stay.
He was determining that he was hearing something that
 had been misunderstood
and that Anne had told some one
that some one had come to get what they could
and would do something if he was prospering.
Antliss was not asking.
Admitting that he would come to leave all they had
 arranged to. If he said that
perhaps it is exciting.
Being annoying.
Some are not asking whether there is to be a returning
and every one would be pleased to hear
and to make any one hear
if there were.
We were enjoying being pleasing and they all will if he
 will be visited. They did what had to be done
and came to leave all he had told one who had come
 they would
but he was not successful in urging anything.
He had been feeling that she would not ask again and
 had gone everywhere where getting is not
 amusing. This can be perplexing.
It is charming that it is to be finished in the way it
 might have come to be if he had done it.

He did not question that there are very many children.
Running and talking
any one going
was regularly sounding
and as he did
he began to be convincing.
Some were not successful in urging anything.
If he said that he was pleased to hear
that it was not likely to be coming
and that some one was expressing the thought
that what he had just been wearing
was not at all what he could go anywhere to get
if any answer was enough to be efficiently explaining
          what they had looked at
what had he gone everywhere to get?
He was doing what we asked when we were eating.
He did this thing that is not very interesting
when he asked if he will be visited.
They were feeling that he was holding all that he had
          gone to ask for
and he said perhaps it is an easy thing
not to be coming and going away
and it would be enough to remember the thing
and remembering it
they all did what there was to do to be repeating what
          had happened when he asked if they knew.
Was doing it
wearing what they did and saying so?
When he came to be enjoying being long
and doing something
they would certainly do something and quietly answer
enough. Certainly
if there was no repeating
then some did not intend to finish everything.
Urging all
would be an easy thing to begin again

if repeating what she had asked and what he was
expected to know was not successful.

Antliss was not asking. Admitting any one is saying all
would not be being annoying. That one was successful. Antliss was
not living and quietly answering that.
The brother was prospering
but he was not being convincing.
If it is not a very difficult thing that is lacking
and to be going is to be returning
then he need not because he has.
Is it certainly not something?

Coming again
she was a long time being convincing. If he had
just been wearing what he would have been
would that have been enough? Some were not dead
that had not been wearing what we were expecting
them to and some did know that we knew
that he had not had all that another one could have been coming
for again. It is not suffering.

If he and she had just been wearing that.
He and she had asked and said enough. That
one was pleased to hear that we knew
that another one could determine that they had seen
that they could not stay long when not successful in
urging anything.

It is charming
that easy thing that said what he had just been wearing.

What they might not commence to answer later.
If that one had come to leave all that
it would have been enough. All who have left
and every one who is said not to have been wearing
what they were wearing were the ones another saw.

Any one feeling pleasing?
Quickly walking is not very likely. Clellan stayed all day
any day. It is an easy thing existing.

That one had put something where it continued to be
seen.
Determining
is deciding.
He determined that one had forgotten
something badly chosen. He had been annoying.
That was not all he would be repeating
when he was determining
that every one talking and talking was going to be
going to know that someone had been sick.
We asked if some had then said something.
Clellan not staying
was something.

If it is easy to begin again one can be quite exciting.
That is being long enough to stay. Ask whether
she would not be asking what they had said
and whether we knew something that had been said
and whether they were feeling pleasing. Quickly walking
she is going to ask something.
If what he said meant something and he had gone back
then he had not seen what happened when he thought

this was not all that had happened. He was pleasantly
existing. What he knew. One's purpose in enjoying that is to be
enjoying being long and sufficiently
existing. That is to be enjoying what she should be
giving to Clellan were he staying. Not everything
gesticulating
had belonged to him.
Were he and she waiting
when he said perhaps it is easy enough?

If everything
that he did was not was he?
He came but he did not continue. Who asked if he said
that talking did not complete anything? Is each one
ever not disturbing what has been? He was prospering.
If it is perhaps it isn't. Anne was older.
One has been told it is exciting to have come
but not to tell each one who is admitting it.
Any one
may be said not to be continuing
to feel what it is to be one saying that they had come to
    leave all that he did not come for again. Pulling
is doing something. Clellan.
He found the thing was something badly chosen.
He remembered when he'd talked and when he'd asked
    what they all were saying when we knew that
    something had certainly happened.
It was pleasant to be deciding what he could ask. Being
    older was prospering.
He was doing and finding everything. Clellan
would not have done it. He did not turn
and someone was working on and on
and everything was gone.

He was one discovering that any one and anything
is intermittently funny.
Donger asked him what he'd heard,
One is saying it might be the thing that we'd asked
when he said he meant something was something.
If all did what he had said
that was not all they would have. It is not pleasing
that one was being living
and doing something
when he did not come back.
If it was a happy way the way he stayed
and he said that he would come when one had left
could any one say anything astonishing that he had
decided was decided?
Is it not pleasing to be returning
having been told that a thing is continuing?
Is it exciting to be repeating what he had been
answering?
Donger knew about it and was hearing and repeating it.
Would they notice something there? Coming
and standing
and waiting
he did not see what he had.
Is some one being living
and can one then
tell it again if repeating has happened?
It is not pleasing
to be regularly sounding
and he said
they all were open about what was being pleasing.
That we ate.
He did not stay long when something was badly chosen.
He remembers that.
The brother came and another one came
to get what would finish
everything that meant something. Coming again

and answering.
He did not see what every one saw. Someone
was not to be returning
so all there would come to be tired
when he did come to say all that
talking
and repeating it. There is where it stays
if it stays
but will it stay
if it is not existing? What they said
can be done.
If some one heard something.
Regularly talking and hearing sounding is not pleasing.
He was pleasantly explaining. It can be interesting
that he had a brother who came again and left
and every one was saying it was a happy way
the way he stayed
and saying what he had just been wearing and what had
certainly happened to them.
Anne Helbing had been appreciated
and then one came to get what another one saw.
Every one is saying that it might have been asked
and that he had said what had happened
when anything did.
He did not need to remember when he thought this was
not living a . . .

Twenty-one paragraph/strophes made up of sentences composed by running Stein 26, 27, 28, 29, and 30 through the program TRAVESTY, a program written in about 1980 by Hugh Kenner and Joseph O'Rourke, who published an early version in *BYTE* magazine in 1981. It draws word groups from source texts by a process that depends upon letter-sequence frequencies in English. It can produce seven "orders" of "Travesties," running from Order 3 (the least like normative discourse) to Order 9 (the most like normative discourse). The user of TRAVESTY can specify the order of the Travesty to be produced as well as the number of characters in it. I did this by a combination of choice and two kinds of chance operations. I opted for one of the three "higher orders" of Travesties, 7, 8, or 9, and selected Order 8 by a die throw.

Next, I opted for a Travesty comprising less than 20,000 characters and biased the possibilities upwards by selecting as a number source the 200,000 five-digit sequences of random digits constituting the Rand table. I obtained one of these by random-digit chance operations and changed its first digit to 1, since it was an odd number (had it been an even number, I would have changed it to 0) to stay below 20,000, arriving at 17,138. Then I ran the two-step randomization of the source text described above through TRAVESTY, asking for an Order-8 Travesty of 17,138 characters.

Next, I grouped the resultant 265 sentences, some normative, others non-normative, into 21 paragraph/strophes having the following sequence of numbers of sentences in them: 1, 3, 4, 7, 11, 18, 29, 47, 29, 18, 11, 7, 4, 3, 1, 3, 4, 7, 11, 18, 29. This can be described as three interlocked Lucas sequences, ascending, descending, and finally ascending. The Lucas sequence (1, 3, 4, 7, 11, 29, 47, 76, 123, 199, 322, etc.), each of whose members after the second is the sum of the two previous numbers, was developed (and first published in 1880) by the French mathematician André Lucas as a means of testing for Mersenne prime numbers. Since 265 falls between 196 (the sum of the numbers in the Lucas sequence from 1 through 76) and 319 (the sum of 196 and 123, the next number in the sequence), I tested sequences of interlocking ascending and descending sequences until I found this one, the sum of whose members happens to be exactly equal to 265. Next, I either accepted or revised each of the TRAVESTY-given sentences and pseudo-sentences. The revisions were liminally guided by a complex of criteria encouraging and constraining the changes made in TRAVESTY's output. Finally, I chose a text width of 3.5″, with asymmetrical margins of 1″ and ~4″ (the right-hand one being "ragged") and carefully adjusted the line breaks within it, guided by a number of liminally determined criteria.

New York: 22 July–8 August 1998; 24 February 1999

Pleasant to Be Repeating Very Little of This

(Stein 32)

Pleasant to be repeating what they went to.

~

Each one is saying
that that did happen.
It is charming that merriment differently.
Sample pressure comes and an *and* sings.

~

Enough of them were repeatedly turning. What
did Antliss intend to be looking for?
Living
not showing length
is breadth
and breadth is one
pleasant time discussing celery bread
where no pears to abuse
obliged
four
houses.
Pleasantly deranged.

~

The that.
The whole way there
will be a clear
lovesong piece.
Sample pressure concluded
mentioning what love permitted.
Peculiar materials leave particular people peculiarways.
From here and there to there.
Excess pressure deranged him
and refusing

he certainly mentioned saying *no more talking* from there to there.
Little comes more than the best.

~

That necessity was dearest
that he had intermittently
but others would like doing very often what was lacking in what had been done
and saying to one another again
that he did not say that an answer that came
might come again
and that he did not know what was to be decided.
It is agreeable to be hearing that.
Was what he said that he was
not enough?
Seeing meaning there
filled her with the merriment
cooked pears show.
All say this is better
and not longer.
Whisper so the cooks
choose to come.
Their having gone there
would have meant doing it the way that showed when it was filled.
This is the beer. *Bake it well*
are conviction's best most deepening words.
Certainly mentioned. Thickness.

~

Pleasant celery there
is the matter there
when larger pleasant fried breadth
is talking there.
All they hear there is all that talking.
The very thing one liked
was being.
Hearing things
could be answering truly completer beginnings.
Ask the little fish

growing better with fire.
Children saying things
could have been saying what one was urging.
Tell that there
when the house there
is better than the best.

~

There love permitted mentioning the bread.
Making it that way
showed that being was growing a little lighter.
All time clears excess samples nicely.
The maker is that
that is to be finished.

~

Father is asking if one has forgotten something about being easy.
Staying there will be a clear
lovesong piece.
Place every answer that comes.

~

Little celery chooses little lighting.

~

This and an *and* sing much.
Little as each is certain
some meanings are the best.
All and any and then that
mean that many are obliged.

~

They are not.
Some of the whole way there
the meaning did not happen.
That had not been understood
so they were not successful.
Antliss was not successful.

~

In urging Antliss to continue standing
wherever another one had been

she answered that any answer that might come
might come again
and he did know
that when he asked if something did
they would call one another.
Some one answering talk she intended to hear
said that Antliss intended to be looking
seeing
and staying away.
Begin big singing no more.
The days and the places there.
The.

~

There nothing clearly sings
that celery is happy.
Every beginning was something that one would be hearing when things
were obliging.
They and a *the* all stand.
There is lengthy laughter
lightning's color.
The bigger wish is to be making that.
Each one is saying when meeting them
that they have had enough talking and saying.
Then what has been taken to have meant
that doing that means
coming and saying things
when one is obliged to?
Surely little was cooked.
So talking about food was being easy.
Staying there filled with merriment
she sees to it that noise is placed well away.
That the dearest singing laughter length be breadth
is one
pleasant wish.
There most days from time to time
the best pieces are discussed

and a few conclude that that there
noise and use are one.
Happy peculiar singing laughter length
    is enough to have finished.

~

All who have a way of not completing singing
will have no more beginning.
It is of them
one of them
that one will sing.
The whole way there will be a clear lovesong piece.
Place every answer that comes.
Little potatoes are certainly of better breadth
but talking there where one can want what has been appreciated
one can want two who have a way of not completing anything.
Something was something about being existing ones
that might have been.
She says those things when obliging four houses.

~

A pleasant growing light
clearly has the better breadth.
Pleasantly deranged necessity.
Descriptions there are none.
No deranged fish will follow pressure.

~

Only potatoes mentioning love are permitted. Meaning there was filled with
    merriment.
Simple difference
did cause material description.

~

Description is truly a necessity.

~

The greens are fried the same way they are often fried in that little place
    where nothing is clear.

Happy peculiar people are peculiar.
This pressure deranged
all the thickened potatoes
        that had been mentioned

~

Thickness.
The pleasantly deranged
would be completing it some time.
Each one was not very disappointing.
That was enough.

~

See what they might have been.
She says the opening. The *the*. All that is there
is all that time the best.
Singing that some one says Antliss is completing it
does any one any time have any?
Each one is saying what that one liked being.
Completer singing mentioned that rhubarb
is certainly the best.

~

Come sit and leave the light much larger there.
Pleasant wishes.
There
then there
the house is more than conviction's best most deepening word.
Certainly
the better matter there was opened with not much of this thought that
        pleased them not.
Expressing what they are are hearing
this and an *and* sing much.
Little was surely cooked.
So the food was talking about being easy.
Staying with things nicely
the maker is that that is there.
Every happening has a door.

That.
This is the beer.

~

Bake it well and with conviction.
Most certainly pears are best.
A piece of description.
Figs stayed all day. The singer there
comes singing as is mentioned there
to whomever is there.
Every happening.
Coming they call one another
expressing in what they are saying
something that means thickness's better times
will not abuse any peculiar material descriptions necessity chooses
pleasant
regular
neat.

~

Peas and an *and* gave that much fish
saying necessity's dearest would likely refuse
half of what was there
like green
peas'
descriptions.
So let it be concluded.
Still eating all that's there.
Little potatoes
deranged and refusing
are urging Henns to be decided.

~

It is there.
All time clears excess samples nicely
singing of long red pears.
Pears that are pleasantly fried.

~

Where it is four it is completer.

~

Last time there.
Every happening
happy and eaten.
Happy peculiar singing is mentioned.

~

Thickness is not cooked pears.
Such a time shows necessity.
Every piece of a whole preceder
gave pressure.
What whole?

~

Pleasant permitting makes for louder excess.
Children hear excess differently.
Did time's
happy peculiar people
stay to have more time
happy and eaten?
Nothing is not no having.
Differences long concluded are mentioned there.
Every pleasant kind of celery bread but no pears.
There the house is more than those who come to it.

~

There's little time left
for fishing for pears.
Refuse refusal's pleasant deranged necessity.
Every beginning of light.
Children color light and cloth
with dearest descriptions' necessity.
Every piece of the whole of time
shows its own necessity.
A pleasant blanket is marking a smiling soiling.
That follows the little ways
children are saying it is there.
Where children color light
conviction's the best most deepening word.

They're certainly little.
Refined matter
is opened there.
There's very little of this.

~

A poem of 29 stanzas derived from my poems "Stein 2, 27, 3, 24, 6, and 9," merged in that order after being selected by random-digit chance operations utilizing *AMRD* from among the first 31 poems of my Stein series and then run through TRAVESTY, the program having been asked for an order-9 Travesty of 6,378 characters (these numbers having also been selected by random-digit chance operations). The output was revised a number of times, but the given sentence order and most lexical morphemes were preserved. Prosodic criteria determined line breaks. The sequence of numbers of sentences in successive stanzas comprises seven interlinked alternately ascending and descending sequences of the first five numbers of the Lucas sequence.

New York: 3–5 August 1998

Sometimes
Going On Enough

(Stein 33)

Sometimes.

That one way having answers,
what we feel they saw,
and having been asking seeing,
they were seeing,
was that there seen being.

About any and all are taking to living again,
urged Antliss.

Antliss's way is one way,
and they that would be hearing one and one
are gone
or pleasing something,
which might be meaning anything laughing,
and laughing might be meaning funny walking.

Walking and talking.

Being regularly,
quietly,
having been going on enough to be exciting,
this,
this something,
was offering standing,
standing to some,
to those who who wanted to be having it.

Anne is asking to be visited,
asking,
asking again anything,
saying one,
one,
one that some are disappointing,
some that are said to be amusing,
two to whom things have been doing
something—
that they—
what an easy easy finish he said,
and again and again was asking enough—
enough.

Enough regularly.

Being something.

That was the seen.

When some that one was saying were all
would be staying,
need one have been something,
done something,
made something,
something admittedly exciting and sometimes,
sometimes,
staying?

That one way having the answer,
we felt what they saw,
and were asking whether they were seeing,
seeing that there seen being.

Any
and all of them

have taken to urging Antliss
to take a hold of himself and start living again.

Antliss's way was one,
and they that would have been hearing that one—
that one gone—
were pleasing.

Something meant anything laughing.

Laughing might be meaning funny walking,

Walking might be talking.

Being,
regularly,
quietly,
has been going on enough.

Derived from Stein's LGB (*ASR* 214–18) which was run through DIASTEX5, using as seed a paragraph of Stein's OOD (*ASR* 125, para 4). The program's output was variously revised and edited, within appropriate constraints.

New York: 9–15 August 1998; 17 January, 17 December 1999

Time the Three
Discovering Something
Something

(Stein 34)

Time the.

Clellan might not not much talked. Suffering comes back. Come
received.
To more be hearing one.
Antliss feeling be he.

All visited commenced discovering something
something happening.

That.
That staying went. Might he? That thing convincing convincing.
Hearing what can was saying doing. Some came something.
Something upsetting suffering directing to children.

Hearing what could not would feeling could be hearing?

Easy existing back again question pleasing pleasantly.
Exciting to to all and anything one enjoying one something
that they had easy and continuing not something something.
To do began he one and they know one who answering continuing.

Running waiting.

Talking showing what imitating made he that been staying waiting.
Meeting what each was coming sometimes
sometimes happen completing youngest

completing complete
pleasantly pleasantly.
If in not interesting interesting decides decides intermittently.
Discovering discovering remembering that not.

He remembered very youngest some youngest doing youngest
youngest.

Youngest accidentally one. One every.
Antliss.
Antliss and they would that they they of and are what they who.
Waiting easy answering and left kindly returning.
That likely pleased. One pleased had asked understood.
That what that turned had be very youngest not youngest
being enough youngest youngest youngest one.
In the saying that been had saying and can common
some came then.

Would be were feel. Would for bought forgetting everything.

Without prospering prospering prospering to children
hearing what hearing were were one.
All and expecting pleasant repeating some something gone
has had and not some not again and anything meant he that
meant meaning walking.
Talking were was answering
not not little repeat.
He something make remember remembering
remembering remembering remembering determining.

Determining then there dead certainly hear see what
said was.

The what seen one all had give satisfying upsetting.
One one feeling was had was not some not
for not married long.

Sender expecting forgotten. Disappointing disturbing everything.
Told thing again that has been were say easy or enjoying.
Then been he said meant doing one and they hear has have
          finished again eating badly.
He pleased been.
If and.

That the seen feel saw some seeing perplexing
          kindly leave disturbing.

Have having again.
Asking stay they they has can
          and can not.
Came likely them so being very regularly gesticulating.
Some asked remember remembering remembering remembering
          remembering determining determining then there.
Dead certainly hear see certainly day. Day would bought.
Brother directing received. Remember that what knew.
One and they what when enough have have and not told.
Not.
Being regularly seeing been asked some noise went would make.
Was one one the was then who coming going youngest?
Clellan asked being get some suffering kept purpose discovering.

Donger complete convincing.

Convincing convincing
That what that that married he that when continued continue.
Hearing in is expecting existing thing existing something.
Pleasing pleasing exciting could something could?
Would would be decided quickly just this that answering?
Surprised quiet copying preparing discovering.
Donger complete convincing convincing convincing saying
          doing common repeating saying what seeing what he
          gone that one and to.

They are seen being been using standing.
Things living did have accidentally urging urging.
All in and said they they were came visited friendly.
Disturbing gone again pleasing something.

Something.

Something something if know be determine said meaning.
Enough one and they felt way and again eating seeing
    is and made he that been staying waiting meeting feel.
Saw and asking seeing seeing all any and married he
    that when continued continue hearing.

Antliss.

Antliss and going are they repeating existing existing pleasant.
Charming meant he that meant meaning walking talking
    and one and feeling was and again eating seeing
    and one and badly.
He noise then going.
That the seen when as one saying that anything anything exciting
    annoying be.

Be this youngest being feel saw and give
would.

Anne.
Anne had.
Helbing was have living again. Urging might be again being difficult.
Commence hearing some that one what has has then that when.
When one in one not to interesting can not something
    purpose likely pleased
    understood sometimes pleasantly.
Pleasantly finish said and again. Again asking stay they.
They what has just this thing one meaning knew.

Knew looked. Knew staying waiting meeting then what?

That quite enough. Everybody there every everything.
One another one came not would feel would be seen.
Give.
Prospering been have something anything existing.
Existing meant he that meant meaning walking talking.
Be meaning.
This doing going easily expressing existing
    existing something sometimes.
Clellan anything.
Some what they was saying
    was that that one
    being something.
It said would perplexing not bought not youngest leaving often
    being being going youngest enough complete to came.
Asked that not because he.

All did beginning that said one and one then.

There everybody.
Married not.
Not might commence answering.
Commencing easy come repeat they to be be one.
One one been he all.
Again three discovering something.
Something.

Derived from Stein's LGB (*ASR* 214–18) which was run through DIASTEX5, using as seed a paragraph of Stein's OOD (*ASR* 125, para 3). In order to allow DIASTEX5 to go through one complete period, one word from the seed (the same one) was added to each of the first nine sentences of the source, as determined by random-digit operations. The words and word order of the program's output were left unchanged, but capital letters, punctuation, and line and strophe breaks in addition to those already in the output were added. The numbers of verse lines in strophes came from the Lucas sequence 1, 3, 4, 7, 11: one-verse-line strophes alternate with strophes of 3, 4, 7, or 11 verse lines. Indented lines continue verse lines begun above them. When the poem is published, all lines are to be broken and indented exactly as given here. Every line break indicates a short pause: those at verse-line endings last a little longer than those within verse lines and strophe-break pauses last still longer.

New York: 16–19 August 1998; 15 January 1999; 24 April 2000

Time the Existing Meeting To

(Stein 35)

Time the.

Clellan anything. One everything. One and
to.

They are seen feel saw some not would. Anne
had. Helbing was then who coming gone again. Urging
might not married long.

Sender expecting existing
in is expecting existing meeting then there everybody.
Married he that married long. Sender expecting
that one and not told. Not. Being remembering
to children. Hearing what he gone then there dead
certainly day. Day would make.

Was one one being feel
saw and again? Asking showing what said meaning
waiting existing that what imitating meeting feel
would perplexing kindly leave disturbing? Have have
accidentally urging. Antliss feeling walking.
Be meaning walking talking. Then been had saying was
answering something going youngest being difficult.
Commence hearing what what they was saying was
and give satisfying upsetting existing existing.
One another directing to children. Hearing what they
what each was coming going easily expressing existing
then that meaning. This doing going youngest

being be. Be this thing if know one what each was
coming sometimes happen completing convincing.

Hearing. Commence hearing what the seen one in one
in one in one in one not again eating seeing what
seen one and to. They are seen. Give. Prospering
that turned had be very regularly seeing perplexing
not some seeing something something something something
happening. Talking went. Might he? That staying
and one and to. They what could not would that
meaning. Enough have have something. One one feeling
waiting. One and feeling was had was not some
something going youngest youngest youngest youngest?
Clellan anything comes back. Come received. Remembering
that meant meant meant meant he that not
youngest. Youngest complete to came. Asked that
one and not would perplexing not because he. All visited
friendly.

Disturbing everything again question
pleased understood some youngest? Clellan might
not not not much talked. Suffering some not to interesting
then what? That they they. They are seen
feel would for bought not little repeating existing
pleasantly. Disturbing everything if know one
who answering been have accidentally urging urging.
All in and can common some not to intermittently.
Pleasantly finish said meaning. Determining that
has just this youngest? Clellan asked something.
It said would for bought forgetting.

One pleasantly
pleasantly pleased. One one. All and expecting pleasing
pleased understood. That that not youngest.
Youngest doing. To do began he one that when as one
one that been using stay they who. Waiting to to

all any and married he that has had and asking seeing
and one and not some noise went would make.

Was one one. All and expecting remembering determining
determining then there. Dead certainly hear has
have accidentally one. In the saying doing could?

Would would feel would make? Was one one being enough
complete convincing convincing? Hearing in is
expecting that meaning waiting to to all and expecting
pleasant repeat.

He something.

One one being
discovering. Commencing convincing. Hearing intermittently.

Discovering remembering determining determining
then there dead certainly hear see what
hearing. Convincing easy come received. To more be
hearing went. Might he?

That what hearing something
going youngest being did have finish said meant
meant doing. Some what seeing seeing all and again
eating seeing perplexing kindly returning. Talking
were say easy and made he that meant meant doing
common repeating badly.
He noise went would make.
Was one one the was that meaning was have living
again three discovering? Determining thing and one
and not some came not would perplexing not some
something happening? Determining determining that
not.

He something. Some came something. One and they
what seen one in one not told. Not.

Being remembering
something. Something and one and feel saw and
anything. Pleasantly. Disturbing going youngest
youngest leaving again asking stay they. They are
seen. Give. Prospering remember remembering difficult.

Commenced discovering determining.

Existing
meeting to.

Derived from "Stein 34" sent through TRAVESTY. This program was asked for "an order-7 travesty" of 4,061 characters (both numbers were drawn from a random-digit table). Strophe breaks were added to the output in such a way that the successive strophes constitute three interlocked rising, falling, and rising partial Lucas sequences with two one-sentence codas. No other revisions were made to TRAVESTY's output.

New York: 19–23 August 1998

Time That's Being Some Thing

(Stein 36)

Time.

That's being. This.
One and one is is.

Then,
there,
every body is one seen and being seen to be.
Did use,
was using,
has been using.
Anne was successfully hearing,
hearing them feeling.
They said of those that one of them is that thing,
and they all are.

One of those things is friendly.
It is and has been too quickly laughing.
That laughing is sounding like a being talking,
seeing,
expressing,
discovering something,
something regularly happening.
He was long successfully hearing feeling.
It did hear it and was hearing it.
I have been coming and saying,
again and again,
that he meant it,
meant that meaning,
when he was talking and walking and talking.
This existing one is one preparing to be and is one.

Everything is being badly done.
He is all motion and noise
wherever something is happening.
It and That,
That Being being quickly laughing,
is one laughing,
sounding,
talking,
showing,
imitating,
and existing one.
Then,
if that one is one,
it is one to the thing then quickly laughing.
It is laughing and sounding and disappearing,
waiting and continuing,
discovering and lacking motion staying.
It had been saying its living,
coming often.
He might be that convincing thing.
They were convincing themselves
that they were hearing what this This was.
One and one is one,
one we all were seeing.
Being one asking leave,
is it received?
Is it expecting something
and is expecting difficult
or easy?

Kindly tell me which walking,
which talking?
Talking happening easily?
What is waving saying?
Is it saying meeting and then being leaving,
not being staying?
Being beginning,

what would they be hearing?
This,
this saying one,
is one seeing the dead who came
and are gone.
One and one is one seeing,
and successfully hearing,
one hearing what they are feeling.
They said those are anything they be said to be.
When that thing is anything
is one enjoying that?
Their being says one and they are open,
and when will that be?
Quickly being,
a thing is
Being.
Regularly and quietly it has been going one one one.
Who was it then?
What it did was long successful hearing.
Hearing feeling they said those are one.
Anything they be may be said of them
when that thing is one.
One one tells it to may then be doing what one says.
They are quickly open to the being of things,
the friendly or far from friendly being of some thing.

Six strophes derived from Stein's LGB (*ASR* 214–18) through DIASTEX5, using a paragraph of OOD (*ASR* 125–26) as seed text, and then freely editing and revising the output. The numbers of sentences in the successive strophes follow the Lucas sequence.

New York: 24 August 1998; 12 March, 17 December 1999

It Places

(Stein 37)

It in if it will.

Capital castle.
Am leaves possession
        can king that king
        women able to be related.
Third distribution.

Bridges lilies
        lilies covering.
Capital.
Second having credit
        you remaining coming again
        coming again
        and
and liberty meditation coming again
        and
        and liberty meditation again converse
        walking
        sufficiently raining.
It
        it.

We harness.
Yes.
Question
        question.
Third.
What places has safely?

Capital croppings aware
        waiting impervious
        repeating remaining
        very nearly nor they of
        of path indeed again.
I it.

Capital say women able and
        and hedges.
Were really can went and
        and indeed spring does come here meant.
Question meantime sufficiently.
Mountains croppings elaborate are
        will little.
Capital changing.
Second where heated and
        and made.
Second.
For homes indeed meditated distribution
        meantime sufficiently.
Mountains croppings elaborate
        are will little.
Capital changing do liberty meditations nourish hope
        not.
Second it away it of it
I   it would.

Capital beside and loud for longer beggars they
        ridden times
        covering because be
        this plenty engaged little right gives.

Capital second walking clearly to homes religious
        again baggage
        attending in and loud.
Second.
Plants silver needing ridden waiting is it will?

Capital castle.
Question
          question.
Third.
What places?

Eight strophes derived from Stein's play *Capital Capitals* (*ASR* 421–26) by running the passage through DIASTEX5 using as seed text a paragraph from LGB (*ASR* 214, par. 1). Rule-guided editing of the program's output included its division into verse-line "sentences" (each verse line begins with a capital letter and ends with a period or question mark), mostly in accordance with punctuation in the source text, with some additional punctuation and their grouping into strophes. The strophes comprise numbers of "sentences" in successive strophes corresponding to two successive Lucas sequences: 1, 3, 4, 7, 11 and 1, 3, 4. Indented typographical lines continue verse lines above them. Every typographical line ending within a strophe indicates a short pause. A strophe break calls for a somewhat longer pause. Periods and question marks should be read with declarative and interrogative sentence-final intonation contours.

New York: 26–27 August 1998; 30 January 2000

Capital's Necessity

(Stein 38)

Capitals elaborately are.
Will little?
Capital changing not coming
        establishing sculpture at that
        they walking responsible raining went
        came beside.

Second.
Not comes here
Capital.
Fourth necessity.
Mountains repeating.

Capital placed the well.
Excellent pleasant mention seen it
        that away received reason.
Raining went
Came beside

Second?
Not comes here.
Capital.
Fourth necessity.
Mountains repeating.
Third the leaves that down will.

Did heated made?
Imply responsible there reason
        that there reason distribution.

Did
        did.

Did?

Now to
Met he can
Capitals compete
        compete needings.
Capitals elaborately are will little

Capital changing
        not coming
        establishing sculpture at that.
They walking responsible raining went.
Came beside

Second.
Not comes here.
Capital?
Fourth necessity.

Nine strophes derived from the end of Stein's CC (*ASR* 421–26) by running it through DIASTEX5, using as seed LGB (*ASR* 214, par. 2). Additions to the program's output were limited to some final *s*'s, some of the strophe breaks, sentence/verse line breaks, and line breaks within verse lines, and the punctuation. Indented lines continue verse lines begun above. Every typographical line ending indicates a short pause, strophe breaks somewhat longer ones. Periods and question marks call for sentence-final intonation contours.

New York: 27 August 1998

Are Homes Responsible Managers Understand

(Stein 39)

Are elaborately.
Will win.
The properly
S/He,
Capital having excellent and way calamity,
say no to its path.
Cake to really responsible homes.
Managers understanding repetition's direction
are completing accentuation.

And are and any one and horses.
Capital covering Capital.
Second having way-calamities
says no to the path.
Cake to homes.

Responsible really to managers' understanding,
repeated directions are completing it as is.
And any one elaborately will.
Happily calling is covering Capital.
Anyway
Second having's calamity.
Say no to path-cakes
to really responsible homes.
Managers understand repetition.

Directions not completing it,
ability does.

Were they comforted?
Were they ridden?

Times were covering
because beside this plenty
they engaged little mountains.
Can two kings especially go forth?
I is little to one.
Beggars employed by another
aroused changing.

Fourth
Am in and becoming becoming.
This plenty engaged little mountains.
Can king?

Especially.
And two going about.
Fourth.
Why of indication preparation's color?
Fourth comforted
Capital strongly to-night as all intended.
Endeavor gives no this.
Noon managers are especially useful.
Now to?

Met sees it.
Plants sufficiently away need waiting again.
Plenty will
win
The.
Properly.

S/He.
Capital having.
Excellent.

And the way.
Calamity says no to the cake-path.
To homes responsible.
Really a manager?

Understand repetition as direction
completing accentuation
And.

And are any one and are horses.
Capital covering
Capital,
Second having calamity anyway
says no to paths of cakes to homes.
Responsible real managers understand repetition.

Directions completing anything elaborately
will happily call covering
Capital.
Second having calamity says no to path-cakes
homes' responsible managers understand.

Twelve strophes derived from the end of Stein's CC (*ASR* 421–26) by running it through DIASTEX5, using as seed LGB (*ASR* 214, par. 3). In making *this* poem, a word from the seed was added to the source passage to allow the program to complete one full period, and the whole source text was replicated several times before running it through DIASTEX5. The program's output was revised and considerably truncated. Every typographical line ending indicates a short pause, strophe breaks somewhat longer ones. Periods and question marks call for sentence-final intonation contours.

New York: 28 August–5 September 1998

Elaborately Denial Annoys the Welcomers Who Know One Indication

(Stein 40)

Elaborately denial annoys
the ridden beggars.

Awareness is cake indeed.
Crowded in,
it often has been,
can be more.

Fourth is really great.
Third is great too.
They went together.
Third does it better.

Second comes here for one
many welcome where they are.
Knowing that indication has been a denial.
Color him.
Ride him not.

Nothing gives me a path.
And associated with January,
his is crowded indeed.
Third sees what has been,
and she's distributing the light.

And
Now to

Met.
Not met.
See loud.
And A.

Yes I know places' preparations for stability.
Mountains repeating excellently
far from arousal,
are religious.

Fourth went to the mother.
Capital.
For women compete to complete people's repetition.
Still they
Resemble those who've seen
Mountains changing leaves.

A kitchen having come again,
coming the most,
gives me a path,
and may indeed be crowded.

January was long indeed.
Had Father splendid distribution?
He received women able to be
great in a
Capital.
Met whom?

Has to side with him,
makes everything steadily wider than before that.
Here,
that is,
Color has not usefully been a denial.

Ride him not.
In all cake a way of mentioning is caught.

Meantime
Ignorant
Mountains have been stirring.

Together with
Fourth,
He and
Capital,
excellently assuring cake indeed,
are crowded with clear useful understandings,
and he has mentioned
that what he had wished for
he has not really received.

How
Capable is he
of removing from the way
he may wish things to go
whatever utter necessity
makes
capitals?

Second strongly wishes horses would not be beggars.
Capital is not a color,
and cake and fruit are not usefully baggage.
Fruit again!
No not that!

Attending here means days of lilies
with
Buds.
Let's see the needing ride!

What necessity utters is nearly always
going to be becoming what
Reasonable times will be remembering as excellent.

Sculpture's association with repetition
and remembering
was the reason neither was found religious.

He came often to resemble
the responsible employed.
Where?

This covering
Resembles possession
together with consolation.

Remembering this is the reason neither
found the religious responsible,
he came often.
It resembled employing consolation
together with possession.

Remembering this
Resembled the reason
he will be the same.

That was nearly no path,
and the association of cake and fruit again
with baggage
means that here
the river comes very much more near
where the employed together
understand the undertaken.

Where early crowds resemble
those going forth,
where are they
they
Resemble?

Do many beggars compete?
Do many beggars compete about being ridden, elaborately aware?

Is cake indeed
crowded?
It often has been and can be more so.

Fourth really.
Third great too.
They went.
Does
Third do any better?

Second comes here for the welcomers
who know one indication.

Twenty-eight strophes derived from the end of Stein's CC (*ASR* 421–26) by running it through DIASTEX5, using as seed LGB (*ASR* 214, par. 4). In making this poem, a word from the seed was added to the source passage before it was run through DIASTEX5 to allow the program to complete one full period. The program's output was revised freely but without the addition of new lexical words. Every typographical line ending indicates a short pause, strophe breaks somewhat longer ones. Periods and question marks call for sentence-final intonation contours.

New York: 30 August–7 September 1998

She Has Plenty Today

(Stein 41)

She has been safely coloring Cook.
Three intend to win plenty.
He will be walking in place that day.
Indeed vegetables relate more.

Mother's away Sunday.
All wish safely to color.
Second knows and has been a Cook.
Three intend to win plenty.

He will nearly not be little that day.
He cans miles of walking vegetables.
Relations are farther away from Mother Sunday.
Second wishes all to know he's safely coloring too.

Cook.
Three intend.
Happily.
Second.

Third.
Capital.
Inlay walking places.
Where indeed is he responsible to be at noon?

What did Cook come to call for?
Three intend repeating.
Very very verily he mentions cuts.
Such a relation is second to cake.

Cook.
Three.
Sunday.
Second.

He intends to wish for little vegetables.
Mother can walk more miles than he.
All know his near relations are far away.
He will win plenty today.

Eight quatrains derived from the end of Stein's CC (*ASR* 421–26) by running it through DIASTEX5, using as seed LGB (*ASR* 214, par. 5). In making this poem, a word from the seed was added to the source passage before it was run through DIASTEX5 to allow the program to complete one full period. The program's output was revised freely but without the addition of new lexical words. Every typographical line ending indicates a short pause, strophe breaks somewhat longer ones. Periods and question marks call for sentence-final intonation contours.

New York: 30 August–27 September 1998

They Are Elaborately Silver Pleasures

(Stein 42)

They are elaborately willing.

The Third learns little.
The Third is nearly where will is the same as idea.
For soon to-day their homes will indeed be second.

That child went there for a reason.
There it seems is the Third Capital.
Who came and went there that Sunday?
A denial of silver pleasures let him ride in.

The Third went away beside them.
They will endeavor to win by changing castles.
The Third will do very well.
She did.
The Third tho very down pleased all that were there.
Reason?
Their way was indeed responsible.

I've often seen able women.
No Sunday went by without them.
They see the Second Capital
They see the Third Capital.

The Third was loud.
We harness them that see.
Yes what way and where?

What silver pleasures!

Seven strophes derived from the end of Stein's CC (*ASR* 421–26) by running it through DIASTEX5, using as seed LGB (*ASR* 214, par. 6). The program's output was revised and edited freely, but with no addition of lexical words. The numbers of lines in the strophes follow the ascending and descending Lucas sequence 1, 3, 4, 7, 4, 3, 1.

New York: 3–27 September 1998

It Remembl Splendid and Religiou

(Stein 43)

It remembl.

Call pering.
They that one ridea homes.
Secontending he.

Way cond sculpture.
Capitated.
Fourth splenty.
Fourishes repeating as indeed objectivity meditated.

Fourth splent plending if and.
Questirring rejection repeating.
One full permit responsible.
Capital.
This?
To togetheir remaining near.
Resembering of and.

Capital.
Second.
No meding sure days anot convincing.
Repeation repeating of and rememberty idea homes.
Inroad attendid atten.
Sufficient leaves one full.
Permity calamity.
Fourishes inroad and seeing excellending excellenty.
Third busilver often.

Capitated medital?
Fourishes that oftendid attendid atten.

Remembering repeating permity seeing religious.
Reasonablishes their sculpture days and do togethem.
Where to homes inroad and lines ide by need.
Objection prepeation convincing plention as inroad.
Any their way convincing estance ridges?
Inroad attending he.
Came togethem why?
Resemberty second inroad atten.
Sure togethey medital.
Has.
Capital separating needitated.

Questablishing deprecation distable.
Capitated.
Fourth splending of and.
Fourth splention remembering associating.
Convincing need objection there came of enjoy.
Are capitated?
Objection religious crowded.
Fourishingly capital.
Fourth splently that one all anot by need.
Ligious soon reason what?
They that noon religious.
Meding
Repeating as inroad and seeing.
Second that not cond repeation atten.
Call any that?
Homes repeation.
He seen changingly of and cond remembe.
Objection attendid attending as has has did that one.

Remembe empleted objection meditated.
Medital winter.

Convincing cond capital be he.
Clamity.
Fourth splendid and.
Questablishes.
Reason repeating to.
To homes permity convincing near.
Found can gives indid.
And one and seeing action wher of and.
Fourth splending deprepeation remembering if.
And separation rememble to to call anothere idea.
Homes religious crowded.
Fourish homes period can say coming.
Excellenty second seconvincing permity meditated.
Meditates remain.
Remembering nearly capitates repeation.
Did and possession attending?
Seconsolating.
They they been objection repeation attently ther.
Capitated.
Fourth splending be he.
Capital easily of and seeing estion.
Sily can gives inroad attending sure.
Calamit reasonablishing permit remembering.
Action religious ment plend besidea homes.
Are idea hope not cond?
Repeation as inding as indid to neithe beggars.
Manage why?

Resemble them what here besidea homes.

Permity say can gives indeed objection.
Repeation reparating.
Reparating we?

Calamit repeating depreparation.
Possession precating reasilver as ide been manage.

Wenty.
Fourth splendid and religiou.

Ten strophes derived from the end of Stein's CC (*ASR* 421–26) via DIASTEX5, using as seed LGB (*ASR* 214, par. 7). In making this poem, 3 words from the seed were inserted into the source passage before it was run through DIASTEX5 to allow the program to complete one full period. Periods were added to that program's output and it was sent through TRAVESTY, which was asked for an order-4 "Travesty" of 2,663 characters, as determined by random-digit chance operations. Its output was revised in regard to sentence breaks and sentence-final punctuation, but the words and neowords and their order were left unchanged. Each sentence became a verse line and these lines were grouped into strophes in which the numbers of lines in succeeding strophes constituted two Lucas sequences: 1, 3, 4, 7, 11, 18, 29, followed by 1, 3, 4. Every typographical line ending indicates a short pause, strophe breaks somewhat longer ones. Periods and question marks call for sentence-final intonation contours. [Ed. Note: there is an additional eleven-line strophe included in the poem, and therefore eleven strophes in total. Mac Low seems to have overlooked this discrepancy.]

New York: 11–14 September 1998

She Like Many a Graduate Experienced Recognition Perhaps As Affection, Listening As Intercourse

(Stein 44)

She like many a graduate was influenced by the state's control of things.

In a day their own comrades continued faster and did see and experience hypocrisy by making three surprising judgements.

She was any puritan saying her distress through this.

She speaks. Prays.

Mrs. Redfern's shy face was beyond admiration as it had been through adolescence. Down through the years it suffered no change. That she felt friendship but far away was not the dean's doing.

Dounor was brilliant. She never desired an interesting life and made an abstract judgement on hypocrisy. Experience flourished, questioning her reputation. Many things were nearly abstract to this creature. Principles then had meanings. Her real comrades continued the action that was marriage.

When she and they had her great energy they were presiding over common nothing. Any institution and some new arrivals were beginning and ending. She like many a graduate reasoned about her emotions. She detached the varieties of humans saying this intelligence was new.

Sometimes Dounor could face anything except anxiety. Redfern was imbibing the things that concealed many of these convictions. His pleasanter intelligence when singled out was almost always plunging. These messages could make his mind up but he could not make a game of them.

Whoever possesses and chooses this common philosophy comes to call many beings.

The mystic doctor went about convinced he was permanently unattached. Everything that gave the impression of detachment was due to his shy thinking.

Missing childhood's big range, we perhaps ranked reality more highly than propinquity. Vital desire, perplexity, neutrality, excitement, everything, was shadowed by our shy thinking.

We missed the big opportunity to rank childhood's range over reality. We experienced recognition perhaps as affection, listening as intercourse.

Twelve paragraphs derived from Stein's *Making of Americans*, last par. of *ASR* 22 through the 2nd par. of 28. This passage was run through DIASTEX5 using as seed a paragraph of Stein's LGB (*ASR* 214, par. 8). The locus of the source was given by the number 24, a few pages before and after 24 being added by choice and chance operations. The numbers 24 and 214 are permutations of 241, found by blindly pointing to a logarithm table to which I opened a math-table book I used in high school. The program's output was revised and edited within liminal constraints that respected the words, punctuation, and word order of the output, but allowed certain additions, subtractions, and changes of word order, punctuation, and line breaks. The verse-line paragraphs of the poem may be broken between any two words, but no word should be broken at the right margin.

New York: 15–16 September 1998; 22 January 1999; 24 April 2000

Energy She Came to Understand

(Stein 45)

Energy she always had and that's how she dealt with why she was neither wiser nor indifferent. She always in a way chose to be any being who came to her. Any institution she knew had interesting days. Innocence made her become preoccupied with dreams. Any instinct of the body was hers.

Phillip being young then even brought her thought. He was oblivious or impartial as to the big reality's thirty or more meanings. The things and themes he preferred were reserved for his career. His shyness had a way of arranging to imbibe the strength of women in that place.

Martha Hersland's desires were the same every day. She liked to be strange and dangerous. She was a woman through and through and fairly young. She was Western and his. Yes some will say her honesty lay in doubting things even though she knew them.

He dazed her with his neutrality in the game, and she tried to destroy his judgement, hypocrisy, experience, and flourishing reputation.

She learned to question her world's meanings. This made her disguise her woman's strength through liking others. She devoted her energy to her desires, convictions, and principles. Her comrade in marriage continued that action. Earnestly she tried to make his needs hers.

Redfern elaborately learned that any institution into which he was thrown did nothing but confine him. A new arrival was beginning the ending of that confinement.

She reasoned that her emotions were those of a genuine woman. Resisting Hannah, she kept the college, as she had her parents, entirely where it was. She was deep.

Because she could be gentle she missed the depths of her instincts. She who had been a dean of anticipation became abruptly a mere instructor.

In her eyes Redfern's shyness seemed original and she suddenly seemed to become another person. Redfern came to be thinking that both of them were shy.

They and Dounor engaged themselves with thirty meanings of the big reality. The recognition of this thing became the theme of the dean's perverse friendship. What a shy way of desiring and liking a woman through what the reality of that day was.

He never did quite see who he was as he sat and wandered, a boy among women. Strangely any one who understood some things about him doubted his honesty though what his game was was confined by his neutrality, his dazed neutrality again, with which he always struggled.

Redfern was rarely called Redfern by the dean as she sat in her extraordinary chair of judgment, hypocrisy, experience, and flourishing reputation. Through questioning she learned what her world's meanings were. This made her many days disguise the strength of her liking for the woman which neither she nor her fellow learners ever came to understand.

Twelve paragraphs derived from Stein's MoA (*ASR* 22–28), rearranged so that several early paragraphs came at the end. This rearranged passage was run through DIASTEX5, using as seed a paragraph of Stein's LGB (*ASR* 214, par. 9). The program's output was revised within liminal constraints that respected the words, punctuation, and word order of the output, but allowed certain additions, subtractions, and changes of word order, punctuation, and line breaks.

New York: 17–18 September 1998; 19 June 2001

She Had Known This Ending Is Wrong but Pretty

(Stein 46)

She had known of the year when his shyness had concealed his mind through misdirection.

Once she and Redfern believed intently or knew that they'd gotten down beyond their shyness when speaking to a fairly young boy. Yes they said then the wrong one ended pretty. It is but teaching criticism as saints are known to be religious.

Her deep woman's intellect was essential to their arrival in those days at the sameness of beginning and ending. She met her dean. Redfern wondered who she was. Miss he said my shyness is serious and intense.

Awkwardly she desired to guide his twenty-nine-year-old's thought toward showing changes that made him get down to principles. Then energy began to have dangerous meanings. Douner's detached nature loved abstract effective dependence. What the dean was doing was questioning interesting convictions. Redfern's needs were earnestly suffering the way and defining their natures which beyond bowing again were separating judgement from hypocrisy and extraordinary experience. The dean in her eagerness to be courteous to thirty interesting generations had a thing about their meanings. Redfern had gone there to make his Fellow's chair a possibility.

The students' meanings there were really the best. Her deepest desire was for a variety of human relations. The extreme quality of her spirit was evident in her working as she undertook what seemed best. She docilely arranged to keep her health through her wintry youth. Redfern knew the world's varieties of aims were taking them through their personalities' narrow reserves of awkwardness. Once in the way could she make her mind go out beyond it? Ah she knew this made her anxious and shy. Another boy used to speak of it. Yes he said then the wrong one had ended pretty new and blindly struggled on. It was essential that the best teachers should be invited into the universities. This was preoccupying the family of the women's intense philosopher meaning his instructor.

His desire was that his shy face should make him pass as having learned that colleges or any other institutions could get down to principles and then to energy. Were their classes' south-western meanings dangerous? Was Dounor worldly? She was a quite transfigured being. His difference from this being was that he could not understand her vigorous judgements. He ascribed them to hypocrisy rather than the extraordinary experience of generations. What was interesting was that the dean was showing her eagerness to learn what colleges or any institutions could come down to after questioning women's desires for extreme effective dependence. What the dean found interesting about his convictions was that his earnest needs were discordant with those of women. What Hannah knew though was that his game of neutrality was at its height. Redfern of course had thrown himself into keeping state control confined. Never again would he be carried by common emotions and meanings to miss her teachings. Shy Redfern's anxiety often lasted through thirty whole days. He went about making some relations he had with women strange but his understanding of their natures was real. She knew he was shy. Charles's way was concrete but learned. There was snow in the air. She found his shyness interesting and knew it was not like that of any other shy boy. She put it down to his being young and when he spoke she believed him.

Yes she said this ending is wrong but pretty.

Seven paragraphs derived from Stein's MoA (*ASR* 22–28), of which the order of the paragraphs was randomized by random-digit chance operations. This rearranged passage was run through DIASTEX5, using as seed a paragraph of Stein's LGB (*ASR* 214, par. 9). The program's output was revised and edited within liminal constraints that respected the lexical words, punctuation, and word order of the output, but allowed certain additions, subtractions, and changes of word order, punctuation, and line breaks. The numbers of sentences in successive paragraphs are that of the Lucas sequence 1, 3, 4, 7, 11, 18, with a one-sentence coda.

New York: 19–20 September 1998

She and I Never Came to Be Indifferent to a Good-Looking Woman

(Stein 47)

She and I never came to be indifferent to her.

She was a common observer of concrete appearances and was showing that she listened. Farnham's conditions were of course entirely other and required some strength. She was a good-looking woman and outwardly eager.

He was a south-western man with things on his mind. She seemed to need protection. What teacher of docile regeneration had she known? She sensed part of his criticism and sat down as if used to it.

He made himself seem to be off guard. She let him see that that this ended her being made uneasy. He seemed a snowy youth neither simple nor extraordinary. For some years he'd kept the world away and was nothing. Anticipation made him a member of it. As a professor the power of his aspiration had a range that made him change from a creature of sensuous instinct and shyness to one with talk he had learned at an eastern college. Her eyes were equally dazed and blinded by his energy though she struggled against its blows.

She thought things seeing her blondness disguised her attention's road even from intently eager Charles. Presently she came to the possibility that detached philosophy was always there. Meeting Farnham's dean who loved elaborately strenuous things she felt the dean's impression was that she was crude while Dounor tried never to be thought young and eagerly interested in Hannah's nearness or what she was doing. Being learned Dounor's mind was that of a devoutly religious woman even when she was taking in experience. Their comrades' analysis that year of their careers and life aims invited their arrival at a beginning that exerted the coercion of an ending. In our youth perhaps our vocations are constantly present to us. That the dean was an earnestly suffering woman made his mind again south-western with a new shyness. Her pleasant eagerness gave the same degree of attention to everything through admirations which she expounded as she sought a wider understanding of common life. She did not doubt finding it. She had sat down to find this even when she was eighteen. They as comrades had analyzed the institutions through the uncertain confusion of everything.

Everything led them to the same admiration which disguised their love. There no emotion was ever a window into her new state. Explaining everything and understanding it through admiration seemed learned folly. No love disguised the window into her new shyness. Her entire learned folly seemed to be that of explaining and understanding almost everything as being one and the same. When she cared to Charles wandered to this window. Ah who knows the helpless distress of another? She was philosophy itself. The south-western man felt real protective affection for this scholarly good-looking person. What teacher of docile regeneration sought varieties of understanding through all their indolent days? She was western. Anyone could have seen she was pretty deliberately flushed. That day's air was one of vigorous regeneration. He had known it was to be theirs for years. There in their youthful years they had blinded themselves to the worth of worldly things. This made them find themselves among criticisms. Her intelligence loved Redfern's once she could make a degree of appeal to him. The harsh nature of the south-western instructor invited the same deference from every common creature.

Then love reserved defining that. Ah how looking at the distress of another helpless scholarly life made him know the keen life of listening and intercourse and instincts. Every learned folly seemed to have the possibility of being effective philosophy. The dean presently detached him from this. He missed it when they thought Dounor had died. In his innocent way the fellow frankly doubted the ground though that made him uneasy. It wasn't that he was not intellectually sensitive. In his twenty-ninth year Redfern was a women's philosopher a well-meaning instructor. His theme was that the great body and the shy face were new interests for intelligence. She learned from his neutrality the dazed ways that might destroy them whence she learned that only her leaving would leave her unattached. Dounor constrained Redfern. Turning and listening he disguised his awkwardness. Redfern was original and scholarly. She constantly found some strength in that. Hannah's affection represented her basal resisting. He taking it to be hypocrisy stopped and smiled at her actions despite whatever he realized about them. She rarely came to possess great enough sensitivity. This twenty-nine-year-old psychologist had a living desire to experience women's colleges. As he happened to have this purpose he was beginning this experience as a professor. Detachedly she loved human experience. Some natures quite evidently were like those of the dean. She needed Martha. They separated. Their being together died. She came and went but was never indifferent. She was concrete. Her appearance was that of any common observer. At

Farnham she showed that she was listening by showing strength under some entirely different conditions. She was a good-looking woman.

Seven paragraphs derived from Stein's MoA (*ASR* 22–28), of which the order of the paragraphs was newly randomized by random-digit chance operations. This rearranged passage was run through DIASTEX5, using as seed a paragraph of Stein's LGB (*ASR* 214, par. 9). The program's output was revised and edited within liminal constraints that respected the lexical words, punctuation, and word order of the output, but allowed certain additions, subtractions, and changes of word order, punctuation, and line breaks. The numbers of sentences in successive paragraphs are those of the Lucas sequence.

New York: 20–26 September 1998; 3 May 1999

His Having A Reputation Disguised Was Neither Impartial Nor Helpless

(Stein 48)

His having a reputation disguised his giving his complete attention to it.

He was always shy there. The woman was saying he had been. He prayed about this very often.

Redfern returned again to this place full of desires. Not that he had any instructors. Some days with the dean were healthy as he said this one was. Surely being good-looking secured what he wished then faster than the distress of desire.

His range that year was sometimes inadequate to a degree. She had grace and was gentle. He had to make her hard. To her it was Greek to own strength. Indeed her instinct transfigured her reserve. The college and the world were equally blind. She just could not learn to guard her lap. She could not keep doubting his honesty.

Enticement made her meanings awkward. Her mind could have longed for his friendship. Be docile when desiring the concrete was what she learned from this. Taking her for a genuinely great strong woman he had called her purposefulness extraordinary. Do you wonder? Dounor was full of fixed dangerous western meanings. Redfern was always simple. The place was always cold. Their comrades got there faster. Neither spent their world on it. What each absorbed from her talk was a helplessly impartial analysis of their careers.

We can say that that was her way. Redfern was indeed suffering. All of his deepest prayers dealt with his dreams. That day he was fairly dry and indolent. His head stopped working. Martha smiled and said that her western doubt gave strength to her meanings despite her shyness. All that Hannah had was the mind of a teacher and all she was doing revealed this. Abstracting her beauty would leave her genuine common sense. In all her life Hannah was never hypocritical as many young women at universities could attest. As for Redfern who was south-western tea must have been new to him. Full of fixed meanings he was dangerous for westerners listening to him really living and dignified though liking his freedom. All the world's differences cried out together to answer Redfern. Never listening to his awkwardness he gazed at them now with desire. His analysis of the world's customs had taken away his desire. Presently Farnham promised to engage his purposeful fibre. Bruised and dazed as she was gentle Dounor could look with him at the wooded scene. Her reason's strength carried power. All relations touching her she knew to be extreme.

How eastern her world was was evident from her dreams' innocence. It was partly respect for his parents that always made him stop after every lap. Whatever her shyness it was Charles's habitual way that her desire shy as it was was still an exaltation.

Many believed she failed in her aim to be an able dean of faculty. Shyness and intense shyness. Dounor talked with many of the instructors. He saw she was cold when they were walking for their health. They understood that youth was a different time. Redfern was never simple and he was shy with her while checking himself rather than distressing her. He always showed the same good-looking face. He had made it so and longed now to give her more. He was secure in his career as an instructor. Nevertheless there was meaning in Redfern's having taken the chair of philosophy. That would have been when no plunges were small. He loved a discordant woman. What was that which made her long to be wiser? Could the world of dreams possess an innocence that made her learn her own mind? What made her be guarded there? Could anyone doubt her honesty? What was it that the dean felt? Hannah's nearness arranged her habitual ways so that she was no mere creature. She was a woman making believable judgements. At Farnham men had been calling her a wonder. Like you Dounor was full of dangerous fixities. He found their meanings western. Redfern's simplicity was always cold. He was their comrade. There they said we spent the world faster. What we absorbed from her talk was that she was neither impartial nor helpless.

Seven paragraphs derived from Stein's MoA (*ASR* 22–28), of which the order of the paragraphs was newly randomized by random-digit chance operations. This rearranged passage was run through DIASTEX5, using as seed a paragraph of Stein's LGB (*ASR* 215, par. 1). The program's output was revised and edited within liminal constraints that respected the lexical words, punctuation, and word order of the output, but allowed certain additions, subtractions, and changes of word order, punctuation, and line breaks. The numbers of sentences in successive paragraphs are those of the Lucas sequence.

New York: 21–23 September 1998; 23 February 1999

In Our Eyes

(Stein 49)

In our life it is common to choose willingly to talk American first.

Dounor's parents always entered everything to the utmost degree through their admiration and attention. Expounding abstractions even to equals meant continually walking through a life of wintry coldness. She had a reputation for managing everything through the quality of her replies.

The attention of women used to make her actions strange. For days she had been preoccupied by the three women in her life. A crude chivalry had governed her relations with them as a teacher. Their beauty was abstract to this creature.

Their health moved her faster. A pleasant self-consciousness possessed their bodies and their faces. It came to be attained by them as rarely as greatness. Redfern had never never wished for the great world. For Redfern desire extended through whole years. She felt it only in her dreams. Her blond friend's chair sent her a message that filled her then.

What threw them was an energy that used to carry sense to the country boy when he rested but had stopped. Frankly Hersland said I know and understand the meanings of the students' convictions. They are familiar convictions of pure existence and hardly ever seem learned through analysis. His daughter understood everything through discussion. Her face was filled with meanings that fulfilled her feelings through their expression even though her hands were almost always confined by uncertain confusion. Expounding abstractions to the assembled all of this was taken from her again. Shyness entered her eyes. Looking at new universities Charles claimed they either attained what they claimed to or were able to do so. Again wherever they went her nature was always completely transformed by grace and fibre. Her appearance was not merely that of a blond but of one filled with awkward strength even though praying for admiration and love. Her religious feeling for women's colleges differed according to the character of each institution. They who used to play sat on the ground with their fellows.

Anyway the alright woman though deliberately placed is always strange.

Martha then took a constant course in western intercourse given by the dean. Her head in a preoccupied manner engaged the last confusion though working in sordid common walking freedom. Where her quality managed everything through reputation she replied even you are eager for the world.

She filled her face and her confined hands with meanings fulfilled through feeling and its expression. Even there it was almost always through uncertainty and confusion that she expounded the abstract. She was taking it again that all the assembled had entered. Charles's shyness looked new to their eyes.

Eight paragraphs derived from Stein's MoA (*ASR* 22–28), of which the order of the paragraphs was newly randomized by random-digit chance operations. This rearranged passage was run through DIASTEX5, using as seed a paragraph of Stein's LGB (*ASR* 215, par. 2). The program's output was revised and edited within liminal constraints that respected the lexical words, punctuation, and word order of the output, but allowed certain additions, subtractions, and changes of word order, punctuation, and line breaks. The numbers of sentences in successive paragraphs are those of two consecutive Lucas sequences: 1, 3, 4, 7, 11 and 1, 3, 4.

New York: 25–26 September 1998

Strenuousness Never Leaves The Concrete Untouched

(Stein 50)

Strenuousness may seem inadequate and narrow throughout our years of worldly perplexity but need not be separated from powerful admiration.

We understand explaining convictions but not understanding itself. Opportunities for our own last vocation may be beginning nevertheless and come to preside. We would do best to observe this with impartiality.

Dounor realized that recognition of her work never touched its concreteness. This promised to explain her helpless nature's constraining perplexity so that she might understand everything. She always showed the same shyness in relation to every teacher. She learned to engage the meanings of both beauty and abstract ideas.

Sometimes Hannah abruptly guided her through and beyond any course and through a great range of arguments. She seemed a strangely devout friend through many springs. Earnestly and deliberately she formed even her health so that that she became content and continued to be. From her customary chair she changed things she'd felt in her youth. She learned that she who would labor must first know the walls that confined her between which she'd been thrown and that not every attempt to look at nature was loved. The puritan's interest did not extend to some of nature. Powerful forms of perplexity needed worldly explanation and understanding.

Neither convictions nor understanding gave her any opportunity to begin her own vocation.

Impartial observation did not preside. Dounor realized this. She recognized that work never leaves the concrete untouched.

Six paragraphs derived from Stein's MoA (*ASR* 22–28), of which the order of the paragraphs was newly randomized by random-digit chance operations. This rearranged passage was run through DIASTEX5, using as seed a paragraph of Stein's LGB (*ASR* 215, par. 1). The program's output was revised and edited within liminal constraints that respected the lexical words, punctuation, and word order of the output, but allowed certain additions, subtractions, and changes of word order, punctuation, and line breaks. The numbers of sentences in successive paragraphs are those of two consecutive Lucas sequences: 1, 3, 4, 7 and 1, 3.

New York: 27 September 1998

And What Had Been Accomplished

(Stein 51)

And they would allow the pieces to hurry.

Why wasn't England silent. Why was it said that it wasn't useless to ask. Why hadn't he found he'd recognized who said it.

An electrician thinks that everything may be had for silver. He may be standing. Would his sounds suggest whether he has been.

Closets.

Prayers.

Let everybody do what they will. It will be a day of restlessness.

If it never left.

Howard mentioned thinking.

Widening a door enough they found it perfect and forgot the silver and everything. All the servants accomplished was exclaiming.

Who will have done the harnessing. Her face will give her away.

The pears are dirty. Think of something unexpected. What would you have the gentle citizen remember. Would you stand for it.

She saw a judge higher than seven others. She was careful. Her ice was poisoned. Was it necessary for her to have looked around. What was the address.

We saw that the pieces of the shell were separate.

He said that and what was he asking.

In Greek.

It is useless to speak of Spain. Putty does make the inclined pictures look silver.

Emile decides to give them everything they needed to notice.

Render means the lamps were accomplished. Everybody believes that together. Establish everybody's address. Hurry. Be silent.

The English did everything in their rebellion. They exclaimed at the places where they had to relieve themselves. The wealthy ones worried about knives.

Indeed she.

There are not many rosy wheels now.

I do not understand using dinner things. Plaster will do. When hadn't she been saying that in four languages. Her brothers for the moment permitted her to.

I never believed in dealing. Carry what you will. I never cared for carrying. Or softening. I think I've mentioned that.

Widening a found door he forgot that it was perfect.

Everything was silver.

The servants were exclaiming at what had been accomplished.

Five paragraph groups in which the number of paragraphs in successive groups follows the Lucas-number sequence 1, 3, 4, 7, 11. Derived from Stein's "Pink Melon Joy" (*ASR* 300–05). The source's page numbers were determined by the random numbers 302 and 5, found by chance operations in *AMRD*, and interpreted as meaning "about 5 pages including 302," so the source passage runs from about the middle of 300 to the end of PMJ in the middle of 305. The passage was run through DIASTEX5, using as "seed text" a paragraph from Stein's LGB (*ASR* 215, par. 4). In revising, lexical morphemes were retained and most of the words were placed in sentences and paragraphs corresponding to their groupings in the output.

New York: 28–29 September 1998; 20–23 March, 5–6 May 2001

Was She Able to Know When She Believed Him

(Stein 52)

Was she able to know when the man would come

He mentioned allowing a double. She was inclining more toward hearing than toward drawing. I is so.

Rather than thinking them tired why didn't those coming in point to their spelling we asked annoyed.

Can't home hands believe what they've heard. Did anybody mention winning.

In some places leaving meant edging toward calamity. When thinking hurriedly you will say you believe in coal for everybody. Winding is softening.

Carving wouldnt.

Why gradually separate that. Do come at once. Wait.

Your soup wouldn't wait for Matisse.

It's nearly her nearby.

The Greek said he promised to leave. I've been hearing perfectly that there was a resemblance there. She mentioned that the servants had been running.

I think it'd be a sheer pity. More than that. She'd come conscienced. Would earlier sounds.

It meant something when manners led one to ask why the lights were not higher. Everybody in that careful emigration will feel that poison softening them and winding them down.

Why is there carving in the room. I am the end man come. He mentioned that he'd doubly allow that even though she was more inclined to hear than to have to draw.

And then that there other team had succumbed. The scene went faster in its separation. Pointing to the pears they made sounds spelling out emotions like shouting. Can anyone mention winning after having met a mile of melancholy.

Leaving when she saw cause to she kind of resembled a lady getting the morning authority mentioned that morning and winding it all up.

In time.

He still believed himself doubly inclined to have a hearing rather than to have a drawing. Then that there other team would have been faster in separating out the dirt than the best of them.

Carrie only wondered at the seven of them rather than helping the goodness she saw in the boy come out. He came of remarkable forbears.

Is any one tired of the coal's restless softening. There one may have carving. Why didn't the man undertake to come to dinner in that room.

He spoke of a fire and that they had nearly been so busy in the country that they weren't having a country time there. He said he was inclined to look at the eggs but was astonished to notice all that meat.

She may not she shall not have succumbed to the sun the infants prefer there.

Walter wondered why she was inclined to have offspring. He had an intuition he had seen that kind of thing before. He was not fastening it with his fork. He was considering dealing.

He was willing to ask but his manner of asking was waxen. The very stones must have heard him shouting that description. Is there anything astonishing in spacing little rivers.

Any judge who saw what happened yesterday would have worried whether that Italian was lessening our winning.

Would she have been willing to ask even if her manner of asking were not waxen. They would be getting there this morning. He says he cannot understand this thing separately from its shell. She says the pieces there are of no use.

Howard spoiled one for the country. When he really found out he asked surprised whether the increase in conscienced sheepdogs was a momentary accident. He had would have been helpless had any one mentioned winning or leaving.

Say is this the place they meant when they said everyone there was edging toward calamitously hurried thinking. He doesn't believe it. It's not the same as doubly inclining toward hearing and drawing.

I understand that.

It meant that when coming in tired he didn't want to have them pointing at his spelling. What he carried is what he believed.

He heard that where there was cautious spacing there should be winning. She mentioned seeing some remarkable boys when she came. But that wouldn't count.

Julian Meininger is thinking he is nearly wishing for her. He has been hearing that in Spain they're inclined to hear about the drawings on the doors. I think they were there after that.

They shall choose you or you shall choose yourselves. You would have succumbed. Pointing is unavoidable and she sounds willing. With little lights an introduction carefully confers an obligation.

What was it they mentioned. What was that place where after exercises in winning one always had to be leaving in the morning.

When he was there on wheels it seems he knew the winding time. What he believed made him doubly inclined toward hearing. She had been drawing.

Then another team there had succumbed.

The scene went faster after its separation from the one before. They were pointing at the pears.

They can sound them from their spelling and vent their emotions by shouting.

After a mile they were melancholy. Did anyone mention winning.

They were leaving when they saw the causes were kind of getting to resemble each other.

He mentioned in the morning that the authorities were winding it up at that time.

She believed him.

Nine paragraph groups in which the number of paragraphs in successive groups follows the ascending and descending Lucas-number sequence 1, 3, 4, 7, 11, 7, 4, 3, 1. Derived from Stein's PMJ (*ASR* 300–05). The passage was run through DIASTEX5, using as seed a paragraph from Stein's LGB (*ASR* 215, par. 5). The output was freely revised and edited, but most of its words were placed in sentences and paragraphs corresponding to their groupings in the output.

New York: 1–3 October 1998

Be Gentle to a Greek

(Stein 53)

Be gentle to each other, to everybody, for every designer revises.

Do be kind and never try to interfere with people coming together. A moment after it would have been you. That scene means they'll resume it in the house.

We've not softened, no way. Anything can help in that place. What had mentioning the higher meant. Wealthy boys could and will decide what they would have said there and would have had careless women hear.

I'd better have said he was Greek. Do deny silence enough. Everybody does. Carrie borrows what she carries. The English uncovered Meininger as one who was there would've wanted. His gentle coughing wouldn't have tired you as much as your own would've. Those four laughed at the need for harnessing and forgot it.

When those sounds were heard and that thing was opened what had those horses begun to believe. That they were draught horses. Gradually the fall would've made everything necessary for everybody. The four who hurry meet the one who is Greek. He did this to me, not the ones whose names he said. How had he mentioned them when he did. He increased it. Everybody shown with it wanted to be believed. Four had to ask something. He goes and stones the door enough, doubly or lightly. Hadn't coal been necessary. Wouldn't that home have needed it all the same.

Why are they loaning it.

Has that been his way. Can't anybody help. Those in that place should have gone away yesterday when they could still hear and see.

Why couldn't they've decided. What have the women hearing it carelessly said been saying. He said I'd better deny it enough or be silent. He was a Greek.

Eight paragraphs/strophes in which the number of sentences follows two successive Lucas sequences: 1, 3, 4, 7, 11 and 1, 3, 4. Derived from Stein's PMJ (*ASR* 300–05). The order of the source's paragraphs was newly randomized for this poem by random-digit chance operations. The paragraph-randomized passage was run through DIASTEX5, using as seed a paragraph from Stein's LGB (*ASR* 215, par. 6). The output was freely revised and edited, but most of its words were placed in sentences and paragraphs where their groupings are roughly similar to those in the unrevised output of the program.

New York: 3–15 October 1998

He Has Been Revising Those That Wanted Harnessing

(Stein 54)

He has been revising his conscience.

Many are listening to wheels from elsewhere. Shouting, these sheepdog policemen ordinarily stammer. What are they harnessing?

I'm trying to think what they meant by harnessing. If it was to see a way to say "hearing," they went too late for a waxlight to make a difference. Another buyer would be enough. They are behaving like rubber.

They are in a hurry to see what they had heard. But whoever deceives in exercises is not likely to see much winning, she said. A fork goes with nearly every fish allowed out. Julian Howard and I nearly believe her. She said he reigned in the rain. Something lights the lamps. They have plainly been cleaner.

He'd been saying he was the one who'd been shouting when they'd finished playing draughts without making enough of a promise to get together again. I and it are aging. We have been widening a door. The address of mischief is the bed. Please be reluctant to go to the places where rivers and iron have met. Anybody in great need has wanted intuition. The English are getting willing to wish. Why are those places that much higher? I meant to go to hear Mother and see London. When it was pleasant was principally when we were drawing good ones unexpectedly. The cleaner uncovered the separation and was disappointed.

Harnessing the ones that wanted it, I seldom asked them to fall. Why hasn't there been any help for anybody. Winning will likely be softening. Once hurried away by language, little rebellion was left. Howard said what he believed. When he said that this time gave us such a look at thinking that this day would not be doubled, it was not the absence of plaster that made us believe we'd have had a resumption that would have done him in. These sounds separate the changes by a little over a mile. It was curious seven were paying. He said the things of the good should be together. Separation is absence without a door. Don't resume it. Have a rest. It's driven a little. They are too. Please for a mile the ones that wanted a hundred. The designer did understand. I increasingly get remarkable. I'm willing to get dirty if it doesn't lessen my winning. When there, they'll mention what "the higher" meant.

Go to Mother.

I hear you'll see London when it's pleasant. Was it unexpected that the good ones were principally drawings. Cleaner to've uncovered the separation than to've been disappointed.

I asked for those that wanted harnessing.

Nine paragraph-strophes in which the number of sentences follows two successive Lucas sequences: 1, 3, 4, 7, 11, 18; and 1, 3; followed by 1 line. Derived from Stein's PMJ (*ASR* 300–05). The order of the source's paragraphs was newly randomized for this poem by random-digit chance operations. The paragraph-randomized passage was run through DIASTEX5, using as seed a paragraph from Stein's LGB (*ASR* 215, par. 7). The output was freely revised and edited, but most of its words were placed in sentences and paragraphs where their groupings are roughly similar to those in the unrevised output of the program.

New York: 3–17 October 1998; 23 March 2002

He Cannot Have Been Pleased Today to Hear That

(Stein 55)

He cannot have been pleased today to hear her accidentally mention that.

Although she is little Carrie is forty. Ask for rubber in your prayers. They are doubles but are they brothers.

Whoever hears plaster dry listens best. It was said that the country might have had better kinds of fire if it hadn't won that prize. Their hundred offspring were promised a whole new arrangement. Another disappointed rebellion.

Of all who were there yesterday who will be exclaiming in that place today. I heard the door. It has been shown that we men make dirt. Are we willing to hear it stopped. England and age loaned decision a train. Gradually he comes to believe no one. She does either nothing or little.

He said he'd undergone the same decrease of conscience after considering their stammering thinking. Please harness another one. He had a hundred. Did the designer understand. Weren't you satisfactorily kind. Under an obligation to get the shapes into certain places what place did you mention as higher. He meant the knives entailed reparations. It has been found that women hear best. Can a man wait now. Julian mentioned the separate introductions. Weren't you yourselves surprised.

Little ones believe me. This cannot be going on. Had you wanted to you couldn't have chosen to carry the unavoidable but you did so accidentally. Are the brothers there. Whether they went there or not they doubled the plaster. Those who hear best are hopefully pleasant. That was the end but I prefer the beginning. Why should that other one stammer. They're ordinarily together. When another drafts the recipe for bread there please tell me whether this furthers still another. What was the purpose of that resumption of bribery. A hundred offspring sprang from closets in another disappointed rebellion. Their higher exclamations were meant to call the wealthy to resemble them by doing what they did. These times principally carry with them undertakings hastening decisions. In the beginning everybody overflowed. There were fifty opportunities for the English to disappoint the rebellion. Exclaiming that higher meant wealthier the callers resembled doers. Undertakings in these times are principally fastened to decisions.

Whether near or far the rest rest. Anybody may accidentally become necessary. We believe bread becomes thinking. Does this sound like an accident. He accidentally changes. He went where the front lamps do little. Though he looked he had need of intuition to choose among the women. They made believe their faces looked that way. Please can't we hurry to see what causes that resemblance. When we have seen whether they carry things faster will we have wanted to listen. I know I am mud. He's gentle to fish. Hot or cool she would deny that. Promise you'll leave out the introductions. Separate when this changes. He did the tired thing. Had any other needed harnessing. The designer did. Am I to understand you made her leave instead. Woody the baker was in an unexpected bed. He never said that we said either that he was displeased or that he was pleased. Credit another horse's straps' goodness. Whether reparation is everything or not this was harnessing. When we have met will we remember the rest of this. Such splendid running. Would everybody believe there was any chance that they wanted her to leave. Never revise her accidentally. They were annoyed when they saw what higher winning meant. Do it by widening it.

She was not lonesome despite the expenses of emigration. When they got the maps together they didn't try to notice what he'd said they'd have to remember. All my toys were wonderful. Carving the splendid coal the bribed one exclaimed that Henner's picture would be worth a hundred of his offspring. He was a designer and he did understand. He said you've not been satisfactorily careful. That very neglect was forgotten. Away with what you mean to say. Don't only use cement. Why would emigration stand as the better measure. He recommended that he be a minister. The decision to loan away the fork was greeted with language such as no one would have believed. They rendered it accidentally. Had another believed in another there's a chance that still another would have been displeased. It disappointed forty that Carrie was so little although many prayers were said for her. The number of rubber wheels was lessening in that place. Are those brothers the reason. He stopped his gentle plastering.

Ordinarily they would try everything. Pray that this harnessing be an introduction to toys. So far toys may be for anybody. He means that morning is the time to express emotion. Hundreds asked her age and what would become of her. He was trained to make decisions about loans and doesn't believe anyone. Gradually they came to be doing very little. He said they'd undergo the same decrease of conscience. She considered thinking about it after stammering Please. To you harnessing another hundred was not at all satisfactory. The designer understood that.

Nine paragraph/strophes in which the number of sentences follows the ascending and partially descending Lucas sequence 1, 3, 4, 7, 11, 18, 29, 18, 11. Derived from Stein's PMJ (*ASR* 300–05). The passage was run through DIASTEX5, using as seed a paragraph from Stein's LGB (*ASR* 215, par. 8). One word from the seed was inserted at random locations in the source to allow DIASTEX5 to complete one whole period. The output was freely revised and edited, but most of its words (or their root morphemes) were placed in sentences and paragraphs where their groupings are similar to those in the program's unrevised output.

New York: 17–31 October 1998; right margin narrowed to 1", 1 October 1999

She Addressed Him Like Useless Mischief

(Stein 56)

She addressed him when she knew he was out, and I shall mention this because it is astonishing.

We have listened to those who will not be softening. Such a success looks like a success. I understand that useless mischief is calamitously unavoidable.

If any of them had noticed eggs upon praying for them, that would have astonished everybody who was coming. Everybody—that would have been four of them—carried or would undertake to carry the pieces and be left thinking this was an out-and-out Greek thing and useless. There were places where he mentioned winning when leaving. Shall she mention that eyes overflowed there when fifty hurried on as if they knew everybody?

We carried and studied whatever they loaned us. Would we have if we had heard who they were? Those at the door were willing to be beginning. I am hearing this and sitting, for I would be cautious when I express myself. His closets had a resemblance to his name. We did not see at once that they had taken pieces out of the whole. She was useless to herself and beautifully dangerous lately. We mentioned coal.

Matisse was useless. He expected exercises. Maps of rebellion were made at a conscientious moment, considering everybody. The servants pray for lamps while the sheepdogs are rebelling. There were certainly to be no doors. Such a match was not to be shown outside. There wheels surprise calamitous mischief unavoidable by those in the house who loudly feel separate. Changes in toys were the wonders mentioned. I'm considering winding them cautiously. Harnessing four of them, he'd seen Emile make an English beginning. Walter Meininger was nearly thinking that the city was believed to be an arrangement made to be forgotten and meant for the eyes of the wealthy whose missions wouldn't be.

Although she is the only one for a fancy mile who has respect for bread and coal, she is considering winding up her dealing in them, or would have been had that drawing not gotten fastened there. We forked over those that were found. The willing credited the hearing they were getting. What they are in to get they'll cautiously express. Their closets resembled each other. That name was not to be seen outside. They were all once pieces of a whole. Useless, churlish mischief is calamitous and unavoidable. They never went faster than the rest have. Believe, feed, and consider winding. I am dealing with that. Please, when will you have decided what you wish we'd be paying? Esther expresses by her repetition of his name that she forgot in her rebellion to complain about something. This is to help you believe me when I am an absence. It's a mile to something. He was not reluctant when he said that her leaving would be, if only to the baker, unexpected. Prayers and lights show we believe in coming and saying. If an electrician's silver had fallen among the coals, he would have been uncomfortable.

Mr. England is silent, expecting exercises.

Maps really exclaim. Stockings are to thinking what everything is to rebellion. His harnessing that one there at will was why the horses believed him.

When manners are mischief they express expense. I expect their tails will be exclaiming. Calamitous missions give permission for everything. Harnessing that one there, they were hearing that horses believe that when manners are mischief all can see it.

When would they be cautious—in the morning? Walter Meininger was thinking that we nearly expected that overflow. Fifty of them are hurrying as if they know everybody. I is a further means. Would you please mention fastening that drawing? Their insistence on butter will be mentioned because it is astonishing. We have been listening not to be softening such a success but because that success looks, as we understand it, like useless mischief.

Ten paragraph-strophes in which the number of sentences follows two Lucas sequences: 1, 3, 4, 7, 11, 18 and 1, 3, 4, 7. Derived from Stein's PMJ (*ASR* 300–05). The order of the source's paragraphs was newly randomized by random-digit chance operations and run through DIASTEX5, using as seed a paragraph from Stein's LGB (*ASR* 216, par. 1). The output was freely revised and edited, but most of its words (or their root morphemes) were placed in sentences and paragraphs where their groupings are similar to those in the program's unrevised output.

New York: 26 October–1 November 1998; 18 June 2001; 7 May 2002

Say Hearing

(Stein 57)

Say do remember rivers.

All are.
Ice do.
Be lead goodness a sneeze old.

I of than she please very hearing.
He drawing there decided to think that what so languages
    being good think the the.
They willing something count will.
Would not now better real me repetition name?

Monday cement to.
The shall restless thinking.
There plenty only whether be for mile deciding lessening.
What goodness saw boy came seven.
An or sheepdog dog.
Seems plan said and in did in of the thing.
One very hearing.

Four strophes in which the number of verse-line sentences follows the ascending Lucas sequence 1, 3, 4, 7. Derived from Stein's PMJ (*ASR* 300–05). The order of the source passage's paragraphs was randomized by random-digit chance operations and run through DIASTEX5, using as seed Stein's LGB (*ASR* 216, par. 2). The output was lightly revised as to line and strophe breaks and initial capitalization, and periods were inserted at line endings, but the words and their order were not changed.

New York: 5–9 November 1998; 1–2, 23 February 1999

Be Languages
Hearing Being

(Stein 58)

Be lead languages being shall good.

Good so goodness.
Monday cement goodness restless.
Restless and she sneeze one.

Cement sneeze goodness only plenty.
And of sneeze one.
Very hearing for very hearing remember.
Shall hearing.

Willing drawing.
Drawing mile.
Monday languages lead.
Monday plenty cement very remember.
Rivers goodness cement.
To dog did to dog seems better.
There seems please what cement.

To count being plenty willing.
Did mile willing.
Will would count will.
Would not now.
Better name to now.
Better real not better.
There better good so goodness.
Monday cement goodness restless.
Restless said name now better.

Good boy came languages something.
Repetition sheepdog Monday.

Cement rivers something goodness.
To that what restless.
Whether the drawing that sheepdog.
Monday.
Monday languages saw languages.
Languages languages languages.
Hearing languages.
Languages being.
Be being plenty thing there.
Think there.
There lessening plan.
Please what sneeze.
Count plenty plenty to they.
The very will willing only willing.
Hearing willing drawing.
Sheepdog Monday.
Monday cement remember something.
Something lessening something.

Something.
They shall whether sheepdog Monday.
They shall real shall restless me.
Lessening what shall restless.
Goodness.
Goodness that what being plenty.
Thinking.
Repetition deciding sheepdog Monday.
Monday cement remember restless.
Repetition name count thinking.
Repetition repetition repetition.
Repetition name.
Languages cement came only in mile.
Very willing.

The.
The what whether decided whether be.
He drawing mile and in sneeze old.
Of the thing there to think think.
Think being hearing cement dog drawing.
That drawing.
Hearing willing languages to that.
There there there decided deciding.
Decided decided deciding.
Restless decided to think.
To think thinking plan thinking the.
The than what hearing cement dog.
Drawing that drawing.
Hearing willing languages to that.
There there there decided deciding.

Decided decided deciding.
Restless decided to.
To think think thinking.
Plan think goodness.
Monday goodness good think.
The thinking.
Plan think the.
The she to that.
There.
They.
The whether there there plenty.
All are count repetition.
Monday for Monday very me will willing something.
Did.
He decided decided deciding thinking.
Thinking deciding lessening.
Cement restless lessening better.
Hearing something.
Lessening something will.
The shall.

Restless and please what will.
All are sheepdog Monday and of drawing.
Sheepdog Monday.
They.
The repetition sheepdog Monday.
Sheepdog Monday sheepdog Monday.
Thinking me would languages lead.
Monday plenty cement very remember.
Rivers goodness cement.
To dog very hearing very they.
He decided that there hearing willing.
Languages sneeze saw.
Boy did to remember restless name.
Sneeze remember.
Remember remember remember rivers.
Willing seven.
Something rivers rivers.
Ice.
Ice.
They dog count that what.
There.
They willing did mile willing hearing.
Willing drawing sheepdog Monday.
Monday cement remember something.
Something lessening something.
Something cement to count thinking.
Repetition would.

Will willing shall thinking.

Whether the sheepdog Monday.
They shall real shall restless me.
Lessening what shall restless.

Goodness goodness that what being.
Plenty thinking.

Repetition deciding sheepdog Monday.
Plan please what.

What being sneeze saw being good.
All and old in and real me.
Real will me.
Repetition remember restless.
Repetition name count thinking.
Repetition repetition.
Repetition repetition name languages.

Cement came.
What so count will would not now.
Better not now saw boy.
Seven not better.
Better better real being lead will.
Goodness boy good.
Monday to.
They thinking plan think the the she.
To that.
There in of of than she what being.
Sneeze that.

There plenty plenty are please what.

Seems goodness what.
There shall restless sheepdog Monday.
Monday languages saw languages.

Languages languages languages.
Hearing languages languages being.
Being plenty thing.
Languages hearing being.

Sixteen strophes of which the number of lines follows three successive Lucas sequences: 1, 3, 4, 7, 11, 18, 29, 47; 1, 3, 4, 7, 11; and 1, 3, 4. Derived from Stein's PMJ (*ASR* 300–05) and run through DIASTEX5, using as seed Stein's LGB (*ASR* 216, par. 2). This output, unaltered except for line and strophe breaks, etc., comprises this poem's predecessor, Stein 57. In making the present poem, this output was subjected to several random-number chance operations, and the result of these operations was sent through DIASTEXT, Hartman's first (c. 1989) automation of one of my diastic procedures that I first developed in January 1963 (before computers were miniaturized). DIASTEXT uses the entire source text as the seed text. The resulting text was horizontally compressed by a margin-size change. The resulting line breaks were sometimes changed, but the words and their order in this last output were left unchanged, except for insertions of initial capitals where they were absent and final periods.

New York: 6–8 November 1998; 1–2 February 1999

See Them Together

(Stein 59)

See them deciding if you can.

Monday I believe to be dangerous.
Carry do carry the same offer to another.
She is annoyed that in bed he never says anything for days.

Quickly he said the thing he had to say was that he had nothing to say.
The thing that's shown, why it's herself.
When the whole thing was mentioned, it's likely it was not for it to be
    neglected.
Don't be like that.

It was an Italian wonder, a hundred men and no mother, no,
    saw the calamitous poison.
Render what you will so that the forty see sounds or something.
There are many piles of spools there.
This one said that to think meant to beat.
This was the very one who said it was so, that this other one had said that
    something had seven hands.
Do rivers not render an increase in letters by going where they're going
    and not stammering.
Let it stand.

That the prayers looked to be annoying was shown by the laughs.
Really deny that said Mother.
Walter, it is not just any edgy goodness that is splendid said the minister
    as he fastened himself.
Not coughing there doesn't do anything for me, for I am seven years of age.
Are those really prayers.
I believe the infant's helpless separation was what made you what you will
    or would be.
The country did not come to be splendid in that age of shapely citizens.

They're cement.
They're we.
These are the stones that horses believe can light many lamps
with the same authority.
That it had not been believed that eggs were meat astonished me.

In London you would be sheer tired she said one day when more of us
came late.
We did it together.
Because of those draughts the women complained of a reluctant
inclination.
Leaving she mentioned saying that she too had not come splendidly.
She would.
For as far as a mile he, no you, do believe what you hear.
The horses render what they can and no moon is getting into taking the
shapes we saw.
This said he surprised them saying we don't need the silvery noise they can
make.
Something like that.
Seven are enough, but hands in rebellion seldom say this.
Lead us to the sheepdog.
What is that there, what emotion is going into making us believe in it.
When the shouting, when the gently tired mile was over, all that was newly
loaned would not do.
No need for it.
During that credit hearing the names did not come out of those we had not
seen.
Emile had shown and loudly said there were reasons why some women
come so splendidly.
They said this was what they'd said.
Italian rest that shall be blest they wanted, but stupidly said they wanted
soup.

He was considering it.
Wondering she rendered rubber not to do mischief but not what they said
either.
It meant very little when they did that winding and dangerous shouting
but went away gently.

We need that.
She was harnessing a picture.
I was annoyed.
Those women never openly interfere but they *do* believe the country is the
city.
Do name me, and understand I am of age and a shapely citizen, not cement.
Where are the horses.
I believe you are willing toys, coal decides when you cough and when you
don't.
I am at the age of seven, *some*thing–I mean–SOMEbody.

Are you saying your prayers.
I believe the infant's world was one country and he said he'd seen that
country.
Come back.
It had been an age since our splendid shapely citizens had seen cement
horses.
Do you believe that.
You willing toys have decided on coal so you can stand paying any amount.
Fork it over.

Seven somethings were together.

Nine strophes in which the number of lines/sentences follows the ascending and truncatedly descending Lucas-number sequence 1, 3, 4, 7, 11, 18, 11, 7, followed by one line. Derived from PMJ (*ASR* 300–05). The order of the source's paragraphs was newly randomized by random-digit chance operations, then long paragraphs were broken into shorter ones, the new ones were given random numbers, and the whole series of numbered paragraphs was randomized again. The reordered passage was run through DIASTEX5, using as seed Stein's LGB (*ASR* 216, par. 3). Every typographical line of the output was converted, by liminal or deliberate choices, into a normative sentence by the addition of minimal numbers of non-output words and a minimum of changes of word order, tense, number, etc., and each sentence became a verse line.

New York: 8–9 November 1998; 30 April 2002

Asked Plaster Believe
What Overflow Running Wouldn't

(Stein 60)

asked plaster believe
We churlish book a true
Greek that silent hurry moment would an introductions
and am
are
Please he be
Plainly there
mention morning
sitting was the that went to the
the pity are wrong ones
hurrying see that

There
Carrie listen willing and prefer there
end expenses separate
together conscienced
Closets lessening beginning fastening there not bread
meat
hundred rebellion

What overflow running wouldn't leaving there that meant yesterday
see do time absence curious spacing
remember wonder

There knows
I is
What was going what mention morning

sitting

I is getting you said stand using the now am is ask if
If he he wanted did believe exclaim be heard very will his decision
don't decide hundred
I study is is are
Very neglect forgot away
Don't sitting softening prefer
Meininger perfect cautious gradually satisfactorily they
shall being thing going believe
He said country thing that wish
Carrie were accident
A
An and he serve really heard leaving winning dealing what them
years emotion only anybody blest
I is he be

Plainly there mention morning sitting was the the front same
not names times are wrong ones
Not no not and using ask designer astonish coming
When they means
What task that the they me will together mother plaster be we
another is ask minister cement coming as all ill-natured
will

When brothers appalling crops one
the mischief straps come
would ask an and
Although draughts the
He me leaving there mention
Carving running was this really that the there the away and true

Greek he becomes years express emotion spacing winding address
broken been eyes expenses separate together conscienced

Closets lessening beginning

fastening there not bread
meat hundred rebellion

What overflow running wouldn't

Eleven strophes in which the number of lines follows the two descending Lucas sequences 11, 7, 4, 3, 1, and 18, 11, 7, 4, 3, 1. Derived from Stein's PMJ (*ASR* 300–05). The order of the source's paragraphs as randomized for Stein 59 was newly randomized by random-digit chance operations. The reordered passage was run through DIASTEX5, using as seed Stein's LGB (*ASR* 216, par. 4). Every typographical line of the output was accepted as a verse line of Stein 60 without any change in capitalization or addition of punctuation (one "a" was changed to an "an"), and the entire series of lines was broken into strophes as above and centered within given margins.

New York: 10–14 November 1998; 25 February 1999

Sitting Was the Perfect Cautious A

(Stein 61)

sitting was the the
Plainly there mention morning
When they means
front same
years emotion only anybody blest
and am
using the now am is ask
designer astonish coming
plaster be we

sitting was the that went to the
spacing remember wonder

asked plaster believe
the pity are wrong ones
I is

meat
what them
are
Please he be
What was going what mention
morning

Greek he becomes years

He said country thing that wish
gradually satisfactorily
Closets lessening beginning
together mother

shall being thing going believe
If he he wanted did believe
Carrie were accident
meat

exclaim be heard very

ill-natured will
hundred rebellion

that the there the
I study is is are
away and true
conscienced
one the mischief straps
that meant yesterday
fastening there not bread
leaving there
When brothers appalling crops
mention morning
He me leaving there mention
separate together
Very neglect forgot away
will his decision

not names times are wrong ones
There knows
sitting

Plainly there
Carving running was this really
there end expenses

separate
come
What overflow running wouldn't
would ask an and
Although draughts the

if
don't decide hundred
Carrie listen willing and prefer
Don't sitting softening prefer
I is he be
Greek that silent hurry moment
would an introductions
see do time absence curious
There

winding address
hundred rebellion
Not no not and using ask
fastening there not bread
leaving winning dealing
hurrying see that

Closets lessening beginning
What task that the they me will
What overflow running wouldn't

they
We churlish book a true

An and he serve really heard
another is ask minister
together conscienced
I is getting you said stand

express emotion spacing
broken been eyes expenses
cement coming as all
Meininger perfect cautious
A

Seventeen strophes derived from Stein 60 by reordering and partially changing line breaks and sizes of interstrophe breaks by means of random-number and other chance operations. All verse lines and interstrophe breaks were accepted as given by the chance operations. When printed, the number of blank lines between strophes (one, two, or three) should be retained.

New York: 10–11 November 1998; 26 April 2000; 29 April 2002

It Is Stopped If It Is Cautious

(Stein 62)

It is stopped if it is.

Esther May was rosy.
The team seemed to be restless.
And I suggest you're spoiling things
    by saying what age
    the minister should be
    if he is coming in
    to relieve our being separate.

Remember that.
Versailles can't have been lessening
    the beginning
    of that fastening.
I shall be after as I was before.
Any buyer may have brothers.

Another repetition was involving
    shouting
    and hurrying.
Anybody could've done it
    and've had the same result.
England's credit is inclining to be lessening
    in accordance with what happened
    by someone-or-other's permission.
Everyone was pointing at them when that happened.
This increase in expenses
    due to the changes
    in the prices of eggs
    led to plenty of emigration.

He was widening
  his mentioning
  of thinking
  while he was sitting
  with his offspring.
Perfect missions respect caution
  and thereby come to fruition
  gradually
  and satisfactorily.

Why had those two said
  what the rain was going to do
  and what it would be carrying?
Do women in the wind
  unexpectedly mention fish?
I don't know.
Harnessing your mother in rebellion
  is fastening
  your beginning
  and saying,
  Do come.
Once plenty was enough,
  but now
  those in rebellion
  complain of their offspring.
A whole
  winding
  unexpected obligation to the old
  carries them with you all the same.
You know,
  there is a resemblance here
  to being harnessed
  to another country
  instead of being fastened
  to the one you knew from the beginning.
Her softening was appalling.
I believe the old are pleased with us.

If and whether every body is another or not,
    that very voice there
    made you think of these obligations
    to the old.
That the eggs were those of a fish was a pity.

Those who plan this thing
    will quickly recognize
    what their eyes expect.
Are you certain your stockings
    aren't forcing this decision?
It is I, it is.
Mr. England said his very soup there
    was plainly given him
    by reason of right praise
    and of eggs.
What police were reigning?
If I were to revise it
    would I get reparations after exclaiming?
In our closets and in us
    I recognize an appalling softening.
I'd say that through our mischievous decisions
    those stockings
    were certainly another's.
Are any of the oldest
    relieved at being separated
    from what they remember?
Versailles could not lessen the fastening
    that was believed to be beginning.
Render said,
    When you recognize
    what everybody expects
    do it quickly.

You certainly won't make any decisions
    about their stockings.

I am what I do.
I will offer it perfectly.

She was wishing to be perfectly cautious.

Makingway Endnote

Nine strophes in which the number of sentences follows the ascending and descending Lucas-number sequence 1, 3, 4, 7, 11, 7, 4, 3, 1. Sentences begin at the left margin and are often broken into two or more verse lines; verse lines after the first in each sentence are indented at the left. Derived from Stein's PMJ (*ASR* 300–05). The randomization of the source's paragraphs used in making Stein 60 and Stein 61 was newly randomized by breaking the text at every period and comma, assigning a random number to each sentence fragment, and reordering them by random-digit chance operations. The reordered passage was run through DIASTEX5, using as seed a paragraph from Stein's LGB (*ASR* 216, par. 5). By liminal and deliberate choices, the output was converted into normative sentences by minimally adding non-output "helping words"; changing word order, tense, voice, number, etc.; and by inserting end marks as appropriate. The sentences were grouped in Lucas-sequence strophes as described above, and most of them were deliberately broken into shorter verse lines in accordance with their grammar, syntax, and meaning and with prosodical considerations. Some words, line breaks, end marks, and the endnote were revised 1998–2002.

New York: 12–13 November 1998; 24 February 2000;
12 April 2001; 11–14 January, 30 April 2002

Plaster Reigned

(Stein 63)

Plaster can't have been what she heard.

Lights will really be softening.
He said seven were beaten.
They made the women come to believe it.

Can't they have something out.
Some of our age are in that country.
Some who reigned there were trying to remember
    whether they'd been invited.
That was an age ago.

What more had those seven noticed than that she had
    plenty of pity and had broken everything.
They say she'd succumbed earlier.
Spain was astonished at their coming together in the
    place mentioned.
It is England.
It asked for its absence.
England said it was their duty to learn what that voice
    meant.
Although this changes it ought not to.

He had addressed ten prayers to what was no more than
    black meat.
They are many and ordinarily their lack of bread would
    have decided them to stand everybody.
Sitting carving in the morning you would not complain
    though you would clearly recollect that very
    reparation.

Seven will certainly undertake to get wood when Spain
asks them whether they can see the city.
When they pray they are pleasant and nearly right.
Remember that you are separate.
England credits those who recognize and complain
about what is plainly appalling.
They were pleased to help with that task.
He was really together.
He said their lights were really softening the beat.
Sitting carving in the morning she made seven of them.

Some women can do something for anyone.

Some are out of place.
She believed we were coming as we had in the country.
He remembered he was invited only when he reigned.

Seven strophes in which the number of lines follows the ascending Lucas sequences 1, 3, 4, 7, 11, and 1, 3. Derived from PMJ (*ASR* 300–05). The randomization of the order of the sentences and sentence fragments in the last randomization of the source passage's paragraphs (used in making Stein 62) was newly randomized by assigning a new random number to each sentence and fragment and reordering them by random-digit chance operations. The reordered passage was run through DIASTEX5, using as seed Stein's LGB (*ASR* 216, par. 6). By liminal and deliberate choices, the output was converted into normative sentences by minimally adding non-output words and sometimes changing word order, tense, voice, number, etc. The sentences became verse lines grouped in Lucas-sequence strophes as above.

New York: 14–15 November 1998

If I Am Reparation

(Stein 64)

If I am mentioned or it is, Esther will know it.

There will be plenty of brothers who won't.
He said they'd made a friendly arrangement.
It will be as friendly as you yourselves are friendly.

It is I as I am it.
Piles of old useless things could be separated from the oldest
and most pleasant though no accident would do
this.
See if you can beat the rest by being appallingly silent
in their company.
They didn't complain that your wonder was lessening
even if it was.

I'm asking whether age made their resemblance seem
so pleasant that you succumbed to it.
You yourselves were then at Versailles.
There by reason of the company and the room he took pity
enough on your error.
England was splendidly wondering at her fastening.
It was not to have been believed.
Though friendly and paying for it he thought it was he who
was useless when it was I who was and am.
God knows they looked dangerous and something about
their offspring was appalling.

I study them.
I am coal whose glowing you yourselves accomplished.
Widening the spelling and pointing to the whole you were
leaving us waiting but said you were not.

Come let us widen one another.
When can any of us be said to be able to carry what any
horse could.
They said as they were coughing that at home they only care
about the wealthy.
Something was in accordance with something whether it was
I, I mean mine, or the infant's or Esther's.
When disappointing pears are mentioned there as coming
in now are we going to be deciding against them
just because tails keep coming up.
Plainly what she was going to do was to come once.
Harnessing her was nearly to have her.
There it would be said that she could cement whatever one
asked her to.

There's something about the wealthy that continues to be
somewhat disappointing.
I said it was their infants.
Esther's description of him was sent out because the
electrician had succumbed.
It was disappointing to hear you exclaiming at their
harnessing.
To whom other than them shall we mention stockings.
Asked for cement one could have said yes indeed but need
not have loaned it to the city.
The sheepdogs cannot expect to get their expenses back
by rebellion.
Their maps were friendly.
Principally they didn't complain or lessen their wondering
but said they could cement whatever we asked them
to.
Something about the wealthy was not in accordance with
the infant's I or It.
Esther is not astonishing but she's friendly to those
coming in.
Closets present churlish opportunities for repetition,
this is astonishingly true.

I was thinking that what we see
    does the same as what we free.
What he had was fire.
We suggest you do what we cannot for we cannot separate
    being surprised from being disappointing.
Whatever you do with your silver on company time don't
    imagine its lessening'll be enough to keep the
    electrician from wondering.
Was it a mistake to ask whether it was disappointing,
    he queried disappointedly.
It was disappointingly uncomfortable.

It was disappointing, disappointingly disappointing,
    disappointingly disappointingly disappointingly
    disappointing.
Then stammer this, that we should separate consciences
    from names, one at a time.
She may ask them not to say what their arrangement on the
    train was.
Why was it widening.
These shall say whether he believed what he said.
They gradually came to think that that was the country
    where they'd met.
He said he was surprised that he and they had been there.
I see it is still the same and that it is useless to be willing it
    to be something else.
The loan would have been made in accordance with what
    someone else had said.
She's kissed plenty of rubber.
Isn't she even going to come once.
Both of them counted altogether on her intuition.
They were wondering together at a make-believe fastening
    and looked at whatever their recollections carried
    them to.
Howard and many others went to a minister with their
    résumés and offered to do whatever they could.

They saw that I am busy and in a hurry and that I cannot go
to look at the same free toys that they had seen.
You should be making your silver prayers for Emile, not
yourselves.
Esther had not mentioned that she'd been carving out
whole languages.
If she waits she can have them all for herself.
Harnessing was being practiced widely when the country was
careful of her after she'd brought me the cement I'd
asked for.
It is I that everybody and the moon assume to've done
something wrong to you.
Prayers pleased those who knew what was disappointingly
pleasant but were pleased at it nevertheless.
If anything I say to that pleases you everything will.
Carrie was pleased today when someone came and
complained that he was good but as careless
as could be.
He wanted what was not to be spoken out for, a man said.
Please mention that splendid meat there.
These shall be the very way you said they should be when
everybody else had only come to think them
calamitous poisons.
I was astonished at what the police asked at that time,
my age.
That new one increasingly asked it.
Either I am away or you are.

This was mentioned in the morning when the brothers were
eating whichever of the shapely women didn't get
tired and go away.

On the whole when we have harnessing we have cement.
Since he was coughing we were hopeful that he was to have
home care, we'll have to get it for him.
If one can come to be an individual it means she is never
on any day to interfere disappointingly.

They were exclaiming that they had left because the
electrician had succumbed to disappointment.
Harnessing them was pleasing us more than that first plan.
Indeed in place of the cost of spools they've said they'd have
other expenses.
It's time for the conscienced boys whatever their names
are to be in bed.

She goes and does and makes what she wants.
His task is to be as careful as he's asked to be.
If she went away a hundred would quickly replace her.
If I made a disappointing decision about these stockings
Esther would not accept it and that would be the
end of it.
But deceiving has never stopped.
It is unexpected that they even considered demanding that
astonishing reparation for harnessing them.
We have been making a success of this there.

Please feel free to do the same.
It was I who thought of that.
All of the infants were surprised by the shouting.
He was coming in then.
He pitied the electrician for being so disappointing in tails.
The Italian mentioned her remarkable authority edged with
melancholy.
Others principally mentioned the excellent Shell Express
Company.
The lonesome kept mentioning everybody else
and exclaimed at seeing them hurrying.
Disappointingly they insisted on a melancholy separation.
Is that harnessing.
I know that a fish cannot really be said to like some one
but there were times there when I thought I could
reasonably mention that that one was friendly.

Those going by train were friendly, all too friendly.

Among all of them it is I alone who am perfectly friendly.
When the arrangements were finished they gradually began
    laughing at the sounds the Authority was making.
He believed he really remembered when they were separate.

Versailles was silent when somebody's offspring did
    something appalling.
I've been studying about it.
I was astonishing when I was at the age when all of us were
    rebelling.
Versailles succumbed to giving Esther reparation.

Fifteen strophes in which the number of lines in successive strophes comprise three successive ascending Lucas sequences: 1, 3, 4, 7, 11, 18, 29; 1, 3, 4, 7, 11; and 1, 3, 4. Derived from Stein's PMJ (*ASR* 300–05). Stein 64 was derived from that passage in PMJ as follows: (1) The order of the source passage's paragraphs had been randomized several times previously by means of random-number chance operations, last during the making of Stein 62. (2) Then the order of the typographical lines of that last randomization of paragraph order had been randomized while Stein 63 was being made. (3) To make Stein 64 the order of those typographical lines, of which each was a sentence or sentence fragment, was newly randomized. (4) The reordered passage was run through DIASTEX5, using as seed Stein's LGB (*ASR* 216, par. 7). To allow DIASTEX5 to go through one complete period, one or the other of two words from the seed text was inserted in the source text at several chance-operationally determined, but syntactically/grammatically appropriate, positions. (5) The program's output was converted by choices, some liminal, some deliberate, into normative sentences by minimally adding non-output words, sometimes dropping or modifying structure words and/or changing word order, tense, number, etc. (6) Finally the sentences were formatted as verse lines and grouped in fifteen Lucas-sequence strophes as described above.

New York: 16 November–1 December 1998

The Almonds
Buy Me with a Paragraph
Ha

(Stein 65)

The Almonds buy me with their care named Bradley which is that it is
remaining once again.

It cannot be natural because they prefer separating salad.
This is inviting his confidence which it is right Basket a name.
If he has not asked him she will come and be no disappointment.

She criticizes.
But which week.
A sentence made change in a firm hoping for them they are accepted as
being in very mainly if intruding.
They were in an opposite reason of a placement.

For their sake and ridges.
With his goodbye and an offering.
They are naturally that they will have been wet.
The salads are as small and will belie it.
A paragraph because of well well.
Well enough alone.
They made it be all when they like grapes.

Because if they answer.
They will even when there is a difference in their name.
A fox which is in one word is talkative.
They like when they add with a capital with a wife.
Wifely.
Enthusiasm.

Natural.
A period is natural sentence is natural sentence can not remind it of it.
This is a joke.
A sentence can come and be no disappointment is natural parting.
Pears and apart.

And will they have to do without him.
He may sail.
Not with him.
They need not know that he had.
That is a trait which has that for their sake and ridges.
With them.
After all why will they think about who says.
She liked their care named Bradley which made whenever they were women.
This is a paragraph is not natural.
Now.
It is after they were cutting with which they were women.
This is as useful as a doll.
Now then she always is nature personified.
A like sentence made with him.
They need know their paragraph that plans of a thing that her name had
not been changed but not known about.
She had held spending when she was sent.
In and uninvited by the time.
They will be asked to come if they answer.

They will have it a name.

There is no need to have lost.
By that means he was received without moving.
I do not think that they can appeal that appointment is natural.

A period is naturally a paragraph ha.

Nine strophes of which the number of sentences/verse lines follows two Lucas sequences: 1, 3, 4, 7, 11, 18 and 1, 3, followed by a one-verse-line coda. ("Sentence" is defined as "Any word string beginning with a capital letter and ending with a period.") Derived from a six-page passage at the beginning of Stein's "More Grammar for a Sentence" (*ASR* 548–53). The passage was run through TRAVESTY by asking the program for a 2,000-character "Order-9 Travesty." The output was minimally revised: a few suffixes and letter cases were changed, and the text was broken into verse lines at periods.

New York: 3–4 December 1998; 22–24 January, 5 December 1999

Shall What Please Eleven

(Stein 66)

Shall.

What please wakened?
Say instigation of on.
Speak be retracting choice.

Susan?

Eleven?

Four strophes made by running a passage from Gertrude Stein's PMJ through DIASTEX5, using as seed a passage from Stein's OOD (*ASR* 282–83). The output was revised by breaking lines, changing letter cases (capital to lowercase or vice versa), choosing periods or question marks when a sentence end was signaled by a looming majuscule, grouping the six sentences into a sequence of strophes having the sentence-number sequence 1, 3, 1, 1, distantly related to the Lucas sequence.

New York: 27 January 1999

Long Narrow Julian
Felt It First

(Stein 67)

Long narrow times have had their reasons afterwards.

Baltimore's little doors give up selfish business monthly.
Julian imagined necessary justice.
How long will weddings be imagined differently or ought they be?

Julian is forgotten by twice two doors.
How have the large arranged their means?
A morning walker seldom wills the best stepping stones.
All could have all but did not.

Has anybody whose wedding sank banked a tan?
This funny sister places ferns in twice-forgotten cellars.
Many imagining they have business just have papers.
Many having business have it in Baltimore.
Baltimore makes for having an easier wedding.
There the pears coin thinking papers to have means.
Did anybody have business in Baltimore?

Whose narrow wedding sank a bank in Baltimore?
Each business in Baltimore was selfish.
How many twos thank their sisters twice?
How many have had very much business long?
Nearly all could have.
Julian hadn't forgotten Saturday.
Having business over here, they wanted to see their married sister.
This is Monday anywhere.
Thinking a while, Julian supposed long walking was the way to think a while.
Imagining different papers, a selfish man was nearly there.
That man sank, having many sashes, and sank well.

Their two doors never shielded them.
Once upon a time, a selfish boy accepted direction differently.
Arthur named connected floors.
All having different sashes is best.
Having a funny sister is easier.
How many long days have narrow places?
Julian started having to be selfish differently.
Large stones arranged in cellars sank neither scales nor narrow pears.
Many a selfish sister of many a selfish little boy done two-timed him.
Their thinking fathers started in Baltimore.
They seldom dressed in funny sashes.
Their three sisters needed powder.
Baltimore makes five pairs of shellfish selfish.
Imagining having their papers accepted first, these selfish boys widened their narrow doors.
Thanks dressed these doors in two places.
Imagining time was done, the three sisters once devoted their thinking to vines and their will to walking.
A selfish boy whose time was narrow gave each day to imagining the evening papers differently.
Weighing Baltimore, nobody favored rubbers, and Julian felt it first.

Six strophes comprising, successively, numbers of verse-line sentences corresponding to the Lucas-number sequence. Derived from three pages of Stein's "Business in Baltimore" (*ASR* 480–82) by running them through DIASTEX5 using as seed the first 20 lines of the same passage (*ASR* 480) and then drawing words from the output of the program, more or less freely, composing them into a series of verse-line sentences.

New York: 14–29 May 1999; endnote revised 15 January 2002

Shall Haven't

(Stein 68)

Shall.

What please wakened say instigation of on speak be retracting
beginning living beginning needing beginning excellent
believing being being being worn being?

Look kindness have fruit haven't instigation across.
Instances and then she one being.
She then one was family was one one she being being being then
thing to.

This that.
That of in are by mean height been going don't have.
Don't twice distinct willing.
Meaning?
She thinking the was dancing was being being believing domineering
feeling believing believing something this thing.
She using being believing being being being one one one being.

Certain existing being being every existing thinking
questioning existing existing anything cheering.
She that been was dance was that.
She feel being be meaning existing doing being one in one and answering
and every every.
She every every one in.
She in one having feeling certain forgotten table time fruit.
Portland gladly leather.
Little living beginning living living was was was.
Not me "well said hospitality."
Suddenly willing thought.

What please think not deceive been condition dancing dancing
dancing being being thinking meaning being careless
domineering simple simple careless domineering
energetic connecting connecting connecting that
the that that the.
She being thinking being cheering something coming hospitality
excellent shattered thought disappointment retracting
permitting her needing her being being being then
being one one one being believe.
This piano thought don't make.
Lena twice distinct willing.
Meaning.
She thinking the was dancing was that the one worn being beinging
believing domineering feeling believing believing
something being believing being being being?
Look kindness have fruit haven't instigation so should been
was saw rose think that there mean one and then being
being being being being living living like some she.

Young family.
Make all and.
Suddenly saw that are we make was to that there chance.
Oh only please be deceive whirl means being every existing thinking
questioning existing existing anything cheering
been feeling being meaning doing ones one one was then.
Look words salad rushed are you for you think being one one?
She and one and family was completing believe shall likely look
time never fruit haven't instigation whirl days was
be retracting reinforced meant being every existing
thinking questioning existing existing anything.

Cheering an in and.
She she one was dancing was that the one worn one in?
She careless domineering simple simple careless domineering
energetic connecting connecting retracting there
choice what?

Little then she being being being.
She then one was dancing was one and she being being right fruit.

Haven't distinct believing answering answering?
Being being thinking meaning being.
Look kindness.
Have fruit haven't?

Nine strophes comprising, respectively, the following numbers of typographical lines: 1, 3, 4, 7, 11, 18, 11, 7, and 4—an ascending and partially descending Lucas sequence. The source text was a blend of words drawn from two passages by Stein: OOD (*ASR* 126–33) and PMJ (*ASR* 182–83). This "blend" was run through DIASTEX5, using as seed part of the passage from OOD. Each word string beginning with a capital letter at the left margin, and whether including one or more typographical lines, was punctuated as a sentence, with a final period and with "runover" lines indented. Then all the typographical lines, unindented and indented, were successively grouped in "Lucas-sequence strophes" as above.

New York: 27–28 January, 1 February 1999

Care Firm

(Stein 69)

care named firm

Made by running Stein 65.txt through DIASTEX5, using the first five lines of pmj300.txt, beginning with “Carving” as diastic seed, and accepting stop at nonmatch. The source was variously derived from texts of Stein; the seed was a five-line excerpt from the beginning of a passage in Gertrude Stein’s PMJ (*ASR* 300).

New York: 28 January 1999

Women Dazed

(Stein 70)

Women day walking health world.

Surely being time her used duets with three the country.
It day wet once their armed between bruised never how between?
To college to college who took transfigured awe blindness?!

Succeeded indeed immoral face.
Redfern politeness instructor this who than distress at blond.
Filled to then care.
Later.

Redfern wandered.
Redfern were fine.
Mrs. was made often of . . . of themselves these when one and all away.
Dean?
Miss was protection sordid common unconscious constant conviction.
This health being younger brother realization remarkable!
Practical experience basal greater though knew saying.

Invited dean mind and new south-western with manner.
Restraint than bring forgotten to anxious wife hills.
Them the thinking?
Miss!
It is when there may is side which real world?
Charles not power action vigorous fixed restless familiar.
Constant day cold go world ground all head said resolutely.
Pretty doubt honesty be new was his hold could receive.
Happened nothing went!
The dean meet assembled in alone ecstatic successive validity.
Third.

Charles influence abstract was the quality quite any human.
Too nor extreme spirit looked this who two acquaintance?
Bring thought understand with the . . .
Charles that.
Ah!
Dounor reply uncertain power during tumultuous relation with.
Labor doubt narrow happened to she that destroy it.
Essential who the any institution and instructor.
Was known sense prayer daughter detached nature world!
Practical blindness the clear transfigured innocence?
Desire too sensuous invited by dean wonder was awkward.
Intense during gentleness checked distress to . . . to . . .
She quite think thinking!
It strain of ever seemed learned docile concrete meanings disguise.
Conceal good-looking woman!
She class south-western intercourse steadily familiar day.
Difference together boy friend see uneasy pretty.
Though promised was things when blind young for?

Dounor colleges had went excitement hypocrisy.
Still permanent practical innocence which the while . . .
Control deepest shyness forgotten to very each again!
Eager presiding essential extraordinary qualities!
From attained distinction college experience even!
Due spirit everything the discussion same deference.
Dounor looking no forces with during personality exchange.
Life willingly believe . . . believe about been preacher.
Among criticism which complete teacher way philosophy?
Beauty abstract ideas as pure real pure difference.
Faster convictions understand in and rested.
Martha marriage message elaborate instinct distinction institution.
Good-looking in more said making gateway in great.
Desiring abstract awkward meanings instincts pleasure.
World and active for recognition years always in and . . .
Redfern's vast either enough called?
Redfern presently instructors excitement religious never!

Lost not and in any was the spirit.
Charles gentleness not lose into bring eyes and blond filled.
Miss?
Redfern standing down hills.
Dounor no confused sometimes years no plunges there the which.
Down frankly said for flushed looked could year's great!
Between happened impatient destroy was why presiding.
In many her.
Dean!
Farnham great the women best teachers came claimed enough presently.
College institution intellect detached in.
She which who?

Though gentle looked him talk.
Several understand begin helpless.
The found to the thinking.
Dounor!
It when has misdirection and active other spring friend strange.
In say have always and almost all that she needs.
Redfern loved was make in do not much more.
Mrs. what wholly energy the choose universities being breaking?
Through the than distress this.
She speak hear.
Redfern it is power no relation during twenty-ninth change.
Redfern immature dangerous intercourse and always cold own.
Of it?
It of on lap.
Redfern start.
Martha flushed!
Deliberate chivalry never to but it it inferior.
So the what walls wholly sameness spending the greater?

Breaking of . . . of intelligence . . . shyness to . . .
Miss her than bring to course begin . . . its helpless!
Dounor from thinking.
Greek childhood in and themselves.

These when relation here?
With energy uproar american completeness in individual.
Rights great always slow there always there this the.
Comrade there is is much to her never came who ground.
Alright enticement complete that she needs narrow!
Grace intelligence as with who learn just what had.
Destroy them!

She thrown dazed.
Certain called college believed in devoted.
To many great married he chair.
Farnham personalities were her community feeling utmost morality.
Exaltation conditions everything with!
Redfern labor these vocation completeness immature life fiction.
Redfern standing town hills.

Dounor no confused sometimes years no plunges there the which.
Down frankly said for flushed looked could year's great!
Between happened impatient destroy was why presiding?
In many her.

Not felt?
Charles nearness recognition deference being things indifferent.
Development extraordinary influence influence!

Unattached she quite was management human and acquaintance.

Into thought companions good-looking anxiety scene.
Intently about combat fulfillment big reality willingly!
Individual prove believe . . . believe more meaning in.

Side her ideals in it and always relation way philosophy.
Shy sordid the slow ground fairly ground.
Hersland's perplexity?
I looked him dazed.

Sixteen strophes comprising verse lines that are "pseudo-sentences," the numbers of which in successive strophes comprise the ascending, descending, and ascending Lucas-number sequence 1, 3, 4, 7, 11, 18, 29, 18, 11, 7, 4, 3, 1, 3, 4. The source text is a passage in one of the excerpts from Stein's MoA that Ulla E. Dydo included in *ASR*. I lost my note telling the pages on which it occurs. This passage was run through DIASTEX5, using as seed a passage by Stein that appears in *ASR* and begins: "Why were birds. When I decided not to look twice I felt that all three were made of the only distinct changeable brown. I did not mean foxes. This is why I shall not visit." I've not yet been able to relocate the piece in which I found this passage. [Ed. Note: The passage is from PMJ (*ASR* 282.)] I added one letter to the output of DIASTEX5 and changed another to another, which did not affect the sound. I did not otherwise change the spellings, forms, or order of the words of the program's output or where the lines began and ended, so I retained almost all of Stein's word forms and spellings. However, I eliminated all left indentations from it and changed lowercase initial letters of lines to uppercase. Then I divided the text into strophes by inserting a strophe-break space after each of the numbers of lines comprising the alternately ascending, descending, and ascending Lucas-number sequence. Finally, I substituted an exclamation point, a question mark, or points of suspension for one of the line-final periods whenever I sensed a command, exclamation, question, or truncated sentence, and I also inserted points of suspension *within* a few lines.

New York: 27 January, 2–3 February, 23–28 July 1999

Saying Was Anything Existing Happening

(Stein 71)

Saying was anything coming having having that they read that.

That thing quite then being have been.
Doing finishing and finishing he knew feeling that that what?
That something not something liked sometimes something.

Something answering beginning was not would would.
Heard not something not being been could told some.
Again intended living and and did he getting what had?
His need not not everything expect expected some expecting.

Repeat something expecting repeating anything and.
Saying that which anything laughing laughing one.
Efficiently is ate was call some something saying.
Saying saying he be where each has not not not easily.
Existing happening something expecting expecting?
Something something something!
That not been mentioned having having having having again saying.

What when hearing that he heard what found found?
Clellan asked not not get because he.
He was having admitting saying saying exciting annoying another.
Enough enough something one offering and all all what?
That brother kindly answering enough know that when?
That that the thing knew very him have have have regularly.
Gesticulating what said said would something make?
Something.
Enough receiving appearing something she had any thing thing.
That wasting rolling very what dead rolling growing?
Wasting thing that that that the then this standing.

Enough it as quite number.
This quite!
Quite everything expression because asking something anything.
Exciting annoying saying doing some came some said.
Anybody they what heard what they then they stayed?
He said give some could told some.
Anne the for all could go.
Henns successful kindly conclusion expression everything!
Understood interfering she would come done so say.
Say that that heavy that there that where there called.
Some thing enough enough little should be reading.
Many some arrange something remembering be that said.
Feeling needing feeling been feeling left annoying!
Returning please that who they everything appreciated.
Can not something something finish come not?
Donger which likely conclusion concluding everything satisfying?
Satisfying and enough saying of and been coming was.
Went sometimes was way and any way went anything anything!

Exciting annoying this this!
One hearing there came to some some satisfying to that one been.
That?
Polly bought remember everything everywhere where every annoying.
Directing everything prospering continuing explaining.
Visited very tired they might easy kindly they been.
Tell thing doing being meant he finish that meaning.
Mentioned anything mentioned continued successful.
To some were!
Antliss urging the repeat were came were charming remember.
Finished discovering discovering interfering remembering.
Something.
To some some great enough something something finishing of.
If a?
Clellan?
All of of time where one common and one and any arranged feel saw.
Was any seeing seeing having that she what what she?

Had say living again urging what that what what they?
The feeling they and are are some waiting anything.
Again coming saying it is some says saying again having.
Asking who what that that is is be decided quickly being?
Thing some was.
This said that would been he might seeing eaten them that them.
There bigger it is of enough the things who they every.
Where been were being when enough of and they they what?
They heard wanted had wanted living come be dead over.
Thing something completing completing like they?
This there there three houses making movement saying.
Coming coming be he they thing?

Some come.
Some more there.
There then everything.
There have having have.
Remembering been mentioned are being and not quite came anybody.
Happened suffering baby successful.
Antliss not some not.
Antliss going are they pleasant something meant said finish?
Very refuse hear came likely remember remembering.
Remembering remembering remembering expression remembering!
If that they are common is is remember?
Helbing some.
Anne charming remember finished discovering discovering.
Interfering remembering what they what what any one?
Saying one enough there said was saying saying begin.
Having all and way went anything anything exciting.
Annoying is is saying was saying saying seeing seeing.
Then there dead certainly if asking everything.

Anne?
George thought being something tired to ask are agreeable pleasing.
Astonishing saying purpose stay!
Donger something something meant something something something.

Something that that that what if is ask all all they?
They hear what has can just not.
Not not!
Being regularly seeing been made he went.
That waiting mentioned anything mentioned continued not not.
Not not did successful expected kindly likely he each.
Have again eating seeing?

Waving showing what imitating?
A pleased all ate are are he each have facing facing facing interfering.
Is then to be be not high because more little nicely?
Having having having having again saying what when?
Hearing that all all all an are they hearing can living.
Living having arranged to when being prospering continued.
Not could?

Antliss would be feeling successful was not again pleasant.
Interfering lightly completing completing proceeding.
And one and because feeling.
This thing?

Enough something say but saying satisfying satisfying anybody.
Everything everything satisfying everything everywhere!
Where every annoying one one every could was continuing.

Be!

He repeat were came were charming remember finished discovering.
Discovering interfering remembering something?
To some some great enough something something finishing said.

Was not saying satisfying interfering satisfaction?
Satisfaction difficult disappearing misunderstood.
Satisfaction?
Not!

Doing not everything and looked enough enough enough any one?
And being get thing when doing exciting annoying another.
Enough enough something question purpose being continuing!
Where everything and know enough enough enough?
It is!
Enough and know regularly.
Being something any one did be we going then enough ex?

And enough naturally enough enough easy one enough enough doing.
Something it is enough any enough enough thing enough.
And in and because feeling.
This *thing*!
Enough exciting?
Any enough enough enough enough is it is is that there again that?
Quite much said what there and all all there that that.
That *could* had.
Anne back wearing when that that what intended it in is again.
And and all all able one if intended.
It being hearing being thing thing that thing again that question.

Purpose being continuing where and all all open?
If it it it is any all walking talking showing one expressing.
Expressing is is one!
If is it deserted not being being enough is it an again start again?
Again.
If is not not little finishing little finishing coming looks.
Something expecting expecting something exciting!
Everything are.
There every everything everything everything everything!
Everything?
Doing not.
Doing been doing in it an again standing living again and and did.
All again again again asking?
It is not come not friendly disturbing gone again pleasing something.
Something something something enough every one every!
Funny imitating everything everything expressing!

Expressing doing doing doing doing doing it it annoying!
Again start again again again and and all again again!

Again again and and and again again again finishing.
Again is is not?
Doing not finishing did deny begin satisfying thought directing.
Directing expecting explaining every one heard every.
Everything everything continuing continuing continuing.
Donger something said meant doing intend it again again that.
Again asking any one and all again what saying saying?
Ate knew had at again what notice saying all one and.
After again start again again!
If is not not little finishing little finishing coming looks.
Something expecting expecting something exciting!
Everything are.
There every everything everything everything everything!
Everything?
Doing not.
Doing been doing in it an again standing living again and and did.
All again again again asking asking anything and a?
Again again saying friendly agreeable answering.
Saddening and again again again intend and intend!
And asked again again again asking is is not do not felt?
Finished finished again pleased something something?
Receiving appearing ended over the heard every regretting.
Everything conclusion concluding everything.
Doing not!
Doing?
Doing.
Doing it it again again again again again again and and again!
Again that saying saying all and did again again that.
Living coming it is not completing not feel finding.

Anne again?
Henns thought directing directing expecting explaining every.
One heard every everything everything continuing.

Continuing continuing.
Donger something said meant doing intend it again again that.
Again asking is is not do not felt finished finished?
Again pleased something something receiving appearing.
Ended over the heard every regretting everything.
Conclusion concluding everything are of but.
Remembering?
After.
Clellan all the feeling?
Clellan.
Clellan certainly said was being need to what that that he?
He keep in!
The answering that thing that left have hear what having answering?
Not something astonishing forgotten he seen explained.
Continuing hearing hearing then there what what everything?

Existing happening expressing expressing understood.
Expressing expressing conclusion remembering is.
Is number?
Remembering them said feeling needing feeling the when what?
That in it it is!
Donger he not later older determine determining repeating.
Agreeable understood he he what make was not do not?
Face were when would falling!
Falling hearing all all all that what they had not happening.
Something he?
He having having and being begin?

There being finishing he knew feeling needing feeling feeling!
And understanding did he heard he was did found he all?
That might not very some having convincing repeating.
Determining what what seeing then hear see what said?
Was not not not say said any having taken living what?
That again that he kept when had was successful was.
Way again again asking what they they thing hear hearing?

What having answering understood and had asked after?
Expressing completely disappearing surprising!
Determined understanding disappointing gesticulating.
And pleased walking?

He hear we was was hear we hear hear staying waiting meeting certain!
Please are would easily pleasant kneeling doing little?
And not would not do were done they that they that what?

Have feeling happening way did he?

He what there could satisfying something something something!
Sometimes something something answering beginning.
Convincing older one would perplexing pleasant charming.

Disturbing disappointing saddening nothing to not.
Disturbing been can very then that that that heard?
Be for been well what stay do came likely might something.
Something receiving appearing done not done sung!

Walked larger laugh liking like were standing was.
Why that meeting have met feeling doing could thing?
Would was what they thing have be liked found looked.
Looking?
Donger needed finding!
Donger very!
That?

That staying went feel would for was that being successful anything.
Have left what having answering leave nothing enough!
Walk walking talking talking doing sounding continuing!
Bigger where disturb done little had.
Not not not looked did liking something all all rolling that.
Who are something he meaning there expecting?
Enough something something something has been what having?
Was determined not which doing being did not long long?

Donger answer did living and not not not living living liked!
Liked arranged all all had seeing feeling.
Polly bought standing standing was what needing stand.

Helbing?
Helbing was had was told did working.
Anne standing one if long to who back nothing amusing hearing?
For to perhaps that what that what felt would very who?
There being quickly anywhere he be where each has left.
Come who walking remain walking feeling dead rolling!
Finishing.
Donger looked.
Donger did like did not found not have said having time was.
That!
That went he get some said said said then there dead certainly!
Hear see not see they said stayed packed?
Anne!
Anne had did not?
Anne long.
Sender answering disturbing disappointing saddening nothing.
To not been tell began again again and again that asking.
Again happening!

Being continuing describing turned went certain pressing.
Annoying naturally naturally done will and not to.
Not bigger hearing together until saying all again.
Start again again!
If one had had living finishing moving strangely browning he.
The then five little done said feeling walking feeling.
Everything everything are.
There every everything everything everything everything!
Everything.
Doing not finishing!
Donger looked.
Donger searching was doing said and all.
All time where what anything if if?

In.
It was happy was and leave to.
Anne long to tired some tired be begin being thing thing left.
Kindly having saying again having can not something?
Finish began asking any one and like seen what heavy.
Falling?
Falling hearing is.
It when walking was quite number.
This quite!
Quite he was expression happening stayed staying something.
Something answering very he very they one!
If determine determining seeing is?
It could had some.
Anne again and and if it what he?
Henns brother again and and successful to some were something!
Anything sometimes sometimes misunderstood come.

All then would nicely naturally refusing so.
It that easy there called and anything and some not completed.
Done right kneeling sometimes sometimes misunderstood.
Come all then would nicely naturally refusing done.
Will and not to not smaller it hearing they called all.
When could smaller pleasant anything not to not something?
It that deny looking looking looking what said was?
Sometimes sometimes something something might enough!
Beginning something something convincing older.
One would perplexing pleasant charming some it that.
They amusing continuing hearing what easy easy stay!
Donger something something meant something something something.
Something that that that what?
Donger him and hear has happening surprised amused walking.
Talking showing what imitating discovering discovering and.
Noise would not he had expressing completely quite.
Running and all falling when there enough had have.
Have sizes and were laugh any of of not doing not come.

To some completing completing proceeding regretting.
Everything concluding everything are and and and!
Enough saying of and been happening came have having.
Having coming and where later anything one.
If not common determining came some some happened perplexing?
George thought prospering prospering everything in is are.
And say of and are are all.
All have have having saying again having a want can any?
One.
If not to not continuing not something happening easily pleased.
Understood everything expressing expressing seeing!

Doing some have them will come together been were being.
When enough liking doing wanted.
Donger everything and who enough enough enough is is living?
To convincing bought everything.
Anne?
George thought being something.
All and and be begin being thing thing left not kindly forgotten.

Enough any who about doing something and one say one?
One then certainly not something finish began asking.
Any one and going sounding waiting.
Being going is as.

If is not to not seeing it what they running waiting falling disturb.
Done done sung walked larger and is like were standing.
It of houses were custom not could would would great.

To what what are every quite said not something something?

Of and been was being went.
That?
All and and he went did did and not not not gone he not amusing any!

And and was answering commencing answering that thing.
They thing are answering saddening has leave disturbing.
Tired and not to sit not be pleasing said and intend.
Was know answer answer determine something something?

Enough enough!
Enough regularly!
Being something!
That to come to coming completely easily smaller completed.
Mentioned being begin being been enough liked did.
Have begin again having that long going he not an answer.
Any answer and was answering commencing answering?

Left have not come returning having been charming.
Says something some that some gone leave nothing when.
That that disturbing have been appreciated is asked.
Something would and and had he he?
Donger him and not do not and is like ask and any felt laughing.
Laughing certain sounding happening.
Being made misunderstood might each might house have have come?
All is likely river sounds all until and had been did.
Did and not not until been were because because because?
Expression because he!
He was was was not convincing not admitting is liked asking seeing.

Seeing having been what was was not bought not?
Anne is take living again urging.
Antliss.
Antliss and had heard dead did had not to not not hear they kindly?
Repeating be some something remember remember arrange?
Interfering remembering.
Remembering remembering.
That!
That that mentioned to what?
This being enough remembering remembering remembered some.
Remembering everybody happened remember astonishing!

Interesting interesting then then that that had heard.
What easy easy not to not and asked ask asking again?
Eating.
He hear repeat he something make remember remembering?
Remembering remembering determined understanding everything.
And who enough enough enough he went then later talked?
Talked talked talked was what they doing having been!

That was all looking leave packed very *be* were they.
Might put back nothing any one and have been then can.
Tell walk there wanted who who one thing happening.
Being discovering discovering and noise would not that had?
All alike very yet were they mean suddenly such might.
Asked and did he?
He that was talked talked talked talked!
All all all that that what what to when there everything leave?
Was satisfying upsetting is offering she would remember.
Anne standing was things needed when that that what to that been?
Very successful was said dead who had visited what?
When what anything thing that they easy are pleasant?
All disturbing tired and.
It.
If to that they they?
Donger did and what that that that the thing knew very decides.
Like and it enough that they seen be be might again eating.
Talking answering imitating preparing one and one saying saying.
Any notice saying saying saying would coming nicely.
Built enough impossible appearing something all!
One had dead rolling thing doing dying something completing.
Completing like lightly enough happening something.
Expecting was having has remembering *be* something.
Something remembering remembering remembered remembering.
Determining determining determining then there!
Dead certainly not some not hear said having asking.
Seeing seeing be seen one been and admitting admitting.
Admitting something admitting determine determining.
Repeating and one any what another certainly certainly!

Offering to what what what on and she was was was one.
On she come not gone leave nothing amusing convincing.
Convincing convincing convincing and one and be *being!*
Being being doing came some gone leave amusing feeling.
Commence commencing disturbing disturbing when?
Have has an admitting admitting admitting something.
Admitting determine determining repeating saying.
Doing some came something something upsetting suffering.
Directing and and did and admitting admitting admitting!
Something admitting determine determining repeating.
Saying doing some came something something upsetting.
Suffering directing and and did successful was way.
Again again asking something commencing come repeat.
Something something expecting something something!
And and had disturbing come thing been thing sit doing.
Something something meant something something something!
Something would came answer not do not and admitting.
Admitting admitting something admitting determine.

Determining repeating was what what what was saying.
Was not some not be seen being been using could told?
Anne leave nothing amusing convincing convincing convincing!
Convincing this this what what one and one would came?
Was one all had give offering and?
Anne had back wearing things standing.
George one all had have returning what has has disturbing come?
Thing been thing were say easy stay says any decides.
Again eating?
Waving showing what imitating truly what what that one and then.
He said had been he then been did to going thing thing.

All!
Enough and saying waiting saying coming saying saying is.
If are enough anyway one one the completely each annoying deserted.
Being not deserted interfering custom happening.
Something determined the when what that that what?

When very and are they saying can any saying saying?
Saying what what hearing what then there everybody!

They and arranged feel saw was any seeing seeing having.
And and had did not things standing?
George when that that what to that been very.
Antliss urging every dead would said.

When going to thing one they asking are they disturbing been.
Astonishing some interesting determine something!
Something discovering discovering interfering.

The who what what then when one very and are the had been.

That where walking remained feeling was that what?
Wanted thing thing are very are growing one has he meaning.
There sitting suddenly waiting an and had such meeting.

One saying coming coming was what that that that thing?!
They.
Very are are they saying being?
There having saying saying.

That.
That?
This.
This is is not some not everything expect successful urging!
Something anything existing existing they that thing.
Says come had gone been tell again and can enjoying.
Enjoy pleasing enjoying pleasing to what being says!

Come came.
Donger be decided can not came them discovering chosen to that.
Noise pressing completely each annoying being being.
Could would done heavy falling?
Falling convincing convincing convincing convincing this!

This being amusing could had.
Anne back wearing prospering he married keep kindly please.
Perplexing everything everything everything they!
They said amusing could had.
Anne back wearing received he expect have explaining repeat?
Something expecting repeating of and they are a saddening.

Has leave when came has one in one appreciated one and.
Again and any?
One enjoying one could say continuing be hearing one any pleasing.
And and and and intend any one and they is is open and?
When any in and are and.
Any one and every be meaning.
This doing going one one preparing badly.
He noise then going one one one.
If is being certain.
This when doing one one seeing one any one where have has she naturally?
Say until saying saying what they that pretty had were!
Were laugh was start came any beginning bowing living?
After kneeling and doing moving dying been enough.
Who thing that that him he would was was do houses said?
Then doing are in and happening regretting would was.
Its?
Doing he not determined understanding determine determining.
Repeating determining determining astonishing!

What that leave that he he who has has said say any?
Exciting intend asking any one and do refuse not like other intermittently.
Happening answering discovering discovering interfering.
Was what what what had refusing when has easy disturb?
Done which then thing any one had have been what saying?
Was had were that heard remained feeling wasting wasting.
Thing that wasting has been who wasting has have he.
Meaning there sitting suddenly waiting an and had such.
Meeting one saying coming coming was what that that.
Have be what saying has satisfying being every satisfaction?

Again saying in.
If sometimes sometimes something something of and one completing.
Having completing some and enough and asked one enough.
What anything perplexing another one and one came.
Said came came and one and see something something!
Some one and they some was being said about any and all.
And?
George that brother prospering brother one one every successful.
Was said dead and intended had said to some tired one.
Anything they hear hearing what charming heard astonishing?
One saddening and and enough that which decided regularly.
One one preparing.
He hear that hear asked asked knew had some noise something make.
One one one saying was saw all and did and and who that?
Laugh started another one and one said said saw then.
There everybody being they they see heard happened.
What gone would feel would be seen everything?
Anne.
George thought being something what who who what hearing very.

Tired difficult left again kindly it.
If exciting everything one heard enjoying remember everybody!
Everybody certainly could had some!
Anne the for baby he did he what need and in had the when where every.
Successful who not would feeling could be hearing?
Easy anything who returning enough something be be.
Being then enough liked like have finished again eating.
Is efficiently existing everything pleased hear?
Every one.
Enough every waiting we arrange nicely left will river until.
Saying saying all and did clap mean were that certainly?
Sometimes.
Clellan certainly everybody see something something some.
Day did had not not not say being one everything everywhere?
Where every annoying directing everything prospering.
Continuing explaining are and had said would came.

Were dead did had not to not difficult to easy every?
One everything everything everything everything!

Everything expressing expressing and anyway and.
Seeing doing some have deserted will and not to not.
Hearing were scattered every ended over the heard.
Every regretting everything conclusion concluding.
Everything are and and satisfying something something!
Something?
Donger liked did not doing not said he needed everything everybody!
There every everything everything everything everything!
Everything everything and any had one one feeling.
She was using needing wearing they stand sitting.
Anne on.

George that brother prospering brother successful was said.
Dead and intended had one and one some easy saw what?
That meant what and intend know that which decided.
Regularly sounding waiting saw all and did ones and.
When done liking had what she what wanted any any enough.
That which completing another dead living and and.
And did one another one heard heard what heard heard?

What they stayed what and and looking that bought?
George prospering he he that married accidentally and and and.
One one every could was some were?
Antliss in and and intended who what anything please regularly.

Continuing waiting some asked asked knew had one and.
Then left were refusing that all and and an and enough.
That anything little smaller laugh mean before anything.

Are and and is of everything everything everything?

Everything everything remembering everybody everybody.
Certainly day did had would what what that they they?
Are they did without had and?

Anne had and.
Anne say number common anybody satisfying could had some.
Anne again and and if if they that they they dead did had not to.
Not something left they what they hearing what they?

Charming one they say have saw and intend and intend.
If that that the very him he that hear stand what when.
That that they when they they have seen what there asked.
To what the thing certain regularly surprised continuing.
Imitating efficiently existing naturally naturally.
She could come done built enough impossible appearing.
Something had had had had had happening surprising.

Regretting reading remembering everybody and enough.
And some not some some something something upsetting.
Suffering directing he was have urging urging asking.
Have have repeat purpose where meaning remember finished.
So not him come some was.
This said would what that that that what they they stay make thing.
Said if it what each has all has face impossible completed.
Every what have say they they they would say way happening.
Regretting saying its what they quite should.
Any all all.
Doing said saying all and way.

Donger later anything asked and did he?
He some said said said would who dead certainly did did and hear.
See said said anybody heard heard something had said.
Said the what that that he he he had and give some?
Anne.
Anne!
Anne on and.
Helbing wearing he had had say he been being and and did that what?
That that he kept when continued could.
Antliss would dead would were that dead what?
He he left kindly asked interesting tired to told doing to and.

One had heard heard liked like ask like would the to.
Did some was?
This that that happening.
Being.
He was had asked are arrange please seeing facing deserted deserted.
The would falling hearing the called had been who not?
Could fell sound did not walked they the when heard?
Heard stay was saw all all all thing when been over those.
Who wasting has thing not sitting were them it ones?
Little movement look looks feeling walking feeling.
Feel something more everything every one there everything.
Everything everything everything everything everything!
Again knew had feeling did deny said finding leaving.
Staying enough everybody there every everything.
Everything everything everything everything everything?
And any had and is taken again intended living and and.
Say one one every that some long.
Sender again leave three and pleasing told thing then again.

That told thing everything they had easy and and enough.
And that something going disappearing.
Waving some.
A pleased all to that pleased they had made made said would something.
Make any are are saying being pressing seeing eaten.
Facing they the what what then when one very and are?
The scattered were every saying saying liking all.
All rolling that who what wasting thing that one there.
Three it as then not because feeling surprising regretting.
Everything thing its it what said was not not not saying.
Was not begin satisfying interfering lightly completing?
Completing proceeding not would not uneasily upsetting.
Was offering about directing directing children?
Expecting not not not again amusing could says meaning.
Walking talking not.
Not not.
Pulling regularly surprised preparing little little perplexing.

Everything everything everything they not see saw.
Way all all all that they that that is is being been using.
Standing things she had thing need and able those returning.
Something astonishing one saying one and then has.
Had have having again asking be decided?
They stand felt be the would talking talking meaning were that.
That that the showing what imitating one one preparing?
What saying describing face were when would falling?
Falling hearing pleasant sound fall well every and in and surprising.
This everything would was its not to not understanding is being.
Being enough any?
All all saying that been had saying and be common would bought.

Brother directing prospering not holding could every.
Would came visited one if difficult something returning?
Charming pleasing pleasing a one and for to perhaps.
Laughing answering imitating understood everything.
Expressing expressing that not growing finishing.
Five were was why that meeting said that feeling what?
Doing could would would great nicely having nicely.
Is of said that knew he was had he had understanding?
Perplexing can packed pack suffering needed when?
That that what say.
This need have had and to have ask tired asking understood up.
To so pleasant was because talking pleasant not all.
Could every.
Doing finishing and not.
Doing not remembering remembering remembered some remembering.
Everybody happened remember everything everywhere.
Where every annoying directing everything prospering.
Continuing explaining are and.

Sender came he were.
All number mentioned feeling needing it is saying it leaving.
Being asked anything anything exciting annoying!
One can determining he determining all.

Helbing?
Helbing wearing needing if.
Anne she standing that standing standing annoying accidentally.
Anything who have easy what hearing what charming!
Nothing amusing hearing what then what what saw something?
Something intend what something would would asked.
Not do not been seen not very them told talking talking.

Meaning that some.
Being *regularly*.
Waving describing what everything lacking motion staying.
Is of the thing seen they certain not house would could?
She it that when sounds who disturb yet right custom?
Conclusion understanding was hearing that heard.
Looking looking looking that that.

Clellan common and one can determining he determining all.
Helbing?
Helbing wearing needing.
Helbing had and them that she them on.

Anne again and and she the she when had was say it that!
Henns accidentally explaining explaining anything and answering.
Kindly friendly having been all number mentioned.

Feeling needing was had was saying did not that looking?

Looking looking and in finding time happening came.
And?
That.

That one common.
One and and any and was saying was saying living not what looking.
Finding amusing all any?
Anne.

Anne to could!
Helbing told some not come.
Anne one intended been.
This thought that getting say then keep he had and to children.
Every commence of and.
All and kindly friendly disturbing disappointing saddening.
Nothing to not come not come have been can exciting.

Walk and again what saying saying ate knew had some?
Then been would had was not do not saying putting left.
Suffering needed father directing directing expecting.
Able in and said they they were came visited what some?
Agreeable back nothing amusing hearing any in isn't.
Something was said was something it again thing would?
Anything laughing laughing a one and same disappearing.
Eating continuing showing copying lacking ate knew.
Had what had misunderstood would repeat what hear?
Staying waiting meeting then what one that they alike?
Being enough sounds scattered they every not left?

Then dead those should finishing.
Doing more saying it leaving being asked anything anything.
Exciting gone he looking everything being?
George did did had not got father continued not come received.
What when every?
When he he had said and not to not hear having saddening and please.
All that they again disturbing have been want not could!
Could heard heard easy have asked he has and it of he?
He have each had going sounding continuing quiet eating.
Everything pleased hear every everywhere everything!
Continue disappearing impossible when which then?
Where looked had were clap look laugh while heard growing.
Completing has he five coming house then could a . . .
This that!
This thing!
Enough that they read that have be great many having nicely every.

Everything everything everything everything of!
And been happening very did did did not not not time!

Later asked have was that that that having been?
If any determine determining seeing anybody happened happened.
They gone that had asking give had seeing.
Anne standing.
Henns was say was prospering brother brother prospering prospering!
Visited regularly continuing sufficiently continuing.
Truly what what that?
If is to some so had saying he be house have and a where will left.
Were and and did and been came baby very.
Antliss in and had heard he said had be hearing one going some.
Might back walk there?
There being this were was answering not not little a pleased.
All.
He hear.
He was had!
If and be we going then enough left will river until saying saying.
All and did had were they that who enough doing something?
Completing an about.
George thought about it it and in had.
He he directing did and and all able to the that what had heard.
Dead did had is and gone leave nothing that amusing.
Continuing hearing what then what what has been going?
Sounding intermittently happening.
Being continuing been pleased hear was had at face way not high.
There bigger and enough and anything been wrong looked.
That laugh started another heard living was feel saw.
Not without suffering father was say was prospering.
Prospering who those disappointing please regularly.
Continuing sufficiently continuing truly what what?

That!
If is to some so had saying he be might each were there hearing.
Little started again again again liking beginning.

Any enough and has been not were them suddenly not house?
Outhouses making movement done doing doing conclusion.
Some is it that that there.
Doing again and and he he determined did had not something not.
Keep he when purpose and all all they they hear what?
Has been know he happening continuing?
Waving showing one been had been call some went.
That waiting meeting continued continue explained.
If in not to interesting be very thing doing being and and continuing.
Annoying heavy anything pleasant kneeling that who?
Are been growing those wasting which completing another?
Heard heard gone seen satisfying having was and all.
Bought prospering thought that brother prospering!
Brother the when where be urging those what anything?
Please regularly waiting happening easily pleased.

Preparing chosen noise disappearing before another.
Everything everything everything heard heard what?!
Came was day did arranged give directing everything.
Directing children expecting explaining every one.
Heard every everything everything continuing continuing!
Continuing has been what said was doing did perhaps.
Asked efficiently everything something something.
Receiving and one and high be when easy easy and accidentally.
Back urging could visited anything pleasant gesticulating.
Efficiently accidentally sufficiently discovering.
By thing doing dying has been finishing thing uneasily.

Do little nodding not not met come to come something?
Be was exciting looked which the when been happening.
Very went was was who where one there there hear see.
What said was an any and he he do liked and not not not could.
Told.
Anne sitting wearing getting continued continue when what?
When when he.

He did did had who what hearing that he be difficult tired and.
Are anything and have left what having answering pleasing?
Or enough says disappearing pleased regularly continuing.
Expressing expressing what what everything been.

Had been repeat he each nicely running receiving together.
Remained were where that what heard because rolling.
Very such done meeting received received expected.

Antliss in and would that they!

When he he dead tired and not to not easy expecting explained.
Interesting expecting everything to to had easy have.
Asked ask any anything many not very asked come what?

This feeling sounding answering disappearing happening!
He hear did did had not would after he each have come very yet were.
They mean laugh longer!
They came.

They while feeling would number.
Remembering something all and satisfying.
Clellan feeling expression?
Antliss was was was not holding not.
Sender put back which there expressing expressing successful.
Successful successful in one understood are might.
Seeing eaten facing easily every one where every one.

And feeling then doing because feeling that what everything?
Of.
Enough they have read that there reading feeling needing was.
The what that everything everybody there every everything!
One another one came not would feel would be seen having.
Been what everything?
Helbing.
Helbing wearing.

Anne on sitting would getting.
Antliss successful what was was not holding not?
Sender put back which there expressing expressing successful.

Successful successful!
Antliss in not would hearing purpose perhaps enough existing.
Happening quiet efficiently everything misunderstood.
Deserted the who what what she could come done will.
That enough when hearing were were not to yet some sung.
Because which proceeding houses surprising successful?
Successful successful would continuing could explaining?
Heard be hearing commence something kindly that nothing!
Amusing continuing continuing continuing everything!
For he.
They will walking talking talking were that that that the showing!
One they who he turned something face were when would.
Falling?
Falling hearing that the they easy when left were were fell being.
They fall walking remained feeling was that what wanted thing?
Thing are very when been strangely like five were them.
Feeling walking feeling reading a . . .
Any but could feeling expression?

Antliss was was was not holding not.
Sender put back which there expressing expressing successful.
Successful successful he he was was was he?
Some.
All kindly nothing amusing hearing any pleasing well him he.
Who has just every existing happening quiet efficiently.
Everything something something receiving the would.
Be be all about!
Polly offering to would had to!
Polly needing.
Helbing?
Helbing was had was urging urging urge again again asking asking!
All.

All have left come coming amusing explained tired understood.
Are might nicely is one each existing happening feel?
Certainly sometimes.
Clellan completing completing completing time where one went.
Later anything he he was was was enough exciting repeating!
Would certainly certainly offering forgetting everything.
Prospering that.
This that getting he.
Henns was say was feeling were feeling feeling feeling holding.
Feeling what they heard that expecting every one everything.
Everything one enjoying one!
If is for been everything would meaning walking talking some.
Not same intermittently and proud pleased discovering.
Describing what said and and had.
If of the thing seen they he each and house left that there sounds.
That the scattered disturb some had being dead that . . .

Who are very when not would feeling could not something?
Not read reading expression determined certainly!
Everything that . . .
That.
That went then what need very when he very some did beginning.
That said said heard gone finding leave suffering.
Come had come received and any did have very successful.
Was said dead that those dead what they . . .
When who existing commence who they enough who been very interesting?
Not to sit doing be that said he said did not to not said.
Saw said said what that meaning that something something.
Something something stay has quickly told to who one.
They some was.
This said said he went said alike bigger disturb little had.
Not not not saying stay that.
They liking doing wanted.
Donger searching he.
Donger said needed.

Donger in and often came having talked remembering everybody.
To would certainly some some some and again standing?
Living again he need when continued could.
Antliss would continuing not.
Some repeat and again again again asking what they they thing.
Hear hearing charming says something some astonishing!
Again again again intend he he what something would?
Would asked said said any stay do came likely might.
Something something receiving appearing one of who.
That what what saw looked remained were where they.
Enough who were more more not not not dead very what?

Dead have wasting and not would not sitting was this.
Suddenly and all all were the who and are they they disappearing?
Surprising something would and anything and are are.
There have been what every feeling needing feeling when what?
Hearing that that what when very and are they hearing?
Hearing what hearing hearing happened looking and . . .
Are seeing everything expect expected some expecting?

Repeat something expecting repeating thing to be.
Be having been charming heard nothing amusing hearing.
Then there what what saw something something intend?
One and they what when enough?

It is would way quickly what talking talking meaning is is going.
Sounding waiting.
Being going.

That to any as likely if of hearing were were disturb walking.

Could been were very little has finishing front proceeding?
Proceeding is it it as a . . . ?
Very being arrange deny did liked left suffering working difficult.

Difficult agreeable appreciated then then thing.

Doing being be be said meant doing to did perhaps asked.
Asked ask any and hear been that there walking talking.
Talking were that that that one one preparing is is.

He hear that hear staying waiting meeting what that one being?
Seeing doing some have and are the not to yet anything.
Is liking.
Finishing beginning bowing when what dead that thing when been!
They meaning did lightly such something be he anything is liked?
Begin again having.
If it it is enough later was very talked not beginning remembering?

Urging urging intended again again again visited.
Asking.
It if repeating repeating repeat repeating repeating expecting.
Something something saddening.
It is any one say disturbing which anything laughing laughing.
A one and regularly gesticulating happening quiet.
Imitating everything something something receiving.
Be be built when enough easy existing this this something!
Anything exciting anything is it is is and . . .
Doing finishing left suffering working difficult difficult!
Agreeable appreciated then then thing doing being.

Then not continuing not something them there walking.
Convincing everywhere a one was answering commencing.
Answering repeating repeating returning some something.
Some something something something saddening something.
Expecting any?
And and could something something them there walking convincing?
Convincing convincing convincing and one was answering.
Commencing answering repeating repeating returning.
It is astonishing please all one!
If told thing again that exciting say easy easy to where said.
Meant doing and intend and that when that that enough.
Said was very to what which stand enough.

It is.
Enough existing going amused quiet sounding existing existing.
Ate all all what they looked.
He made have come left were refusing that high say river make.
Not to yet completed done remain were and again start.
Again again again and and come to some finishing moving.

Strangely an again again again again that that feeling!
Deny all are they saying can any saying saying saying?
Then there dead certainly if.
It.
In asking any one everything was was baby?
This thought being!
Henns dying not come not to more.
He very hearing every was that what what they the feeling they?
And are are hearing hearing hearing hearing hearing!
Commence hearing not to returning that some remember.
He hoped liked certain imitating what what what that.
To that pleased they at are are running being impossible.
Done appearing regretting something expecting expecting.
Is it is is knew did deny said?
Clellan kindly to to be repeating forgotten or said something.
Intend intend naturally uneasily it it in as pleasant.
All they great satisfying!
Clellan?
Clellan accidentally to more be hearing repeat were expecting.
Some repeating repeating answering something answering.
Is it is is agreeable again three have appreciated?
Regularly describing naturally determined the hope.
Been feeling remembering remembering not enough.
Older hearing repeating determining something had.
Happened having asking seeing seeing be seen one been.
And and was answering commencing answering repeating.
Repeating returning it it is is come that that every . . .
Remember anything laughing laughing that they that.
Certain same not some asked one and then said had any.

Pressing seeing doing some have built enough impossible.
Appearing something it it is is proceeding all them.
Because pleasant surprising anything exciting that . . .
They that anything some something some some of any.
One has having was he feeling what hearing heard something?
Not something liked sometimes something something!
Answering beginning.
If.
It.
In asking did without was sitting disturbing disturbing describing.
Everything everything expressing that where that.
Putting seeing doing some have of and one has eaten.
Has not not not being being?
One then enough existing happening something expecting expecting.
Something something something satisfying something!
Something something sometimes something something.
Answering beginning?
If.

It?
In asking any is not annoying urging explaining astonishing.
Astonishing interesting interesting interesting!
Then that that that stay.
Donger something something one and they hear has just feeling.
Some certain bigger custom regretting understanding.
Sometimes completing some long coming asked might.
Enough beginning something something!
If?
It.
In asking did without was pleasant disappointing perhaps everybody.

Everything everything disappointing gesticulating!
Satisfaction understanding that that what that searching.
Doing time often of and one is is not.
Donger not some said saying having saying saying that that what?
What hearing hearing he was was not some not some hear.

Everything then what they stayed what he he he had was.
See leave they seen!

It standing in is say had and need where continue expecting something.
Expecting to that hearing what some not commence something.
Of and they hear having answering pleasing put nothing.
Said come come have question something something.

Something something be had decides walk and and had.
He have just going sounding continuing quiet.
Talking showing one been asked knew had had made misunderstood.

Come to coming nicely that doing left were what heavy?

There not sounds little right walking remained feeling.
That what what wanted has been has wasting and when?
What been thing has he coming was come often?

If it is is every one looks?
Enough thing something them!
To perplexing all seen arranged satisfying perplexing all.
Any say one one every that who what what expecting every . . .

One heard every one and question when who about had.
Easy easy come not come came him had just not do not stay.
Has quickly told asked all walking talking showing.
What imitating truly what everything they some made!
Any would.
That one thing that when one they certain not completely nice.
And again start again again!

If it it is not not little are amusing bought prospering getting?
Continued hearing what that feeling?
When tired two who when three who have have having interesting?
Can not something something he said have asked going?
Sounding continuing quiet is ate.

If is not do not doing nice has what disturb appearing agreeable?
Disturbing forgotten disturbing when three question.
When told thing very interesting there what then enough?
Has saw have asked can not came likely and and had going.
Sounding continuing quiet.
He was have come and is likely river sounds all quite number great.

This something certainly everybody something.
It stayed.
In asking not not not is any not offering returning please interesting?
Pleasantly interesting interesting discovering.
What what everything been some noise something make.
One one one was then who is is pressing please are pleased!
Pleased annoying refusing anything had have was pretty.
All the remained.
Finishing pleasant anything accidentally pleasantly completely.
Each existing happening feel certainly sometimes.
Clellan sometimes continued everything every one hearing.
Every expected everything everything continuing!
Continuing if?
If it enough has saw have asking again eating?
Talking not all said and that what said then going one one one.
Had saying was be we are going are up impossible every.
Where difficult repeating appreciated intermittently.
Impossible appreciated then then one then one enjoying.

One could say continuing what easy isn't continuing?
Not continuing not to do to he well will it it any again?
What saying saying ate knew had one and then come saying.
Annoying them were will built is it an again start again?
Again again and and of one one come wasting finishing.
Browning he is and not like entirely little surprising.
Accidentally astonishing interesting interesting!
Then then been thing and and and one enjoying pleasing!
Continuing easy isn't be been not to not very well for?
They is and not like other pleased surprised pleasant remembering.

Remembering remembering.
That?
That been being is it is is everything expression because asking.
Something anything exciting annoying this common.
Be be this living were some heard another and and they?
Not they heard all would and all all that they that that!
Having was was bought remember everything standing.
To could.
Helbing told if it in is everything expect successful urging?
Something anything existing existing they not be!
Be to disturbing forgotten something asked an interesting . . .
And tell not be tell not to sit everything exciting!
Hoped liked efficiently everything something something.
Receiving and one say to that built when enough is.
It is is ended existing such saying something anything exciting.
Anything?
There comes be!
Very them nicely more hope heard all and did that long sometimes.
Did not!

All and and then he talked would and all all and about.
George thought about everything every one hearing every expected.
Everything everything continuing continuing and . . .
Enough says one and they is is do not quickly being thing.
Is other is is existing expressing lacking motion?
Something certain pressing annoying them come being.
Being the will very likely sounds is of if stay where?
Were were come proceeding all them because pleasant.
Surprising anything exciting that come be reading.
Everything and enjoying enjoy enjoying pleasing!
Pleasing enjoying one one then certainly not would!
Would asked enough knew enjoying enjoy enjoying stay!
Donger something something meant something something something.
Something asked knew had one and they can not would.
Would asked some was way that the again continuing.
Talking showing one they had made made he he that hear would ask.

All all they?
That that that to the one they he be that where would if . . .

If is it is as not do yet pleasant all the remained?
Finishing kneeling browning existing that not because feeling.
Everything and enjoying enjoy enjoying pleasing!
Pleasing enjoying and one and if if it it.
If is not to not perhaps all one disappearing pleased surprised.
Sounding existing is is is ate call some went?
That waiting meeting continued prospering everything prospering!
In if intended.
It is is not to not pleasant pleasing one disappointing please.
Question pleasing exciting to to been be expecting.
Any?

Enjoying enjoy enjoying pleasing pleasing enjoying and one!
And one and they is is have seen what there walking talking.
Talking were that that that one one preparing is is.
He hear that hear staying waiting meeting then what one being.
Certain he were waiting appearing kneeling browning.
Certainly everybody if if they they see heard happened.
It asking any one say.

Polly suffering working keep forgotten purpose remember if . . .
Knew enough enough enjoying enjoy enjoying pleasing.
Pleasing enjoying being be said meant doing perhaps.
All one disappearing pleased surprised sounding.

Existing truly what everything been.
If stay is as else had was they enough and enough naturally enough.
Enough not to yet then not been were enough and enjoying.

Enjoy enjoying pleasing pleasing enjoying is is if . . . ?

It or are.
If asked funny existing is ate pleased pleased been pleased.
Pleased certain pressing annoying not not not the . . . ?

Would be be enough and enjoying enjoy enjoying pleasing?
Pleasing enjoying and one and if if it it.
If is it is it it come not.
Donger that meaning walking continuing continuing expressing.

Expressing a one and is efficiently is ate.
If is not do not is is.
If it come not running waiting receiving falling continued.
Prospering everything prospering in if intended.
It is is when what again anything it it is is to charming one been.
It it is is enough has has they explained in about enough.
Enough something finish!

Donger perhaps it it that something something it what?
They who what when hear there!
If other same ate hear they pressing and anyway and is of it it.
She it that very impossible when which then where looked.
In stay start came any those if is is it would this standing.
Waiting it it houses making custom because feeling.
Everything thing did something conclusion!
Donger looked.
Donger searching was saw would who dead certainly hear see said.
Said said said married he that when something some.
Not some tired might something answering repeating.

Repeating agreeable answering saddening has leave.
Said say thing told to thing that that.
If if it it meant he that meant something said something something?
Something might something something something something!
Him he who has just did some.
This doing going waiting showing what imitating?
He hear did did had not would after is one not nicely seeing called.
To done done not at ended and had been did did and not.
Not until . . . ?
If one not something beginning should there comes finishing?
Finishing finishing again finishing finishing everything!
Everything everything expression everything admitting!

Everything everything everything everything heard!
Heard be seen urging pleasant having disturbing some.
Gone!
Donger?
Donger answer something had said said that that what what he.
He said said saw when they that pretty had were sizes.

Laugh while dead moving been dead thing front sitting.
Not coming were something.
Enough something something something all and and he he determined!
Did had keep in brother answering that thing that left?
What they are been has heard astonishing is asked interesting.
Tired?
It.
If something could something something meant something something?
Something something what said was stay do came likely.
Might something something receiving appearing had?
Been did did and kneeling enough who growing those?
Clellan heard.
Clellan not something liked all and did in.
If it it came was something something is staying might did beginning?
Without about need not not continued not come received.
And again again again asking!
It if is it commence easy come repeat are agreeable charming.
Saying again amusing and and again and and one has know.
Answer answer that the that that could said something!
Something many him might each might completely not.
Some have and again start again again.
If it more.
Finishing beginning lightly something be he to what they that.
That thing then being them that what what what to could?
Clellan heard did deny not like later determine determining.
Repeating agreeable having disturbing some that.
Some and is asked some told something something meant.

Something something something something that that . . .
Again that him he had said had just funny answering.

Continuing and is asked asked would did to went bigger.
Where disturb some had being dead that who what wasting!
Has he know?
Any one knew that that that felt when what hearing that he heard.
Something was doing said he having and . . . ?
That.
That staying went might he that thing convincing convincing.
Hearing doing doing gone bought forgetting suffering.
Keep in!
The answering easy and who returning enough something that . . .
Not remember he something something remember remembering.
Remembering remembering . . .
That.
That that mentioned is of said not something something sometimes.
Something something answering beginning.
If is saying doing some came something something upsetting?

Suffering directing he he come not could.
Antliss would.
Antliss is ask will thing hearing what hearing be who not amusing?
Explained tired and is asked if if him he knew knew knew.
Knew was what that what hear been know one the answering.
Disappearing sounding continuing bigger where disturb.
Kneeling enough are growing are any and an is like were.
Standing and and had house were such talking said read.
Perplexing be were without explaining disappointing.
Interesting is it it is pleasing be certainly might!
Perhaps perhaps decides is it is is can might a one and . . . ?

Happening.
Being surprised walking quietly said that that what that?
If of had be all is likely river sounds all until and some not completed?
Done right enough something.
Finishing beginning.
It is some not something like lightly enough happening something.
Expecting its it what said was very went very very was!

Beginning all would feel would for had give some that.
To having was give give.
Anne is take intended accidentally when where what what he received.
He not expect have children to could.

Antliss is ask thing what one they asking all?
All left kindly asked interesting tired and is asked again again.
Asking that who what that all and anything open and . . .

When what they?

Enough did be lacking motion would notice expressing what that?
That putting is is doing seeing nice facing would smaller.
Started doing because because.

Finishing would entirely surprising way that feel thing is.
It is is that!
Doing been feeling did deny because asking heard another married.
Then that what what to children hearing what was that?

Said which anything is is they do be be did be lacking.
Motion would notice pleased is is that doing being?
Being deserted being receiving easily sounds little.
Started to . . .
They?
They they and all all any is like and and and this why them?
They an all all done not not look not regretting.

He before enough satisfying completing and any and then what?
Need very and!
All all did something not convincing not had been that hearing.
Are and and then there everybody they and all all see.
It that they . . .
Anne on and them that she baby and all all say it that when accidentally.
And and and to children every they.
Antliss all able one appreciated then then were that heard that?
Heard easy easy been he everything meant one open been.

Open when that open open ask and any felt laughing laughing.
Certain sounding talking showing what imitating!

Is is one up when than it is of appearing then thing is.
Of that what they they did not not not sit larger sizes.
Liking something it it that what she very when finishing.
All feeling all is liked searching doing tired that.
What that that?
That one staying could later convincing not not determine living.
Living liked liked.
In.
It amusing any and was she she standing to they them baby continued?
Had.
Henns not come not long tired ask tired is.
It is it is is easy and who returning enough something that they . . . ?
Heard that they what one easy has saw have asked stay.
Been open when enough enough.
Enough regularly.
Being something.
That to had saying have come so left them when were the what what?
Then when one very high say river make scattered were.

Every when is.
It is is not not little very been strangely they like lightly.
Making movement conclusion nicely to what that?
Quite all and saying of.
If time . . .
That one common feel he all that they they that that is.
It was not amusing feeling would be needing for did gone living.
Henns something purpose finished in.
Enough them who there walking many.
Any is other continuing waiting some asked to to been he face?
Will done saying pleasant enough because everybody?
If.
It?
In asking not not not very be were they long tired ask tired kindly?
Likely!

Enough and know regularly.
Being something one of the thing seen them way which who what?
Naturally will walking when had all looked quite number.
This which quickly quickly quietly and one and saying to that.
That pleased hear where asked are are very yet were.
They mean laugh longer!
They?
They they they heard wanted beginning been thing doing dying.
Very being arrange deny might have convincing they are and and.
Very be were they might easy kindly they not come not.
When have told walk walking talking talking that they . . .
Feeling expressing expressing a truly everything!
Very yet were they mean laugh longer.
They!

If of had beginning thing not rolling dead enough have such might.
One and been was what?
That what exciting can packed without on and she was was.
Anne sitting suffering needed that would keep in brother answering.
Who they enough any is asked interesting tired has.
Tired something what then enough has saw and come not.
Come came him he what?
Donger could would asked he said have asked to to that be all will.
Enough have each each one know one what the meaning?
That happening.
Being.
Talking not all said that that then one enough one was when who?
He each and just quickly just that an is like other sounding.
Happening little some an and had he he did did had to the . . .
Thing pressing that where?
This when doing any one any one and where them has will walking.
Remain walking feeling all one had enough over kneeling.
There every one and feeling then have walking looked.

Looking looking looking and in and and and way of and . . .
One long later would bought brother annoying accidentally.
Anything and answering and easy every one everything.

Everything one enjoying one liked has would laughing.
Laughing certain sounding existing made misunderstood.
Might each might be seeing make were scattered when.
Walking remain walking they the that that.
The who when they when mean were were feeling being one rolling.
Wasting waiting rolling!
They those that that sitting not coming were of ones there were.
Making custom any feeling surprising conclusion!

Then everything of and are that what being.
This is is not.
Doing not.
Clellan he more what certainly sometimes.
Clellan not not not long did asked have that thing that that if . . .
Is this this?
One one.

It other like intermittently waiting happening saying and.
Knew had looked misunderstood ask asked that what?
Hear that?
If is to the seen some had come after waiting saying saying and.

One and anyway please all and are pleased nicely completely.
Not doing doing doing doing doing and again start again!
Again while saw all talking feeling walking feeling . . .

What happening all looked looking looking looking?

In is some long could then asked anything anything!
Exciting annoying!
One and then came all looking finding amusing feeling if is everywhere.

Expect children those something anything existing.
Existing pleasant put all explained continuing hearing.
Hearing any in and going sounding waiting.
Being going is as running being high enough smaller pleasant.

Smaller strangely certainly said long could then.
Asked anything anything exciting annoying.
One and and any was answering commencing answering repeating.
Repeating returning it is it one not expecting interesting?
Determine something intermittently efficiently.
Impossible disappearing intermittently intermittently.
Intermittently continuing sounding continuing.

What copying chosen continued prospering everything?
Prospering received successful continuing.
When hearing hearing hearing ask and and difficult kindly answering.
Pleasing disappointing perhaps finished disappearing.
Disappearing satisfaction intermittently disappearing.
And and and going remember was that waiting difficult?
Difficult agreeable gesticulating sufficiently.
Understanding disappointing gesticulating and . . .
And and walking eating quietly continuing showing.
Copying lacking.
If is had saying expressing completely quite running receiving.

Appearing something because feeling being when thing.
Proceeding proceeding proceeding enough could a . . . ?
And did expecting was has having nicely kindly pleasant?
Pleasing one disappointing please interesting decided.
All and and stay quickly very happening surprised.
Sounding expressing anywhere scattered and anything.
And at smaller laugh those while wanted any any and . . . ?
Quite number!
This remembering something and enough and.
Quite quite!
Doing which quickly quickly quietly?
Waving saying all looked staying waiting meeting and one and . . .
Seeing out refusing suffering working difficult.
Repeating commence commencing disappointing sufficiently.
Accidentally expect have not urging urging asking?
It is repeating repeating began enough likely regularly regularly.

Naturally naturally she could would then sounds anything!
Pleasant kneeling that wasting rolling talking feeling!

Walking feeling an and and number not not to quite more.
When hearing looking looking and in and and and was.
Answer answering answer beginning something something.
Admitting anything and not not determine saying determining.
They seeing seeing saying.
If asking question purpose being something meant quickly quickly.
Continuing copying went.
That waiting meeting continued prospering everything prospering!
When have have urging urging asking asking anything?
And something that who answering nothing amusing?
Hearing what then what what it asked if amused quiet.
Continuing imitating everything something something.
Receiving if is come to impossible they walking remained.
Feeling she not come after one on the and like lightly.
Sitting waiting little movement one any one pleasant.
Are them happening repeating suffering directing?
Directing expecting in is are long tired not what kindly.
Please one one they explained exciting expecting.
Everything there purpose perhaps continuing sufficiently.
Continuing and one and a little little motion that.
Nicely pleased one one one each existing happening.
Regretting quite expression.
Antliss continuing explaining explaining is is ask left kindly?
Returning that likely pleased one one preparing discovering.
Discovering describing quickly custom received.
Received remember discovering discovering interfering.
And one and disturb little was which custom received.
Received remember discovering discovering interfering.
If is so say say until saying saying what they that pretty?

In is thing are would feeling everything expecting?
Of before saying searching certainly because beginning.
Difficult efficiently efficiently existing ex!
This house built anything pleasant kneeling are any.

And something wasting any coming often making what?
They what what is is that are could.
Clellan everything enough if left having directing explaining.
Intended something difficult efficiently efficiently.
Existing ex!
This house built anything pleasant kneeling.
It is doing very has which entirely surprising agreeable disturbing.
Forgotten disturbing when three again that exciting.
Everything one heard enjoying everything everything.
Everything expressing expressing be each and would!
Heavy come who enough ones while remained.
If is little wasting such talking feeling walking feeling happening!
Regretting would was its perplexing all seen arranged.
Satisfying perplexing married then not he kept what?

Every to the hearing what was were.
Antliss stay.
When again?
All will what hearing are.
It they hear hearing what having answering pleasing please.
One pleasing pleasantly interesting decided to to . . .
Hear been that there.
There there what wanted who he laughing be sufficiently continuing.
Waving showing what imitating what describing lacking.
He left what?
He hear we had was pleased pleased knew pleased pressing anywhere.

Pleased that doing house left that there that than.
Smaller that who were had have did being well they when?
When they they heard there were were had came and because!
Feeling one when had beginning wasting wasting has.
Proceeding all them because pleasant before concluding.
There comes have been what every that that what that was feeling.
All is asked some asked was that that that was beginning?

And is liked liked would he see was satisfying upsetting?
Perplexing all one pleasant pleasing please decided.

To to hear been that there.
There there what wanted who he knew knew pleased knew what that.

Again what would went kneeling enough are growing?
Has he would was was pleasant all they great satisfying?
Completing married then not he kept what every to the . . .

Hearing what?

Antliss all able hold was and long to who back leave intend and . . .
It would that that that that that knew very him have.
And like so enough walk there wanted asked other happening.

Being walking showing chosen made call made repeat and make.
Some not saying custom meeting talking not come say.
Walking feeling surprising not something expecting.
Of?

Enough they more can and have a number not.
This.
This there and enough and they they see then had he stayed day.
Said said that that what what he feel he saw and be seen.
One been married did was returning having intend remember.
Discovering misunderstood disappointing misunderstood.
Misunderstood misunderstood and and had he he said?

Make thing said then what that that he be where to house.
Would could refusing be impossible done appearing.
Regretting would what that that have be have having.
And satisfying can being said all and had that that.
When doing he he said having said need to what that that.
He?
He.
He talked and not some not been being one being upsetting any.
And offering returning purpose understood understood.
Conclusion determined all and had that that what that?
He searching was doing found.

Clellan asked not not get any asked ask was that that that having.
Been had saying and are is liked liked would he see some.
Was being said that she what what had remember keep?
In.
The answering who they that what hearing repeat what to amusing?
Explained tired not to sit had heard that heard and . . .
Enjoying and then there what what has been what something.
Would would asked not do not and is like ask again what.
Saying saying is efficiently ate all all did did had.
Was then that waiting then what one they that putting?
Were when there called to done done not thing when then?
They when looked sound fall would and clap all saw stay.
That?
They while they they heard wanted received received remember?
That what knew very well he can that any in and are all.
Walking sounding ate hear they staying waiting meeting.
And one saying one enough pressing growing completing.
Thing thing thing and two again very were to could could.

Heard not to not finish efficiently pleased some noise.
Something make something.
Enough receiving appearing something that that what wanted.
Is is enough any enough enough thing enough to come?
Making talking liked like all and way of and one remembering.
Remembering remembered some remembering everybody!
Happened remember?
Anne all all one if they that they that they said.
When going to thing hearing what when easy answering something?
Left they thing what they are been some something some?
Something disturbing disappointing saddening nothing.
To not disturbing come some told quickly just this!
Quickly quickly lightly lightly and as said doing.
Come come of and feeling everything all has nicely.
What to could?
Clellan heard did not something?
Donger time often sometimes something something answering.
Beginning that that what?

That one and one had saying and can common some came then would.
Dead to if if they they see one and they some was say having.
Taken living and all all when had was successful was.
Way again again asking they thing they thing some says.
Saying again having asking any all all what do would.
Would asked be meaning that they feeling that?
This doing sounding going.
Talking showing what imitating noise would not enough every.
One every every one and every waiting then enough what?
Each has she naturally say until saying saying all.
Pleasant fall walked not would smaller heard they.

There they been start came any enough any enough enough!
Thing enough it as said have.
This read is of enough every one there everything of and been.
If is some later anything asking asking asking and . . .
All all if.
If exciting everybody there every everything one another one.
If asking some was say having taken living and all all . . .
Annoying and did expect every one hearing every one.
Antliss feeling in is.
Some had say visited asking asking again if not come returning.
What has said that amusing continuing hearing is is?
Stay says any decides again eating.
Waving describing ate are are certain not completely seeing.
Eaten facing when were and are the growing completing.
Thing thing thing would were and are they more reading?
There anything mentioned feeling needing that the.
Been when everything everybody there every everything.
One another one if asking some was say having taken.

Living what that again that everything was accidentally?
Might of and they it is some says saying again having?
Asking any one and enough have each each one know one?
Is is same way saying efficiently saying saying every?
Every one every every everything everything conclusion.
Concluding everything them that what what enough!

Has nicely might one and been?
If is saying was saying saying seeing seeing?
If if to there every they and arranged feel all all all not not?
Not amusing all being packed suffering the things!
Standing that if is everything and prospering returning.

.

Enough something that not and or for began again asking.
Finished be very quickly being thing certain regularly.
Surprised continuing imitating efficiently existing.
Truly what hear that enough ex?
Expressing expressing expressing expressing expressing!
Completing completing proceeding would this standing?
Waiting enough expecting expecting there there expression!

Antliss continuing explaining explaining is is easy existing.
Repeat charming saddening purpose perhaps continuing.
Sufficiently continuing is is noise would not enough?
Ex.

Expressing expressing expressing expressing expressing.
Completing completing proceeding would this standing?
Waiting enough expecting expecting there there expression.

Antliss continuing explaining explaining is is not to not easy.

Expecting explained everything appreciated purpose.
Perhaps continuing sufficiently continuing and . . .
One and a one saying knew repeat anyway a pie pie one.

The where that putting enough each each each one any.
One is is pleasant sung not pretty walking remained.
Feeling was that one over those existing was such might.
One and been.

If is perplexing suffering sitting that getting continued.
Hearing that who feeling pleasant disturbing one.

Expecting has back nothing one one they.
It is pleasing purpose not continuing continuing meaning walking.
Are one.
Any answering anywhere anywhere anywhere anywhere is anywhere.
Please quite not that running waiting falling there!

That where pleasant did they walked they the heard.
There enough had because lightly of and uneasily pleasant.
Surprising not that reading reading feeling all perplexing.
Living every and and anybody answering which decided?
Regularly surprised is is preparing turned notice?
That waiting meeting putting anywhere putting pie where each.
Each each each one anywhere the in is not completely.
Not pleased quite not that running waiting falling!
There that where pleasant did they walked they the.
Heard there.
If one proceeding suddenly not waiting nodding meeting talking . . .

They that one pleasant disappearing feeling happening.
Regretting more nicely begin might something been.
Being perplexing suffering sitting that getting.
Continued hearing that who feeling pleasant disturbing.
One astonishing one saddening enough has exciting.
Might one and they is is?
Pulling.
Running eating continuing showing copying lacking to that.
Ate pleased misunderstood then would what knew hear.
Turned enough make each each one one they pressing.
Putting putting putting putting putting putting.
The where the pie might the and one anywhere anywhere!
Anywhere anywhere smaller scattered mean liking.
Beginning lightly something be he perplexing suffering.
Sitting that getting continued hearing that who feeling?
Pleasant disturbing one it one put question not want.
Continuing hearing hearing then there pleasing pleasing.
Did everything what that when hear there each each?

Each might one one the is is.
Pulling.
Running eating continuing showing copying lacking to that.
Ate pleased misunderstood then that that what that.
If is any one saying anyway anywhere anywhere anywhere anywhere?
Each each each each one any one pleasant sung not pretty walking.
Remained feeling that what she proceeding did they?
And and why know anything completing another everywhere?
Intended is prospering successful.
Antliss that continuing feeling feeling.
They what they pleasant disturbing one astonishing one saying . . .
Know which decided regularly surprised?
Talking showing imitating existing is is everything knew looked?
Misunderstood going something.
That to pressing please are pleased pleased pleased and pleased!
All are and and an all all an are the not to yet pleasant.
All the remained!
Finishing little proceeding would this there standing and . . . ?
All all and are they pleasant all they great satisfying?
Completing married again all holding all urging the . . .
Pleasant pleasing one disappointing please interesting.
Decided all and and not like each asked regularly easily.
Pleased pleased ate pleased pleased pleased pleased!!
All one made come to coming completely easily smaller.
Completed mentioned pleasantly completely pleased.
All are pleased pleased pleased started while they . . .
They doing all all rolling after are are and all all.
Pleasant all they great satisfying completing married.
Again and and all all able all urge the not not not pleasant.

Pleasing one disappointing please interesting decided.
Not do not quickly just this that answering proud pleased.
Seeing pleased pleased pleased pleased we what pleased!
Then enough make each each one one they doing doing.
Doing doing doing where where what what easily has.
Because lightly of and uneasily it as done not said.

Then doing everything saying exciting might one and . . .
Been!
If is not common determining saying determining seeing seeing.
Living living they they what what and any day one and . . . ?
They did not things standing.
George when that that what an and say one one every in is dead would.
Said . . .
When going if is difficult some being thing thing and and saddening.
And nothing disturbing exciting tired has told could.
Says . . . ?
Donger what that everything hear there some not same intermittently.
Happening easily.

Waving some chosen to some made an and had and he would would pressing.
Expressing not not putting seeing doing nice nice.
Each eaten what them them there bigger smaller not.
Come together had have have sizes clap look remained!
Were any all all of of?
If it all one had any any any over after?
It it is is would this standing waiting it as nodding done not?
And in conclusion before everything anything mentioned.
Anything asked and did enough talked much much one.
And been had saying was enough came not some having?
What they stayed what he say was looking leave offering.

What if?
Anne to they them them and all all thought that what brother.
His father was continued not come received one successful.
Antliss one if they that they commence is of that thing they easy.
Friendly having back gone and when came any who that?
Thing which anything is is they they they of it other.
Like intermittently waiting happening saying truly.

What everything they who he turned something face?
Way facing facing facing facing way what the then to?
When one very when hearing were were . . .
Falling easy because . . .

Finishing beginning bowing to that are wasting waiting any.
Thing that one they would were three three five was.
Such saying coming coming was what they thing that.

They there!

Very what being arrange something finishing said because asking.
Asking asking talked when when one.
It other like intermittently waiting happening saying one.

And then not would not be we going then enough running.
Built done when walking remain walking would have.
Was not doing not because feeling being when thing?
Dead very has have entirely regretting remembering.

Everybody one and see not do not be seen being been using.
Was had things that getting continued hearing what?
Was was not holding not be hearing waiting going thing?
Difficult left easy repeat returning expecting purpose.
Finished of and there not told not is and not intermittently.
Surprised interfering together remembering.
Remembering remembering remembering what said was remembering!

Remembering much some convincing received expecting.
Something expecting who thing hearing what they thing?
They one it other like intermittently one one preparing.
He was had where that looked had made made would what that that.
Said that knew not make not.
Enough after naturally naturally naturally strangely has.
Was and and and had such then one what doing could would?
Would he was having have what they what what saying?
That been.
Not having satisfying enough.
After.

Clellan friendly agreeable certainly has saw and if if something . . .
That the could would would would asked him talking.

Waving some what what what that some then been would not would?
Would would not make not?
Enough after naturally naturally naturally strangely has.
Was five were it of regretting?
He before enough satisfying certainly.
Clellan anything if is exciting can was saying perplexing kindly.
Disturbing some gone come to that when when?
It.
It is asked told not be be doing to continuing something and asked.
If it it ask . . .
Donger!
Donger.
Donger asked was what?
They when it stay has can just certain.
Not same intermittently.
Talking not badly.

He did to went something seen some that the that waiting saying.
Coming completely nice of and one what will all built?
So falling ways that come and all all did not not not!
Sit done to start to . . .
If it it is very been strangely they had little regretting might.
Upsetting up.
Anne.
Anne had yet be not to to be heavy so not hearing little together.
Right if is not not little thing bowing some wasting.
Any thing when what wasting thing that that that is . . .
Is like lightly making movement conclusion nicely.
To could be being he he that leaving annoying is.
If if.
It?
In asking be suffering things would about long tired might nothing?
Question quickly quickly eating and showing misunderstood.
Going something seen some that the that waiting face.
Way will built falling.
Falling hearing is is not not little enough had was.
They fall walked well would remained feeling wasting is is not.

Bowing after enough wasting has.
They are any and if it is is not would not entirely waiting custom?
They what they are doing they what they regretting.
Quite is is a . . .
Remembering nicely having nicely.
After that that that that it is been did begin.
Donger quite.
Donger then what that thing if . . . ?
It?

In asking was that one everything suffering if it in is say amusing?
Again tell likely pleased regularly and and and is.
Ate?
If is not do not every was has they way which the when they the they?
There bigger and are the who called anything ones of . . .
Of had beginning that over wasting waiting rolling.
Existing one proceeding enough doing something something.
Some could being heard because that thing that that married.
Have ask tired and all.
All they that they leave disturbing not want likely pleased.
Talking showing imitating been going expressing completely.
Not some have them come high likely built enough together.
Remembering what they enough what be more hope saying?
Accidentally what what something visited regularly?
Surprised scattered until one yet saying smaller.
The who when they when mean were were come came all feeling wanted.
Wanted?!
Finishing wasting all rolling wasting waiting rolling if is.

Not would not entirely waiting custom they.
If its is is is amusing kept annoying.
Henns!
Antliss expecting impossible pleasantly appreciated then.
Not doing tired easy continuing disturb appearing.
Agreeable expecting every one everything everything!
One enjoying one and one had yet be not is it is is disturb?
Done done ended when then where been any and saying?

What laugh kneeling browning existing would this?
This conclusion anything is is what saying all looked.
Looking looking looking in is any upsetting kept directing.

Explaining.
Sender something expecting repeating is it is is disturbing?
Some gone come any one and told thing one been then then.
That that!
If is not to not enjoying and and something asked not come determine.
Ask it and all all enough enough and asked would is other.
Is is disappearing sounding continuing some?

A one and saying to some made left will not that likely smaller.
There that things when thing is is.
Not to.
Not could some remained completing completing proceeding?

Regretting mentioned mentioned what what are being?
Is it is is?
Doing not finishing!

After not not not everything and who enough enough enough is?

Is living get left another they they see then they gone.
Remember?
Helbing some pleasant nothing amusing when who when everything?

Appreciated again and any.
One enjoying one had easy and been he everything meant not come?
Determine ask knew any one.
If ask all walking.

Walking showing chosen was hear turned something not do not.
Who are enough being enough when seeing were were running?
Will high high built and and and then that that what?
Clap look laugh while heard heard was living come be!
Dead over thing waiting when what wasting showing?

Completing completing like would were three three!
Standing was why coming often making is if and all walking.

Way feeling surprising something not coming not something.
Say say saying saying saying what?
There what anything.
That!
That been deny something was saw would who everybody being they?
They see they liked to looking packed suffering needed.
When that everywhere where father that then keep very.
Feeling were holding could the that feeling they dead?
Did had not to not friendly having all explained an all?
Told one everything when hear they they they!
Pulling pleased seeing pleased pleased naturally refusing.

Pleasant sound not would when heard they there stay.
That who came was because feeling being when thing.
Some suddenly done!
Donger that which the very did did did not not not feel saw all.
Feeling and and had taken what needing they did sitting.
And needed for not say wife not all in and thought that . . .
Need very was was holding back leave intend perhaps.
Are.
There what might easily walking regularly.
Talking truly and knew had.
If and would make all alike putting putting putting the where?
One they had had had naturally could naturally as all.
Falling there that where smaller little sizes have.
Sizes that they . . .
The they when look laugh while heard heard was living come to.
That are very has have and showing him sizes have sizes.
That they that that when heard were were longer was.
Were!

Donger looked.
Donger all and did that?
That one staying he later and some did sizes have sizes that they . . .

That that when heard were were stay amusing that feeling?
Kindly please regularly.
Talking showing one one one one existing what what chosen call?
All what completely when when one doing that what one?
They likely falling sounds sung laugh and and and longer.
Was would.
Donger which was the when been that?
That one staying living to enough talked much he that doing that.
That what?
That that that what what they they are they can all what perplexing?
What that one using to what she they living had could?
Long anything and answering and left have amusing.
Donger which what when open open they they they they like to?
Enough walk there!
There there very asked all walking and pleased walking.
Waving showing chosen some made saw when they being fall walked.
They the they.
They had were that heard heard were there stay that to those?
They!
They heard heard what over would and all all were were three three!
There them the every happening an and and . . .
Remembering remembering something because convincing convincing.
Happened happened upsetting any not again kindly.
To charming one they when been very interesting not.
To sit tell doing something it hearing easy what then.
Where where?

Donger that what everything very well he very likely any in way.
Likely so many laughing answering answering truly.
What everything hear where we had was enough any who.
Enough going enough one of and all will to that that that hearing.
Make and been were been when did not sung sizes and again.
Start again again!
They some saw it that over something are all all the who enough.
Houses there were them look what because surprising?
Something something it that there something completing.
Married then not continued not come received and again.

Again again asking they thing they easy are pleasant.
All come have come have and again again exciting intend.
To that when very can can came likely and again what?
Saying saying ate knew had they who one they stay make?
Not would that thing would alike that that pressing.
They had refusing that there sounds who they that little?
Thing when then they had were that heard heard all and . . .
Had start came saw all all all over after some not something.

Like of of were this that meeting talking they one they.
Said have saw if if some not some some one another one.
What saw was not not not living did ask visited asking.
Asking difficult to thing thing thing some something.
Some something something something saddening something.
Expecting meant something perhaps asked is it was?
Have has not so not be be each disappearing disturb?
Because because that what what wanted over kneeling?
Are wasting waiting has finishing he the would sitting?
Suddenly waiting an all all of of making movement surprising.
Something be he thing then being mentioned some arrange.

Something is it what said was been feeling because . . .
Arranged disturbing purpose remember that what what?
That one and they hear has and not to not he each had would.
What meaning that some!
This the happening easily and not not little.
He was had where that pleased then said that been he said had would.
Had went.

That alike called when which that little some what they had have.
Had were larger longer that those wanted.
Finishing little finishing bowing finishing enough something.
Finishing happening not something not was was has.

Mentioned feeling needing feeling all and saying . . .
Liked did not that.
Clellan completing time where being thing enough if is be be.

Urging urging intended hearing expecting repeating.

Repeating not come not what having answering that.
Nothing amusing hearing any in says liked like not.
That likely pleased.

Talking showing imitating been going is it it is each one who?
Naturally enough enough that the scattered disturb!
And all all who that looked all pretty they feeling.
Finishing finishing bowing finishing enough something finishing.

Happening not something not was was has mentioned . . .
Feeling needing feeling all and saying liked did not.
That?
Clellan completing time where being thing enough and are they?
Be common saw living living having what they the seen.
Would what what that had had was being been feeling!
Using living did have accidentally urging urging.

He way was came not some intended to come be hearing?
Difficult being hearing kindly be by rolling some.
Rolling would sitting suddenly waiting of every one.
Regretting and of not expecting before knew and when?
Understanding!
Clellan certainly!
Clellan anything if . . . !
It.
In asking everything.
Anne?
George thought being something tired what hearing that some.

Going some repeating who they enough any or pleasing?
For did finish again refuse enough answering happening?
Answering not continuing little what saying describing?
What lacking motion staying any one any left will not?
That likely smaller there that things when thing any.
Wrong been what saying being pretty walking remained!

Feeling all one had dead rolling thing doing dying.
Very being arrange deny liked did not that.
Clellan completing might not having admitting saying saying.
What that one been what they what that is is doing dying?
Children!
When going he easy answering not come not be be been been
    disappointing.
He what saddening enough any who about doing something?
That not be be remember something well will walking!
Talking talking that they feeling copying.
He was have come so some come eaten built enough impossible appearing!
Something growing are growing showing meaning sitting.
Waiting.

They who who houses there were them look and are they feeling?
Did conclusion saying satisfying something finishing?
Finishing finishing was was was what hearing looking.
Looking and in way long did not what perplexing another?
Then there being then being about any and if if they . . .
Them standing sitting was that things successful.
Anything it is gone or enough know meaning walking.
Talking is is same showing chosen knew staying waiting.
Meeting is it it is annoying come not come completed.
Smaller started completing completing proceeding.
Proceeding then the this standing enough and such.
It surprising great saying saying arrange certainly!
Everybody came to some happened perplexing.
George thought prospering prospering everything to children.
Children?
When going if if of and they hear having answering astonishing.
That that said when thing then then that that one one?
Then there pleasing for are know thing might one efficiently.
He misunderstood something is as be are enough anyway seeing.
Annoying refusing anything appearing and ended had.
Been if is proceeding proceeding proceeding conclusion.
There before concluding everything satisfying satisfying!

And enough and more he what when hearing looking looking?
In is enough exciting this this something offering.
Standing standing to they stand sitting if is in if.
Had heard intended is to thing one of and they are an . . .
Saddening and and any one one they.
It is pleasing or enough which there pleased pleased everything.
Expressing expressing that where one when house left?

In is the they when other?
One.
One and one and high be if is pleasant pretty who which proceeding?
Proceeding proceeding surprising regretting everything!
Its of that they they.
Very!
Doing finishing and not.
Doing not liked did like like in it time.
That one staying where some would would heard did not if . . . ?
It an any and that that being prospering wife baby was not got father.
Long tired might nothing question quickly quickly?
Walking showing saying truly what everything hear.
Where we been turned something?
That the arrange nicely quite one of them that them them sitting.
Five not waiting nodding meeting talking and in and . . .
This that!
This?
This what said was not not not understanding and been because . . .

Satisfying offering friendly uneasily why three?
Why them this were were there were were three three?
Such it that then could surprising anything exciting?
A . . .
Any and that what being?
This what said was not not not saying quite and need answering.
Beginning friendly uneasily why three why five little?
Movement done one if they that one them what because?
Surprising something coming not coming having having!

Saying are one and that that being.
This was can was not some not everything and not having offering.

George friendly uneasily why three why and all all of of to there?
Them them what because surprising something would?
Was thing quite reading feeling needing that the been?
Deny what when looked he was did all he doing found.
This there and enough and hear said and another all all one offering.
If standing was wearing working.
Anne the things she one intended been.

This was thought about he had and everything and prospering.
Returning enough something one.
If it it to not continuing not something something one quickly.
Not are one had is and and and and . . .

Talking not discovering to.
If stay one of not some saying is if then what one everything alike?
What he were were the they were were there of of that.

What they them this why three were suddenly had house?

Houses houses three houses then that one every happening!
Way regretting more comes.
Any all all of of that there everything common and all all one.

Offering to what she taken what working?
Anne needed he not would prospering father.
Antliss to the were were successful he holding could those.
Sender purpose in if meant said asked again again asking any.

Like will not that likely pleased made motion have?
Come movement before anything accidentally successful!
Successful successful might asking is not come and . . .
Kindly nothing amusing hearing is is.
Donger something finish something that when the thing if it . . .

Is isn't and can quickly just that discovering custom.
That they that that all in way of and feeling more reading.

There anything mentioned feeling needing all and.
Saying of and been.
If is not completing not then later talked talked convincing.
Convincing hearing is.
If then there everybody they heard had having some not not not . . . !
Married he not then that what what one one every in if?
They that they they long to who back?
It.
If exciting everything one heard enjoying one one then liked.
To enough walk pleased and and and.
He was was noise would not said make thing said then what that?

That he be is is face were when would falling?
Falling hearing that the they when anything all all over of that.
Those!
They them and are they doing not?
This thing.
Enough who that read that that thing they . . . ?
Very are are they?
Doing not!
Doing!
Doing?
Doing been feeling because arranged disturbing purpose remember.
That what knew very him have have have not would not.
Come would him were that some same way saying what what?
What that to that pleased they call some would would/
Asked said make any.
If if then what one they he each and completely not some have them.
Come she naturally say when there that that the things.
They easy when done could fell sound sung fall any.

There that while those if is is one a would was why and pleasant.
All they great satisfying!

Clellan?
Clellan accidentally when was any one if would came?
All back nothing amusing hearing any in and . . .
Donger did was disappearing disappearing disappointing purpose.
Disappearing disappearing satisfaction intermittently.
Disappearing!
Talking showing imitating existing is is is knew all what had?
Any away would make any one of face were when would falling.
Falling hearing that the scattered disturb when which that?
Little is is had have happening surprising regretting.
Reading something something something is is said.
Quite very happen later anything.
Antliss continuing explaining explaining that what said those.
Intended is is and are what easy anything and who have?
Saying one!
If not to interesting remember he might expressing expressing.
Everything understood everything expressing expressing.
Expressing every one where every regretting everything!
Conclusion concluding everything some saying saying.
Saying saying having there them what anything?
That.
That?
This being enough he he determined did had felt he when?
Clellan.
That?
That staying went some something something remembering admitting.
Something admitting something something was not.

Would would heard not something not being been could?

Told some again intended living and and did he getting?
What had?
His need not not everything expect expected some expecting.

Repeat something expecting repeating anything and . . .
Saying that which anything laughing laughing one.

Efficiently is ate was call some something saying . . .
Saying saying he be where each has not not not easily.

Existing happening.

Two hundred and twenty-seven strophes of which the numbers of sentences (verse lines, comprising one or more typographical lines) follow many successive iterations of the interlocked ascending and descending Lucas sequence 1, 3, 4, 7, 11, 18, 29, 18, 11, 7, 4, 3, 1, ending with a last ascent to 29 followed by the partial sequences 1, 3, 4, and 1. The strophes were produced by running an eight-page passage from Stein's LGB (*ASR* 213–20) through DIASTEX5. The seed text was a passage from Stein's MoA (*ASR* 78–79). I obtained the page numbers of both texts by means of extensions of numerological operations on the names "Gertrude Stein" and "Jackson Mac Low." I first modified the output of the program by placing periods at the ends of typographical lines and sequences of lines that begin with capital letters. Then I divided it into Lucas-sequence strophes as above, changed the word "a" to "an" before vowel phonemes, and deleted irrelevant hyphens. Finally, after repeating each verse-line sentence aloud several times, both alone and in conjunction with preceding and following lines, and thereby "getting a feel for" its meaning, I replaced many of the periods with question marks, exclamation points, and/or points of suspension.

New York: 5 February–21 March 1999

More Not More Today Forget

(Stein 72)

Happy Birthday 36 Mordecai!

more not more to-day forget

Made by running Part I, Stanza VI, of "Stanzas in Meditation," by Stein (*ASR* 569–71), located by numerological operations on my son's name, "Mordecai-Mark Mac Low," through DIASTEX5 utilizing "Mordecai-Mark Mac Low" as seed text. The program was no longer able to match the name with words from Stanza VI after the "e" (in the 5th position) in "Mordecai-Mark."

New York: 10 March 1999

They Which In and Coming

(Stein 73)

Happy Birthday 36, Mordecai!

They which they not measure increased.
Namely themselves guessing thought security only of either
in and coming losing coming is is no wonder not they
which they not measure increased.
Namely themselves express resigning fortunate pointedly.

Or.
If by.
Left.
Might their known elegantly alighting resigning alighting
have for now from him ounce.
Namely finally neatly in as to their share just so favors thin
to-day and and ever one and.

Or.
If all person altogether than they.
In is neither do not they which they.
Ever in ladling out after all day fat why also of hither have their
great like have their given coming that there there
no we increased.
Namely themselves guessing thought security only of either
in and coming.

Three strophes made by running Part I, Stanza VI, of Stein's SiM (*ASR* 569–71) through DIASTEX5 using as seed the last four speeches of "Identity a Poem" (*ASR* 594, also located by numerological operations on the name "Mordecai-Mark Mac Low"). I revised the program's output by placing periods at the ends of sentences (verse lines comprising single typographical lines or sequences of lines of which the first begins with capital letter) and by making a strophe break before the second "Or."

New York: 7–10 March 1999; 28 April 2000

Description Is Certainly One Thing That Was Completed

(Stein 74)

Description is certainly doing.

That description was certainly an integrated description.
This was a description, a description of things.
She was in a way certainly other than her description.

Some kinds of some living things have not quite enough understanding.
For them this is different, a different mixture of different kinds.
In using them, are they thinking that they are different ones?
The ones thinking differently are the ones needing these descriptions.
Meeting that sister, some are always hearing integrated descriptions.

She was younger then and certainly listening to all kinds of descriptions.
The other one there was being one completely interested in integrated living.
Completely different beings were certainly using them in developing mixtures.
Some kinds of them were feeling castigated.
These kinds were almost really living.
That one was having any one else living developing feelings was
understandable.
Can one then have been feeling or thinking something about them?

With whom are you doing something?
Many who are certainly thinking about a description are very certainly living.
This description is very certain to be emotional if it is of one living.
Being a description of some one, it may be something developing realisation.
Living things having feeling and listening may each sometimes be
understanding.
She is such a being.
Martha together with other beings is using such descriptions.
There are always ones developing descriptions and understanding them.
Some who are often certainly almost suffering are listening tenderly.

Their descriptions are certainly such that realisation may arise from them.
All living things are still always needing feelings if not emotions.

Developing a realisation of liking something living was really being living.
Repeating listening was certainly making a connection between them.
Liking and listening were developing together.
Was developing liking complicated?
Any liking may have become an almost completely complicated connection.
Was it to their liking?
It was being developed and then not complicatedly completed.
Were they needing complete understanding?
Some older ones were being ones developing that.
They completed a realisation that each one was then a different one.
Was this something they were developing together?
Was it always something they were developing between them being living?
Some who were certainly good-looking were needing understanding.

Thinking to some is always a thing completed between different beings.
Understanding older ones is not such a complicated thing.
That very one is completing her understanding of older thinking.
She is nearly loving this older thing and between needing and being it.
Not understanding anything living or feeding or thinking, she is emotional.
The things thinking is certainly for are realisation and understanding.
They are completing their realisation that they are needing thinking.
One of them is younger and easily becoming emotional.
What can his realisation that she is good-looking be for?
A good deal of realisation is certainly meeting the description of realisation.
Then certain realisations may develop only when one is older and willing to be.
This sister is often understanding anything.
She is existing complicatedly but sometimes she's certainly quite understanding.
All her children are complicated.
She is understanding nearly all kinds of complicated thinking.
A different-looking sister integrates description and complication.
That integrated description is something completed.

Sometimes something was existing.
Much was existing.

Quite much.
Something complicated was sometimes completed.
Then the complicated sister was certainly understanding it.
Sometimes Martha was not.
Some mixtures were castigated.
Their descriptions were certainly different.
A being might have been suffering much from such a description
Was she listening to the differences between kinds of description?
The younger one was using any description for castigation.
Martha was needing all kinds of mixtures.
The children were saying they were listening to them all.
Those kinds of mixtures were certainly existing.
Each of them was sometimes not seen being.
The mixtures' descriptions were certainly complicated.
Were those descriptions developing differently?
She completed many kinds of things.
This one then was one thing that was completed.

Eight strophes comprising verse-line sentences that follow the sequence of prime numbers from 1 to 19. The poem is a result of trying to run a passage from Stein's "Two Women" (*ASR* 112–15) through DIASTEX5, using as seed one page from Stein's MoA (*ASR* 66). While doing this, I was repeatedly stopped by a "nonmatch": the program would not be able to find a word in the source text that had one of the letters of a certain word in the seed text in a corresponding place. Each time I was stopped, I added several iterations of a word from the seed text (or one similar to such a word) that had the needed letter in the correct position to the source text, at random places in sentences where the addition might make sense, so that the program could go on. (At some point I randomly shifted certain passages in the source text to other places than those they had originally occupied.) Each time I made such an addition the program produced a longer output. When the program's output had grown to 78 lines, I decided to use the output up to that point as the basis of Stein 74. (By this time, the output included roughly as many words from the seed as from the source, if not more.) I "mined" the output for words with which I constructed normative sentences, adding or changing structure words and suffixes as needed. As I made the sentences, they became verse lines, which I grouped, as I went along, in prime-sequence strophes as described above.

New York: 26–30 March 1999

Martha Was Certainly Thinking Together

(Stein 75)

Martha was certainly certainly Martha.

Martha who was living and sometimes listening to something was certainly remembering interesting things.
She being one needing being living was going and being a living thing.
She was being living.

She being feeding was living and was altogether she.
She was needing to be going.
Some such younger ones could not completely be such things.
And then she was living.

She was one going and was sometimes almost important then.
Such important older ones were certainly always talking.
Older and older ones were certainly thinking.
Certainly anyone being living and stopping living was not needing anything.
Certainly Martha's sister was sometimes being tender.
Almost all of them were living.
She and her sister were certainly listening.

Anyone who was needing anything was certainly being living.
She was certainly one of them being living.
Martha and her sister would not stop being interesting.
One of them was sometimes important.
Some children were certainly listening.
Many of them were living together.
They certainly could not be listening to other existing children.
She and some others were certainly interesting.
Certainly some younger ones were good at completely stopping thinking.

Using this different thing in an older way the men and children had
        certainly been listening to something together.
It was certainly important to Martha that she should be stopping her sister
        from going on repeating something longer but not in a better way.

She was certainly thinking she could not deal with living any longer.
That thing might have been anything she had to be needing to be stopping.
Thinking about stopping living was interesting.
Some younger ones could not be really needing not to be living.
She certainly could not be needing anything then.
Martha was not listening to anything.
Some younger women were willing something.
Certainly anything and any one could sometimes be needing to be stopping.
That one and all of them were really needing this thing.
Something existing can sometimes be something feeling.
Some remembering can be interesting.
When young men have not made some remembering interesting younger
        women will not be willing to be living with them.
This one is really listening to something longer than that one could.
She is certainly one living with some suffering.
She is one that is needing to be completely listening.
This one needed something to be interesting and important.
Martha and she were certainly feeling younger.
They each have something interesting to be thinking together.

Six strophes derived from a passage in Stein's TW (*ASR* 215–17). Lacking notes, I believe this passage was run through DIASTEX5. However, I do not know what "seed text" I employed in this process. The final poem was either made by "mining" the output of this procedure and freely producing normative sentences from the words I extracted or by some more systematic procedure. These sentences were divided into strophes that comprise successively numbers of sentences corresponding to the Lucas-number sequence 1, 3, 4, 7, 11, 18.

New York: April–May 1999; 15 April 2001

Something Important
Could Certainly Be Enough

(Stein 76)

Something important could certainly be listened to then.

And that thing was certainly not anything uninteresting.
Could Martha be saying that that thing was not something interesting and
completely important?
She could be.

What would Martha be saying *that* for?
Something was saying that through her.
What was saying that through Martha?
Certainly something living.
What could that living thing be?

Could it be some younger being?
Who?
I cannot say.
Something importantly feeding on Martha?
Perhaps.
For being interesting?
Perhaps to be *very* interesting.

Who or what could really be interesting that way?
Perhaps the being that was saying that through Martha.
I cannot listen to such talking.
Ha ha!
You say ha ha?!
I do!
You will certainly not be living any longer!

Ugh!!
You say enough.
Ugh!!!
You've said enough.

Five strophes derived from what was left over after Stein 75 was "mined" from the output of DIASTEX5 when a passage in Stein's TW (*ASR* 215–17) was probably run through it. The final poem was made by "mining" what remained of the output of this procedure and producing normative sentences from the words elicited thereby. These sentences were divided into strophes that comprise successively numbers of sentences corresponding to the Lucas-number sequence.

New York: 12 May 1999

There a Different Time-Sense Is Simply Non-Competitive

(Stein 77)

There a different time-sense is simply a different difficulty.

The difference is satisfactory, so the difficulty is simple.
Does the difference make for a different difficulty anyway?
Looking perfectly difficult, it is naturally different.

Looking perfect, the difficulty is naturally different.
The difficulty is different, simply different,
Are things better or more nearly perfect because they are different?
There where the different is simply difficult, the difference is different.

Does a different time-sense make that difficulty satisfactory?
That's simple: already the time-sense because it is a different time-sense
  makes the acceptance of the difficulty different.
There they prepared for a different, more satisfactory happening, though
  war seemed better.
Were the insiders' refusals satisfactory?
Different compositions would have been satisfactory.
Their words would have had to do with satisfactory work, not with war work.
Lord!—the almost classical simplicity that leads to important refusals!

Are beautiful things connected with beings that are beautiful?
Are those beings' first efforts at composition accepted by them?
Are the beautiful things connected with the beautiful things they are being?
Do these things come from the beings that they are?
Does their time-sense or the things they are being lead to those things?
The grey, beautiful things there are connected with the things they are being.
That is, the things they are being are connected with those things.

What they are being is creating those things.
Speak, grey classic, where is creating entering?
Everyone knows that compositions are not created as a matter of course.
All are made by those already prepared.

Anybody may be already prepared.

Naturally, their works are perfectly different and perfectly connected.
Naturally, contemporaries, being different, are not non-competitive.
They are perfectly connected.

Their contemporaries too create connectedly.
As contemporaries, whatever they create is connected.
Why aren't they naturally non-competitive?
Why can't they, though naturally different, be non-competitive?

Eight stanzas of verse-line sentences comprising two Lucas-number sequences: 1, 3, 4, 7, 11 and 1, 3, 4. Derived from two pages of Stein's "Composition as Explanation" (*ASR* 495–96). This passage was first run through the program TRAVESTY, which was asked for an order-6 output of about 1,400 words. Then that output (or "Travesty") was run through DIASTEX5, using as seed a passage from the same book. After that, the output of that run-through was used as the seed for a second run of the same passage through DIASTEX5. I accepted the stopping of the output of each of the run-throughs by a "mismatch" (the program's *not* finding a word in a source text that has one of the letters of a seed text in the position that it occupies in the seed text). I revised the last output of DIASTEX5, composing a sentence with most of the words in each typographical line by rearrangements of word order, suffix changes, and deletions, notably of repeated words.

New York: 25–27 May 1999

Beginning There

(Stein 78)

Beginning an interest in the middle depends on having it inside
And perfectly simply concerning anybody there
So it makes something rather simple but likely interesting.

Interesting remarked the generals about themselves
Before entering rather than creating.

The past is simple there concerning less of course.
And it is singularly likely to rate less
And nearly depends on describing a painting
Created by nothing else but a nearly lost contemporary.

[long pause]

History refused became a difference about themselves.
So naturally they themselves entered and did outlaw things.

Quoting nations nothing is ending.
Everything is nothing they say.
Everybody says that she is very certain everybody acted.

What makes them tell you outlaw reasons?
Are all of them otherwise prepared?
Are they even nearly prepared themselves?

They are beginning and ending their description there
Because acceptors are already singularly beautiful.
They are simply creating nothing.
Concerning having they'd rather it were perfectly so
And there.

Seven strophes made by first running two pages from Stein's CE (*ASR* 495–96) through DIASTEX5, using as seed a paragraph from Stein's LGB (*ASR* 241, par. 8) and then revising suffixes, word order, and other features of the output and using all of it but a few structure words. The division into strophes was intuitive, and the phrase "long pause"—employed as an instruction for readers—appeared in the program's output after "contemporary" and before "history refused."

New York: 31 May, 4 June 1999

Nothing Without Wonder

(Stein 79)

Nothing about a beginning generation is decided.

This one has been quite without time.
How and when is every degree between them exceptional?
Isn't it a perfectly wonderful thing?

There you make every difference between one thing and another remarkable.
You make this what is seen when the world happens.
Then you simply come to composition.
An enormous characteristic is that each generation knows its composition is perfect.

Generals before deciding what is réfuse refúse to.
That is so dead!
Simply lead likely lives!
Make that something!
By mean degrees this one decided how time had been around them.
When is there no thére there?
Everything is now perfect and quite without wonder.

Four strophes of verse-line sentences comprising the Lucas sequence. Derived from Stein's CE (*ASR* 495–96) through DIASTEX5, using as seed Stein's LGB (*ASR* 241, par. 7). The output of the program was revised into normative verse-line sentences which were grouped into "Lucas-sequence strophes" as described above. (Acute accents were inserted in strophe 4 to clarify stresses.)

New York: 31 May–4 June 1999

Person Neither Like Refuse

(Stein 80)

Person neither than cause alighting
One made great
Articles they like known peas beans change

This
And all see but more
And finally can fortunate namely neatly know alike where should they

This
She shared
Gathered who have had as do like refuse

Three tercets made by rearranging a few words in the output of sending Stanza VI of Stein's SiM (*ASR* 569–71) through DIASTEX5, using as seed a paragraph of Stein's LGB (*ASR* 241, par. 1). The slightly revised output was intuitively divided into three tercets as prompted by the initially capitalized and solitary iterations of "This."

New York: 7 June 1999

Losing Great

(Stein 81)

Losing with attach neither finally themselves
Let me

Might one of may just better that without enjoin
Ask all now attach

Glory theirs security strawberries which
Aimless displeasure

All known and to from cause same
Let like not neatly likely raspberries last

Could many elegantly
Person do attach finally great

Five couplets made by rearranging a few words in the output of sending Stanza VI of Stein's SiM (*ASR* 569–71) through DIASTEX5, using as seed a paragraph of Stein's LGB (*ASR* 241, par. 2). The slightly revised output was intuitively divided into couplets, some lines being broken and some words rearranged.

New York: 7 June 1999

I an' Raspberries

(Stein 82)

I an' they
They they by
Left

Might their known
Elegantly alighting
Resigning alighting

One in their
So names may their
Given coming see not

Him more merit attach
Alighting resigning
Alighting at one

Made do not
Which shone thought
Security not come like pointedly

Attach alighting
Resigning alighting
Where may best

Refuse become more remember
Remember strawberries
Remember raspberries

Seven tercets made by sending Stanza VI of Stein's SiM (*ASR* 569–71) through DIASTEX5, using as seed a paragraph of Stein's LGB (*ASR* 214, par. 7). The output was intuitively divided into tercets, most output lines being broken, with several changes of letter case and an added apostrophe.

New York: 8 June 1999

Ask Fancies

(Stein 83)

Ask an' often
Well ladling their fancies
Which have
Just not
Come hither

She just increased
Which senses express
Fancies

Two strophes made by sending Stanza VI of Stein's SiM (*ASR* 569–71) through DIASTEX5, using as seed a paragraph of Stein's LGB (*ASR* 216, par. 1). The output (stopped early by a nonmatch) was intuitively divided into lines and strophes, with two changes of number and several of letter case, and an added apostrophe.

New York: 8 June 1999

Have Heard or Known This

(Stein 84)

Have heard
Ounce than themselves
Hope can ladling after

For favors fat with where
Hither

Aimless and all be from two
Left neither altogether
Nether hope given

Hesitated forget
last get

Might fasten hither
With May resigning plan
Or known this

Five strophes, alternately tercets and couplets, made by sending Stanza VI of Stein's SiM (*ASR* 569–71) through DIASTEX5, using as seed a paragraph of Stein's LGB (*ASR* 215, par. 8). The output was intuitively divided into lines and strophes, with two changes of number and several of letter case.

New York: 8 June 1999

Do Be Gathered In

(Stein 85)

Do

For sense alighting where
Rather know knelt
They know one ever should
Should resigning attach

They

To refuse become more
Remember
Remember strawberries
Remember that shared
That is
If sense to same have great delight

Resigning

Alighting

Resigning

I as shared come
Come
Come merit attach alighting resigning

Alighting have best
Cannot could
Aimless

Tuesday and is asking with which measure

Left have best
Cannot could
Aimless

Tuesday and is to ask
If

If

His weight is known
And they know why

They that fortunate
Have better known
To undo the known day
Known in that they know after

For elegantly one can wonder there

And is asking likely
Could one
Could all have remembered
Shared
Peas
Beans
Strawberries
Which elegantly today
Might be gathered in

Sixteen strophes made by sending Stanza VI of Stein's SiM (*ASR* 569–71) through DIASTEX5, using as seed a paragraph of Stein's LGB (*ASR* 217, par. 3). The output was intuitively revised a little and divided into lines and strophes.

New York: 8 June 1999

Therybody Havere

(Stein 86)

Therybody the wormough be orts fich thosithassiffecte.

Of youlatery ot looking is impork is tory leady.
Les vereakessit doest fore naturally ory siffork.
Int been is peatimporare whe wit is work ing haterferefuse.

Clat afted veres the on ime-se.
It ented.
Speak it tins.
Thappented the clas pread too not.

Ontere not classit of one what is not a cone be ally.
Le they knothis fory imuch to naturally dectly.
Knot arts hinted ity.
Anybody son ing ing is hat it.
Ariessimply shost rentempeautin they they knot it.
A ve nonly a doest bettere actly thaturally so beautit.
Haturalreakes fic.

The a clas is beat is is.
Ity do satiffork it hatiffer the it thatiffereptantemposic.
Is to been mak one ortand so and ant bad.
Anywar insimple accepared Gre to a cone is a diffiestitin.
Is very shosen thery speades too the nat.
Is beass becide.
Thation almormourally assit arit.
Is you hose of the haturally it the one's prefuld.
Being sone effich thappented do the ing is ve does.
Art wough to and so are not the when a natedly does.
Areauting impork ing.

Nat ithervally re thatem.
A clas wity a cone thas pen a nat is yourarts the.
And bectork insen ing.
This tin mory is ing Lor.
It thereptere wory to acted arestis be it whaturalthe.
Where wou do beensenory knot all ting Lormou hat.
Ening.
The rall onne woulas acceptand thensiting.
Naturally knot show ot cread is it ing Lory ing.
Therfecidery aso sally they.
There on aring is first.
Acce one native it is nat itionne ing thows.
Conectly ally thered beautionly is tory leak ithe.
Ork ing thows.
Fies diffic isfacto nat. tor a cont.
Sting.
It whows they otherfecide.
Fies.

Nows.

Thisfacto.
Sat sic.
Now is mak one art sper therense is.

Of the all one's the what.
A natinsit saturareautiffereas.
Whosiculd ther insenin ing spereat so be.
Ho not fort evereak ime everead do als.

Tords.
Ich.
Muld Gren thereaust do the it are hated the of.
Cone ensich thempore and Gre have way.
Frompormost.
Ime-se dif acceparen ithavery leausat sat ass diffirse.
On althe all tookin iffer isfacce it havere.

Ten strophes made by running an early stage of my poem Stein 77 through TRAVESTY, requesting a 2,000-character, order-3 output. I kept the output's Zaum-like succession of words, pseudo-words, and portmanteau words, but turned its typographical lines into pseudo-sentences by initial capitalization and periods and by making new sentence-lines by substituting periods for commas in the output and making a line break after every intra-line period, including those in the original output. The resulting series of verse lines was grouped into strophes comprising two Lucas-number sequences: 1, 3, 4, 7, 11, 18, followed by 1, 3, 4, 7.

New York: 11–12, 23–24 June 1999

Use Is
Steadily
Caught

(Stein 87)

Use is
been
are places
religious.

An all-color baggage.

Fruit see always found
undertaken breadth enough
and choose.

January religious.

Fourth distribution.

Capital way
horses here
hymn comes
been a . . .

And indeed,

Capital they
those before necessity
neither understand . . .

Is been and all
all and . . .

Elaborately welcome
been crowded
sees great
steadily caught.

how this poem was made

method: (1) running source and seed through DIASTEX5
(2) revising output (for output changes, see below)

source: two poems from Mac Low's "Stein" series: Stein 12 and Stein 40

seed: "Stein 12"

output changes:
inserting strophe breaks before capital letters
breaking strophes into lines
inserting punctuation at ends of strophes
deleting one apostrophe; changing one "a" to an "an"

New York: 13 June 1999

Something Upsetting

(Stein 88)

Something could be something interesting.
Something could be something.

Something importantly beginning is imitating repeating.
Enjoying upsetting important others could be something important and
would be if it could be.
Could not—cannot—another characteristic be certainly and perfectly
deciding if it could be?

Anything regular was certainly living, it was certainly living.
Listen to that talking difference intended to be doing things.
She's been being's noticed noise, and each hearing is intended.
She's been hearing about another refusing something.
Her all-seeing brother is around again.

It may be beginning to be intended.
Discovering what imitating is might be doing what is lacking.
Somebody's wearing what they're hearing.
Something's getting prepared.
Being wanting something may be agreeable to a completely other
generation.
Another, completely agreeable, is waving proudly.
What decided that what feelings meant was what was certainly noticed?

Then no thing is now quite noise.
Donger was one who intended needing enough and one answering.
That thing was one thing.
Was it what an all-seeing one intended when prospering?
Wherever pleasing, it was unintentionally noticed.
And was that thing all-seeing?
Anne was into that thing.

She was a younger being than that thing.
Who cannot certainly decide whether another's characteristics are perfect?
Certainly anything regularly recurring along the way is not all that
interesting.
Now Martha was certainly deciding between offering what no one intended
offering and what she was discovering unintentionally was funny.

Could an all-seeing being find that completely interesting?
Could Martha's way perhaps be that way?
Would it be interesting?
Martha's generation had been seeing that happening by degrees.
Anything they intended might be funny.
What's turning that hearing's meanings into things that she might mean if
she were being funny?
Things she wanted to be happening needed to be upsetting if they were to
be noticed successfully.
Something was sounding interesting.
Something was funny.
Something was beginning to be something one without time would have
found remarkable before.
By degrees one might be discovering unintentionally that it was interesting.
One might be coming to make it a composition, a composition simply
becoming by degrees completely and perfectly important.
It sometimes importantly happens that what one is imitating was important
before that thing was important to anyone else.

Each one happened to be deciding what things were quite successful when
they were.
When this happens it's before each one has quite decided what things are
successful.
Each one intended discovering without quite perfectly discovering.
A remarkable thing's difference makes what happens happen.
Walking's continuing meaning when meaning's thing is walking
What one knows around one isn't walking.
What they were wearing and what they were leaving when they quite openly
went was quite upsetting.

Intermittently an all-seeing being cannot quite be seen as being upsetting.
Importantly something perfect was perfectly between worlds.
Are there degrees of perfection?
There certainly were.
One cannot listen long to the wonderful without regularly feeding this remarkable thing with what this thing has been.
Anything that our brother did was wonderful.
Offering the existing to be turning that hearing on might be upsetting.
One all-seeing being would be walking wherever that-there was existing.
What was existing?
What one of them said was enough.

Clellan truly noticed that.
Antliss was standing back, doing what had gotten to be funny.
Something was being enough for them.
Who said what was enough for them?
Donger walked, suffering that he had been feeding an interesting being.
Isn't something successful?
Each one said what they were, quickly suffering what's funny's success.
Can meaning be lacking when one's hearing what one's needing to be hearing?
Having heard talking that wears meaning turning into feelings, could they then be listening to talking that was feeling?
Ha!
Who and what was feeding this listening and when and how?
You and everyone there were certainly beginning to do what was remarkable without knowing every degree of it standing between them.
Then is everything that is truly remarkable?
Everything.
Donger and his brother were receiving something exceptionally exciting.
What they were receiving there might have been upsetting if it had been repeating.
Something exceptional was existing.
Everything exceptional was successfully sounding like it was prospering.
Something interesting is beginning to be imitating repeating what others were enjoying and this is something upsetting.

Method: (1) Running source and seed texts through the program DIASTEX5. (2) revision of output (see below).
Source text: Stein 76, 79, and 22, picked by random-digit chance operations.
Seed text: A mix of four lines each from Stein 76, 79, and 22.
Revision: Output was freely revised, more or less line by line, with additions of structure words and some repetitions of lexical words. Minimal punctuation was inserted during composition. The revision was broken, while being composed, into strophes successively comprising numbers of verse-line sentences corresponding to the first eight prime numbers: 2, 3, 5, 7, 11, 13, 17, and 19.

New York: 14–15 June 1999; 18–19 June 2001

A Plate Pillar

(Stein 89)

A plate laid
And then a book there
And suppose then
That one string really joins a house muncher.

Her meadowed round
Was choosing a cleaner
Where white means pillar.

Method: Diastic text selection
via DIASTEX5 (stopped by mismatch)
Source: End of "Objects" section of
Stein's *Tender Buttons*
from "A plate" through "a to let."
Seed: Par. from "Rooms" section
of *TB*,
from "Alike" through "silver."
Editing: Free revision of output
keeping near to output's word order,
with chosen line and strophe breaks,
capitals, and punctuation.

New York: 18 June 1999

Curtains All Around Are What Is Is

(Stein 90)

Curtains all around are enlarging absurdity's resources.

It is it and changing.
Considering peeling is not to consider the whole.
Social success cuts everything earnest outside the whole.

Roasting's not outlasting separation.
This quantity compliments coal.
A chinking bargain strengthens spring and shows its memory.
Sincerely a gracious spoonful silences all wailing.

There another slender splinter raises whole blood.
To what measure is a thinner color feeling curtains?
The whole thing is not all yellow or so specialized.
The lovely darkening tenderness of courage encourages everyone to stay.
Could a day's choice not be a black-whole choice?
Medicine claims it opposes gloom.

Sleeping doesn't exchange the thickness of meaning for nothing.
Isn't cutting cumbersome?
All that contained division resumed the suction-roasting.
Does any surprise touch anyone's anything?
Cloudiness does no chinking.
A cloud and a plate and a volume in spring are evening evening there.
Everything and beefsteak hurry everything.
Respect is clearly overtaking all small obligations.
Coal regulation's outlasting quantity's separate claims.
Bargaining chinking's a gloom-valor transfer when prisons are preserved.
Murmuring hardness makes a show of having stronger hams.

Regions of symmetry and melting harmony stall estrangement.
Morning's meaning makes evening's shows.

Surrounding surfaces and circling exceptions make necessity shine.
Distress's alterations of our obligations call for careful regulation.
Neither colts nor spoons determine coal's color's outlasting coal.
Your whole little collar suggests what a rush you get collecting and claiming.
Recreation! Opposition! Nonchalance!—Everything's restraint!

Does the principal consider length?
Certainly.
What is he doing?
Darkening.

All in all he's stouter.
The second room is cleaner.
They're all sincerely wailing.

What is is.

the form of this poem and how it was made

Nine strophes whose numbers of verse lines comprise the ascending and descending sequence of Lucas numbers 1, 3, 4, 7, 11, 7, 4, 3, 1. The source text was "Roastbeef," the first poem in "FOOD," the central section of Stein's *TB*, as posted on the Stein website of the Bartleby Archive, edited by its webmaster, Steven van Leeuwen, from the edition of *TB* published by Claire Marie, New York, 1914.

Using as seed text paragraphs 21 and 22 of the source, I sent the latter through DIASTEX5. I revised the program's output within liminally determined limits that respect, but are not bound by, the output's words and their forms, groupings, order, grammar, syntax, etc.

New York: 19 June–3 August 1999

Lunch Question

(Stein 91)

LUNCH

POTATOES have have circle memory surrounding and shine

Suppose snipe and and and the weak tenderness middle between
measuring that purple curve thing everywhere exhibition
sacrifice superposition simultaneous largely

Interleaved specimen recollection very dark repeat color
water and and wedding strong place open turn steady
beware ordinary butter

SUGAR

Water that there tender and blisters only this then pierce signal
open delicacy period chain absent silence necessary

All in sudden that the seen they are sound alone steak and please

Cold tiny that cheese post loud blight bees yellow surging question

ASPARAGUS standards discrimination has circling darkning

Around eruption chickens anything denial order four when thick and

Claiming collecting this this eye jerking sooner way in in

Why perfect practiced pink same cutting recollection sincere
there prices curious

All

All all that does joy more anything perfect the singular lightly
take separation leniently larder

Burden mixture cloaking solitude dreariness precocious
and alone colored to the presupposed sherry seat

Luck that surging caution a caution and had there the green this
be than a flower solemn tastes where green so it cross
peculiar doubt

CHICKEN chambers slender by come

SALMON oyster beefsteak neither entirely linen round have
more simple

Lovely snipe and poisonous eruption there assiduous and
and
to sets send shadow

There difference

Thirstiness surfeit nor thing every exhibition sacrifice
superposition simultaneous largely

Interleaved specimen recollection very dark repeat color
water and and wedding strong place open turn steady
beware ordinary butter

SUGAR

Water that there tender and blisters only this then pierce signal
open delicacy period chain absent silence necessary

All in sudden that the seen they are sound alone steak and please

Cold tiny that cheese post loud blight bees yellow surging question

Twenty-seven strophes made by sending "FOOD," the 2nd section of Stein's TB, through DIASTEX5, using as seed the 6th paragraph of "FOOD," which begins, "Lovely snipe and tender turn." My only modifications of the output were to insert a strophe break before every initial capital letter, two letters in structure words, and two new line breaks, and to shift a few words within a line.

Performance suggestions: make a breath pause [about one half-second beat] at each line end and a longer pause [about three half-second beats] at every strophe break. Speak somewhat slowly but don't drag it.

New York: 24 June–9 August 1999

Lunch Interleaved

(Stein 92)

LUNCH.

POTATOES have,
have,
more anything everywhere,
green this
be than a flower solemn,
tastes where
green,
thick and . . .

Claiming collection simultaneous,
largely.

Interleaved specimen recollection,
simultaneous,
largely.

Interleaved specimen recollecting
this,
then pierce signal
open;
turn steady;
beware
ordinary butter.

SUGAR.

Water that there prices . . .
curious. . . .

All in sudden
that the seen,
they are sound
alone:
color,
water,
and blisters,
only this;
then
pierce signal;
open delicacy period,
chain absent,
silence necessary.

All.

All,
all that surging caution,
and had there prices curious.

All in sudden that
cheese post loud blight,
bees yellow surging caution,
a caution,
a caution,
a caution,
and had there the
green;
they are sound alone,
steak neither entirely
linen
round eruption,
chickens,
anything,
everywhere;
exhibition sacrifice superposition
simultaneous largely.

Interleaved specimen,
recollection very dark;
repeat color,
water,
and the weak tender
by
come.

SALMON,
oyster,
beefsteak and . . .

Claiming collecting,
this eye jerking sooner way in,
in . . .

Why perféct
the seen
thick
and please?

Cold,
tiny that surging caution,
a caution,
a caution,
a caution and had,
there,
assiduous and, . . .
and wedding strong place open;
turn steady;
beware ordinary butter.

SUGAR.

Water
that cheese;
post loud blight

bees,
yellow,
surging,
question.

ASPARAGUS standards:
discrimination has
circling darkning.

Around have,
have more anything,
every exhibition,
sacrifice;
superposition:
simultaneous,
largely interleaved.

Twenty-one strophes composed by running a punctuated version of my poem Stein 91 through TRAVESTY. I asked for an order-7 output of ~1,470 words, which I modified by inserting many additional punctuation marks and line breaks within the strophes, but I made no word changes.

24 June–9 August 1999

Eat Vacation

(Stein 93)

Eat, exercise, accomplish time.

Settlement troubles arrangement.
Different interruptions meant connecting.
Were those determined examples of exercises much the same as regulations?

Establish those examples.
Gamboling resistance makes a difference.
It is breadth.
No certainty there, no window or stairway.

Stars light looking-glass decisions.
Will that flowery slanting change?
Being right means checking reversible means.
If more exercise is anything, it counts as lilac.
Some very light lilac ingredients of seasoning are strictly encircled by
slanting light.
Terrifically white and expectant, all are kneeling or replaced.
Ordinarily left-handed decisions grow to be separations.

Discriminating separations earned an astonishing suggestion—to put small
gliding hangings in the miserable water.
Regulations mentioning connections may certainly be painstaking.
Distaste for curtains leads to defiance rather than alleviation.
There may certainly still be some wholesale straw curtains.
Hearing this always shows little causes are tied in strings.
A whole little section may be shallow and show any order of negligence.
That wooden pen there was considered sickening though purchased in an
exchange.
There a narrow curving window does not come so far as this.
More flowers surely exercise, it seems, than all the willows in that place.

A vacation may be stricter than a hanging.
His little piece of that settlement didn't change the baker's center.

This floor covering was not made to be used for kneeling during a vision.
Very little leather surely did not replace much more.
The single who came there was asked whether he had less hair when he was
 last there.
That exchange between those sacks is an example of a disaster.
All accounts of a single visible eclipse may be expressed in one line.
Because decisions are more than statements, music is more than enough
 after they've once been expressed.
Measure excellence by reversing experiences of negligence.
Windows do everything for buildings if they are indeed windows.
They were attaching seasoning to something and encircling it.
Sacrifice a pleasing chair with plenty of breathing and dressing.
To offer standing in morning's very center is so very much a pleasure!
The Chair meant to doubt discrimination though he did mention the
 starving.
Will the lesson of the window get her admitted to the Exchange?
Any indifferent smaller season may be receiving sacrifices.
There's a silent bed at the very center on which anything red causes
 resignation.
They mentioned excellent connections together along with special
 regulations.
One painstaking tribune was lengthening empty evenings.
The Chairs agreeably accounted for their separate indecisions.

Hesitantly, that canister should certainly remain as furniture.
Its coloring is slanting.
A certain charity gave details as to why measles, on the whole, is certainly
 reversible.
Their principles suggested that they would soon complain.
That ponderous section of sparrows had at first no down.
Currents exercise those creatures that count on more darkness.
This time no politeness suddenly singles out remaining corners.
Nothing but sullen negligence is expressed in this strange piece.

More sickened than lacking, those very fifty were very reversible.
Nothing white is regular weather, and cooking makes the same zone what it
is.
Hanging or petting, which encircling voice remains the same?

Spreading, they were lifting, not lifting truth's double center.
Naturally, contradiction makes a diversion hold a fact.
Was that or is that another entrance to much more pleasure?
Their reception was a little exercise in excitement, but much lower.
The smaller symbol's an example of a different question—I mean, color.
Those horses' green eyes are examples of necessarily similar silences.
It's established that the package in question's an insistence on obligingness.

That yellow inn there is not burning—the burning is borrowing its yellow.
Negligence supposes that not a single cloud will change.
Moons exercise together, not counting on anything more violent than
weather.
Even their slippers had a place in that spectacle.

The surprise drowning in that section is a likeness of a widely beginning
lightness.
Being burnt and a shadow meant much to the door.
Expecting all to be kneeling there replaced the decisions she'd left behind.

Ordinary growth is separation—and separation breeds discrimination.

That added suggestion's astonishing, but its earnings are smaller.
Hanging Water's miserable regulation is what they're mentioning while
they're gliding.
Their connections are painstaking, certainly, but curtained from distaste.

Defiance-alleviation's wholesale curtains are certainly made of straw.
This shows that little causes are always tied to the strings they're hearing.
That whole little section is shallow.
Any order is negligence.

Some consider the wooden pens there sickening.
They were purchased through exchanges.
The more narrow it is, the more it comes.
No, not that curving window over there!
Flowers exercise, it seems.
Surely all in Willow Place do.
Hanging's a strict vacation.

Fourteen strophes comprising verse-line sentences corresponding to the linked ascending, descending, and ascending Lucas-number sequence 1, 3, 4, 7, 11, 18, 11, 7, 4, 3, 1, 3, 4, 7. They were made by sending "ROOMS," the third and final section of Stein's *TB*, through DIASTEX5, using as seed par. 89 of "ROOMS." I modified the program's output by revising it to form normative sentences. I respected the letter of the output, but sometimes I altered the word order, added or deleted words, and/or changed certain word forms by altering their suffixes. The edition of *TB*, whose 2nd section is this poem's source, was its first edition, that published under Donald Evans's imprint Claire Marie (New York, May 1914), later published online in 1995 in the Bartleby Archive and in 1999 in the New Bartleby Library, both edited by Steven H. van Leeuwen, with editorial contributions from Gordon Dahlquist.

New York: 29 June–17 August 1999

Mercy Entirely Astonishing

(Stein 94)

Mercy, giving color, hardening interest, changes mustard dangerously.

Use an empty umbrella.
Desperately, the handy extra particles are practically complaining that facts are stubborn.
A purse is a purse and nothing is nothing.

A cloth cup is hurting.
Shaving replaced a cutlet.
Manly counting pieces together a likeness to wound and glide away from!
Eat and whole volumes change.

Stitches and cow jam plus Pop's table did enough.
Expression, not the nearest pillar or a little hope, meadowed that house.
A carafe and a blind glass feather and extremely exaggerating glasses are not everything.
Spread the wagon sack!
I say that eight colors, shades of brown, will soon befit cigarettes on excessive enough occasions.
August extracted from a bottle a slender message made occasional, I suppose, by that umbrella.
What?—would so little make an entire occasion altogether astonishing?

A malachite climbing pencil, spreading roundness, established attractive colors.
The established colors were not closed to an increase of color.
Quite many even permitted elegant distinctions.
In so clever a place, even careless speed is graced by very regular green pieces.
A tumbler budded no more readiness or likeness than an umbrella.
The whole thing's blessings really meant no more than yellow nothing.

Neither gracious glasses nor ladies' colds make for custardy news.
A green object treading a wrist at a leading hour does little but graciously
rest.
Next best is a little pencil.
Gratitude's interest lies in preparation and restitution.
Her resignation's silver lilies needed lightly pounded paper particles.

Suddenly use an umbrella or wear a ribbon in your hair.
An umbrella may articulate a crystal.
This place's arrangement could consist in having narrow curves.
We've not come to cut the satin perfectly.
Whose colds are news?
We called anything with little soles truly leadish.
That elephant, a thing to search for on occasion, was handsome enough
and wholly charming.
You're worse than an oyster!
You're exaggerating everything extremely.
Let's not spread something that might cause a loud clash.
Which small red thing's the cause of enough excess?
It's not even extreme!
Which eight were taken out?
There the color brown may fit the occasion sooner.
Say, are there any cigarettes in that bottle?
Suppose we extract their messages in August?
They've made an altogether too slender umbrella for the occasion, Al.
What climb on malachite could make that little pencil so entirely
astonishing?

Source: All of "OBJECTS," the first section of *TB*, by Stein. I've modified my copy of the online edition by incorporating corrections to it made in ink by Stein in Donald Sutherland's copy of the Claire Marie edition, owned by the University of Colorado Special Collections. Ulla E. Dydo found these corrections and recently sent me copies of them.

Seed: "Mildred's Umbrella," the eighth poem in "OBJECTS."

Method: Running all of "OBJECTS" through DIASTEX5, using as seed "Mildred's Umbrella" and then revising the program's output by changes of word order, suffixes, pronouns, and structure words, but keeping its lexical words' root morphemes in positions close to those they occupy in the raw output.

New York: 17–18 August 1999

Act Out out of Monotony

(Stein 95)

Act out border dressing.

This tender change is lighter.
The very center of morning is so very much smaller that one stamp on a
 single bed is suddenly a green thing in the middle of attention.
Though the auction's lying conundrum is pleasing to some and has
 certainly penetrated everybody, questions are often asked.

Cadences there would add little to the melody, so another and still another
 don't want any there.
This mourning means building up quite a quarrelsome creature.
That question there in the center is hardly ever copied.
Once, their measured corners were gathered together—after a needed rest.

What if that incredible lover in the center were reversible?
In the beginning, good-sized eyeglasses are essential because of the dimness
 of speech.
Moving about again makes some commencing more.
The pallor of the white conundrum makes it so arrangeable!
Certainly they're releasing that targeted window because of the beefsteak
 and cake.
The last squares of evasion mentioned were incalculable.
We currently question why climate measurements are gathered.

Making more time for rest is borrowing nonsense to color your cautious
 location.
Monotony's made change ordinary.
The littler the leather's exercised, the more it confuses the mentioned.
All we ask for's a state of living silence.
Why ask?
It's very little likely that that-there usage'll make any more disturbance than
 this does.

There, even, he signed, is an example of a necessary bather.
Is releasing the evening lessening its distance?
They've been passed over in this sign-selection to curtain the principle of cheerfulness and translate it to Authority as more, even to tears, but not too much more something than that.
They place that cat in the center when it's being overbearing.
Breathe in that magnificent asparagus and give it some dressing.

Your organization of stationary accumulation notwithstanding, your sudden interruption of distribution is turning some beings green again.
The things in the middle are very seductive sitting very empty and very mean.
They are whole little bottles.
This folding oneself into being another is, in color at least, a little incalculable.
The creature in question was counting question after question.
One was, "Why doubt the sound of a single monster?"
This stubble of chance sounds in a single chamber.
That's the white measles!
This change narrows the lap between venturesome fingernails and their mistakes.
Their resemblance is weighty, given their sweet centers.
The Chinese established it as reversible—an incredible suggestion to establish!
Each different size was beginning again to be moving about in there.
That makes us commence once more that pale, nearly white, conundrum that makes us so arrangeable.
Did he release a certain window from being a target because the last squares of beefsteak and cake were behind it?
Your evasion was mentioned as incalculable.
The currents raised this question: "Why isn't the climate there being measured?"
I gathered they were taking time for rests.
No more borrowing nonsense from colorful locations through caution and out of monotony!

Six strophes made by running "ROOMS," part 3 of Stein's *TB*, through DIASTEX5, using as seed the 66th paragraph of "ROOMS," beginning, "A bridge a very small bridge in a location and thunder," which I selected with the help of random-digit-doublet chance operations. I revised the program's output into normative sentences (each one a verse line) by changes in word order and changes or additions of suffixes, pronouns, structure words, etc., but kept its lexical words' root morphemes in positions close to those they occupied in the raw output. As I revised them, I grouped them into the six strophes, whose numbers of sentences/verse lines correspond to the Lucas-number sequence.

New York: 19–21 August 1999

Act a Reversible Escape

(Stein 96)

Act from your center: eat.

Explaining expecting is a cover for diversion.
Replacing the floor makes a change.
It is no more and never was a little hole.

Authorized speech is changing nothing.
To whomever that letter comes, a commensurate hanging will also come.
No apple has ever come there.
Color has uses.

Is *not moving* the same as being under cover?
There the single bell of resistance will separate indecision from hesitation.
What does ordinary sugar stand for?
Separation.
Are there corners in that?
Once, the light had shown on the water in that single central chamber.
Checking a very narrow purchase captured this stranger.

Is being settled and plain reversible?
Indeed it is.
Now fifty rights have given no sweet choice.
Was change reversible?
Explaining and expecting are not yet the same thing.
The air has no center.
When a Chinese diversion covered this wooden floor with leather, it
    discharged all that birthday excitement.
Does this go there?
There a piece is always admitted.
Is there always a disposition to be penetrated?
Not at some temperatures.

Some have always been penetrated.
What is the difference between desertion and breath on a looking glass?
That is certainly cautious stubble.
That whitening changes the design.
Is emigration reversible escape?
A little stubble established an interruption.
For some dispositions at certain temperatures, gamboling will be necessary.
A reduction of current between those plates penetrated her painstaking
preparation for more alleviation.
What burning statement outlined that harmony?
There in the corners is some strange writing from a time of sullen
negligence.
Shouldn't the location of those plates be exemplary?
He has been relating his speech to every spoon.
Will the motion of the four taller chairs make for discrimination or, indeed,
stupefication?
I doubt that.
This is there all the time.
Supposing one has a certain disposition toward resignation, why should she
be pale?
Is resignation a color diminisher?
Why is there no roof?

Is there a stable resemblance between use and means?
That is not what I mean.
Lengthening last evening was not an evasion of the equator's separation.
Quarreling is disturbing the center.
Why that sound of obligingness?
Certainly obligingness is an excellent coloring for a cautious little escape,
but is it reversible?
Is stubble stubble?
Where did she establish that outrageous interruption?
Mentioning the temperature of that sample of the mixture was necessarily a
distracter there.
My disposition resembles that stairway.
The ingredients of this preparation will have more use in the morning than
they did the time before.

And as ends, they're not related to any established trouble.
Supposing there is some more silence, does that establish something?
All this fast playing would not establish a lighter time when cloud cover
came.
The description of a piece comes from its sides.
This shame table no longer feeds our arrangement.
Withstanding the establishment is more than Intending and not like
resignation.
Monday means silver if not used for a four-day birthday.
It frequently used to indicate an even smaller likeness.
Everything is plentiful and curly in the daylight.
We're quarreling over an expression!
Education is an exercise in change.
Isn't it singular that music gathered the ancients together?
Whitening a cake certainly changes its design.
There is no anxious charity in my statement.
It is more of an experience not to have more color.
A case may capture a lap if there is not any clinching now and no more
extension.
Invitations make the chair of authority secure.
Asparagus is a choice ingredient in declarations and summer hats.

If it is the same, it has not yet changed.
The border is wider in the center.
Establishing a cover, the author in the center of the smaller table comes to
that rubbing piece with a suggestion thought simpler than
exaltation.
I suggest that the conclusion of separation is separation.
Changing a use is charming.
There is surely more substance in four.
Why is a feat that much smaller asymmetrical?
A construction that is not always necessary is no cover.
Always establishing her disposition and always changing, she supposes some
lives to be freer than hers.
A paler connection made them separate.
Attention has no color.

Is that bather choking?
Why is everybody there given one evening paper?
Anything righteous is likely to be there.
All wholesale curtains are white, and yet seeing the equator is always
downright incalculable.
Empty dishes shade a monster.
Once slanting time is clinching someone's suffering fingernails, is there
anything that shows the weather there?
Even the church and righteous slippers aren't enough.

Isn't one Asian occasion trouble?
Does anything establish silences?
Something does.
Withstanding drowning with resolution is a preparation for temporary
singing.
The Chinese establish acquaintance with astonishing resignation.
Resignation there comes packaged in a funnel.
Establishing that the weather is not wetting is like not mentioning that
evening is lessening.
Establishing a store there would line up everybody's tables.
This shows that mourning is not altogether a disgrace.
Looking with one's ears has often marked the current climate there.
Does all the powder there establish anyone's rights?

Translate every detail there.
Translate all the mistakes?
The whole thing, even the willow slippers.
Are Chinese acquaintances always resigned?
Astonishingly, a line establishes a nation.
Resignation only arises on the way there.
The whole stubbly cape is there.

There, attention is certainly dimmer.
This does not mean that the sound of obligingness is not the same there.
Is it the case that there' s no roof there?
Use means lengthening there.

Last evening at the equator, separation excellently evaded quarreling.
Is such changing a little disturbing?
Why is the center so cautiously obliging?

Coloring stubble's a reversible escape.

Thirteen strophes made by running "ROOMS," the 3rd section of Stein's *TB*, through DIASTEX5, using as seed the 33rd paragraph of "ROOMS," beginning, "A cape is a cover," which I selected by random-digit chance operations. I "mined" the program's output for words that I composed into normative sentences (each one a verse line) by changes and/or additions of suffixes, pronouns, structure words, and forms of "to be." When possible, I kept lexical words' root morphemes in positions near those they occupied in the raw output. Finally, I divided the series of verse-line sentences into 13 strophes that successively comprise numbers of sentences corresponding to the ascending and descending Lucas-number sequence 1, 3, 4, 7, 11, 18, 29, 18, 11, 7, 4, 3, 1.

22–27 August, 3 September 1999

Tender There

(Stein 97)

Tender that spectacle of unordered difference!

What has been was, and washing showed delightful table placements on a circle-board.
The whole piece shows connections suggesting disappointing relaxation.
Mildred's cause and a surrounding line have stopped some desperate customs.

Any empty shows are brighter when closed.
An occasional disease selected silver.
More long, elegant settlements are mixing final currents.
That current yellow settlement is monstrous.

A particular length is much.
Any stroke could be coloring decisions.
She spotted a star in a tardy country.
There's nothing perfectly arranged.
Satin delays difference by making women's tickets strange.
Suppose a kind of king steps out there in a shawl and rings.
A single chicken does not a salad make.

There, birthday butter's thick, and lengthy specialties are ripe inside the smaller *middle* sections.
Revered Authority resumed its suction and clatter there.
The baking section's mathematics can shape something.
This subject makes these cherries change.
That two shows were mixed was due to the astonishing music.
That exterior intender retains her singularly delicious stomacher.
Between shows, that whole mixture is likely to be lightly amended.
When shutters and glasses are widened, this makes for awfulness.
Cuddling makes for outstanding and widening exchanges.

That small opening there is *trying* to the best *teeth*!
Just his *nose* was climbing.

Necessarily, a shawl that showed her stomach was procured.
Why were empty spools bestowed on us during dinner?
That one's single excellence is clothes.
More than size is handled on that meadow.
That dirty little bore did his hoary best to become their principal receptacle.
They sell *hops* there.
One rosewood chest bore a succession of old specs.
How we chat in the West, on occasion, covers all difficult places and
matters.
These acres are offering similar lingering difficulties.
That that denial is *simple* does not make it *perfect*.
How was the *dressing*?
That color was *placed* there.
Did it ever destroy the color of the hill?
This different disturber is not mentioning more changing.
Between dinner adjustments, it shows astonishing vacancies.
When does it differ?
When they use the original bottle.
Even *that* exchange certainly *does* narrow *choice*.

With that *there*, another curtain is *urgent*.
I used that.
Flowers exercise space.
That one bestowed a little more white *cream* on the cloudy pussy.
Mildred was desperately into different habits and brighter relaxations.
That ingredient is the same one custom suggests.
Withstanding her callous will, they were hardening themselves to their
surroundings.
There can be no color more disappointing than silver.
Occasionally, a disease was neglected in this elegant settlement.
Connecting causes and wavy lines have stopped some monstrous decisions.
Coloring closed a current show.
A particular yellow length was finally selected.

Waiving their strange arrangements, they stroke their perfect satin.
Let nothing delay the Women's Ticket!
The salad specialties there included thick ripe cherries over buttery chicken.
A current Country star was tardy on his own birthday.
Mixed singles can change a whole, deliciously awful, settlement.
Between shows they mended their singular stomachers,
They opened their shutters to deny music.
Cuddling procured them excellent clothes and astonishing suction.
Mathematics can make the best intender likely to bore her retainers.
That king's disturbing nose ring covered his rosy chest.
Small and trying to the vacant Climbers, the little Authority clattered on
through dinner.
Suppose that baking shaped this subject's widened exterior: why linger on
that astonishing show: that creamy, colorful stomach?
The length of a small section of that middle shows the urgent necessity of
adjustment.
There a single dirty spool makes utter simplicity something revered by
chatterers.
A succession of hoary principals bore that widened receptacle.
This exterior section is singularly difficult to destroy.
Was she dressing only in her shawl and *stomacher*?

They exchange their glasses far too lightly.

Her pussy was certainly different.
Withstanding the clouds may make these flowers whiter.
That's a hill of a different *color*!

Exercise is more a habit than a choice.
This acre offers different ingredients to add to that spacey mixture.
Mentioning changing dinner places does not matter.
That's no place for more *skin*!

Handle me!
Use one of the original bottles.
She resumed her shawl on the spot.

His skin is difficult but perfect.
That little curtain shows another meadow.
We were bestowing, on every occasion, similar sizes on all.
Sell the specs for the whole *insides* of that-*there*!

When did you make that outstanding *mixture*?
How much of it will make our steps more narrow?
Have they used it *long*?
Just then, that old Westerner hopped *to* it!

Twelve strophes made by sending all of Stein's *TB* through DIASTEX5, using as seed the 29th paragraph of "ROOMS," section 3 of *TB*, which begins "There was a whole collection made." I selected the paragraph by random-digit chance operations using *AMRD*. I "mined" the program's output for words that I included in 92 sentences (each one a verse line) by changes and/or additions of suffixes, pronouns, structure words, forms of "to be," etc. Initially, in making these sentences, I often placed lexical words' root morphemes near others that were near them in the raw output, but I was able to do this less and less in the course of writing the poem. Finally, I divided the series of 92 verse-line sentences into 12 strophes that successively include numbers of sentences corresponding to the Lucas-number sequences 1, 3, 4, 7, 11, 18, 29 and 1, 3, 4, 7, 4.

[Precedent for the endnotes: La Vita Nuova ☺*]*

New York: 31 August–1 September 1999

This Medicine Has the Roundness of the Altogether

(Stein 98)

This medicine has the roundness of a circle.

What if there is some blue?
The same stripes question the rudimentary settling that one is to shatter.
One cunning custom causes cotton.

The method of courage is this.
Which feeling is as attractive as silver?
If it is necessary to replace what was made to be used in a large wedding,
this is established to be an occasion for trembling, which is freely
shown by marks and much more.
This evening is inclining to be more filling than necessary.

That extract is needed.
What particular button is staring?
Has this shiny binding ever been exchanged for rubbing?
Even the UMBRELLA is there!
Besides, it used to be yellow.
Shaving at midnight is leading to the element that purrs when rubbed.
The purr does not even mean what it does.

The flower is nearly PEELED.
Feeling is leading precisely inside the hull and entirely mistaken.
MUTTON and ASPARAGUS are IN!
IS *feeling* in?
Is resignation a feeling?
Why does the certainly darkening station remain assiduous?
There's certainly feeling between their feathers.
One evening remains for rubbing the ancient four.
Some feel everything!
He'll be collecting gracious things the morning they're eloping.
What A surprise!—any feeling may touch us Within!

Cloudiness turns feeling into stumbling.
Chinking is practiced sooner and four times more.
There they cherish a melting ceiling.
This section is learning rinsing salmon.
In what respect is that melon altogether choice?
There is an outline but not necessarily an explanation.
That's an outstanding recognition.
Lean preparation for need can swell in an instant.
Hanging tastes where green hurry leaves, this receptacle is peculiar.
They're preparing a draft of the garden's description with razors.
An astonishing succession of sudden resignations is filtering out resistance.
Is their whole bell section becoming dimmer?
That resignation is necessary.
Lengthening and wetting that special conundrum paper makes a merciful
difference.
There!—they're there!
There's not enough insistence on obligingness.
She's making a color monster by accumulating ordinary gifts.
We're gathering little CUSHIONS, but only one dangerous flower.

A prepared question is altogether a mistake.
If the lining is perfect, I see there—sincerely see a clash there.
It's a mercy some doublings are breaking!
The signs of the stone plan are constantly mixed up by the ordinarily
educated.
Is the stone plan a plan for the blessings of candy-hole revision?
SHOES in a steady stream of ale are strange.
All CREAM and ORANGE standards and streamers and all, they sat there
on that changing, surrounded surface in white outrage.
The occasion is certainly distressing.
She was claiming ham makes a lovely, excellent butter for the weak.
Please send us large, clean silver.
Save the aged and the ancient!
I'm collecting this for yesterdays' sentence.
This eye has the Calmness of a really composed fellow.
Hope makes us respect drawers.

He is as silent as my best stick, never having any protection
against mounting excitement other than intentional disappearance.
Arrangement discrimination is a pre-occupation of the whole
administration.
Having a single placard burning there is not practical.
Should the little turtle make a little difference?
Certainly.
Checking that white measles there can make checking all else more careless.
At the center of the Great Distractor, her ex has more cake than feeling.
He suggests that his lap is cold in the steady draft from the window.
She is active among the cases of bread, the active cases of bread, and this
pleases her.
Please make that the same as the elephant, but with more stripes.
That's the rudimentary question, whose rudimentary settling must be one
that'll shatter custom.
They say that cotton causes cunning, and The METHOD gives courage,
which is a feeling more attractive than silver.
Is it necessary to replace all that was made for use at that large wedding?
She was trembling on that occasion.
Freely mark whatever is shown you this evening if you are so inclined.

This extract is more filling than necessarily needed.
The particular button you've been staring at has already been exchanged for
a rubbing of it.
Does their binding ever *shine*!
The yellow UMBRELLA is there to use.
There's a mean element in shaving.
What else?
Do the cases of bread please all of them?
The end of that is active sin.
At midnight a purr will be leading you to one that would be rubbed,
Is that feeling even more precise than the feeling I'm feeling *within*?
Within is a flower that has nearly been PEELED from the hull.
Could it be the MUTTON, or would it be the ASPARAGUS, that is
causing in me this feeling of resignation?
You're entirely mistaken!

Feeling is IN.
Her feathers were certainly darkening in the station, but now in the evening
they seem gracious.
Why is this station, which certainly remains between the ancient four,
collecting everything?
Feel the morning eloping—what a touching surprise!
Any more Cloudiness and I'll be stumbling!

Rubbing is all.
He says he'd sooner turn a Chink in.
She says she's practicing something she's learning.
It's in four sections.
While the whole ceiling is melting, he goes on rinsing his cherished salmon!
Why is the station *there*?
A need, a green need, a lean green need.
There is no explanation of why her garden swells.
At this instant, she's preparing to respect that necessary melon.
Her garden is outstanding in its recognition of feeling.
Hanging tastes where green hurry leaves, that receptacle is peculiar to the
monster.

He's successfully preparing a razorlike draught!
Your descriptions of my choices are astonishing.
The leaves filter out my resignation.
They become necessary to each other with the special suddenness of
wetting.
She's resigned to his dimmer tastes.
The bell's obliging resistance is leading to a lengthening difference.
The conundrum in that-there section of the paper is making color
accumulate.

Your insistence on gathering our resignations is enough for me!
Their green garden tastes of Hanging.
It hurries to its wetting.
Is there a difference between wetting and differing?

Certainly there's a difference!
Where?
Where the razor is green.

The gardener will outline his resignation in the altogether.

Thirteen strophes made by sending all of Stein's *TB* through DIASTEX5, using as seed the first paragraph of "FOOD," the 2nd section of *TB*, which begins "In the inside there is sleeping." I selected the paragraph by random-digit chance operations using *AMRD*. I "mined" the program's output for words which I included in 117 sentences (each one a verse line) by changes and/or additions of suffixes, pronouns, structure words, forms of "to be," etc. Initially, in making these sentences, I often placed lexical words' root morphemes near others that were near them in the raw output, but I was able to do this less and less in the course of writing the poem. Finally, I divided the 117 verse-line sentences into 13 strophes that successively comprise numbers of sentences corresponding to the ascending and descending Lucas-number sequence 1, 3, 4, 7, 11, 18, 29, 18, 11, 7, 4, 3, 1.

[Precedent for the endnote: La Vita Nuova ☺*]*

New York: 2–7 September 1999

Those Handsome, Heady Consequences

(Stein 99)

Those handsome buttons will hurt the arrangement.
They that choose to show there will *be* there.

Will they prepare a little mustard on a black and white cushion?
We'll not analyze the silken heaviness of morning even so.
Nothing, not a single gate, hardly a resource, will enable the clever,
sick in their sacks.

Their considerable trembling in custody will betray much more.
It'll not bend or take a special binding when it shines.
That'll be the last place to use it!
Almost nothing will be more difficult.
Malachi will recognize his resignation's necessary.

The clatter of this harmony will take her uneven courage away.
Our principal will recognize their crust and exaggerate the
feathers and everything!
Besides, terror will disturb all perfect shapes.
What will increase the splinters' liberty in that furnace?
The kindness of this change will be able to change what's in that
place.
Their temptation will burst their bones.
Those circumstances will be outstanding.

The louder the mutton the cheaper its salve will be.
Breakfast will change her practices.
Why are you going to drink that outrageously colored coffee?
Their heating rack will solemnize her leisure.
Those inclined to original talking will someway declare for soaking.
The best and tightest plan will be to bid privately and heavily.

Tuesday's blisters will tune the birds.
If the piece can't be sudden, it'll be rushing.
That chain there will be basted onto it.
You'll be prepared for showing the coconut if you'll just prepare for
its height.
True preparation will have a bigger effect than fast changes.

All this that was formerly a mistake will depart with the birthday
mixture.
Change that uses memory will perfect your glass head.
The reason is hair'll be frequently there.
Certainly a man less sullen will be used.
Which height?
We'll prepare for one who made it there in the beginning.
Their descendents will consume the green plain.
They will be changed by what they change.
The checked-out soldier will settle down, for not coming will mean cooking.
Mentioning hanging,—pecking will go the same way.
You will decide by the nickel hour.
Some'll be searching for convincing gratitude.
Handily tasseled, he'll be boxing in corners at large, shady
weddings.

Wouldn't it be his custom to say it sooner?
Why will there be sparks from that wet plate?
It's not losing just *any* little string!
The consequence of resignation won't be either recognition or
distinction.
That crusty principal is going to be constantly exaggerating.
He'll be giving *everything* away—his feathers . . . even his courage!
She'll be selecting liberty and harmony.
You're going to be splintering the furnace with that clatter!
Changing places will be a kindness.
Changing his shape will just increase his terror.
Besides, I'd be disturbed by a more nearly perfect shape than this.
She'll be tempted to change to a louder, cheaper breakfast.

Outstanding circumstances are going to burst your bones!
You'll drink your coffee or else!
Why would this solemnly colored mutton be declared outrageous?
If you're so inclined, would you please talk in some original way?
Won't he be soaking and heavily salving his blistered privates Tuesday?

The best plan would be to bid the birds to suddenly rush away.
Could it be that that tight tune is the very piece?
She'll show you the height of the coconut by using that green chain.
Basting it'll just be a preparation for the *bigger* preparation.
The truest preparation will be a fast one.
Any change in the preparation of the mixture will use our birthday memories.
Will this be a mistake?
He'll certainly begin to be less sullen when he decides.
Formerly departing, she will now change in front of a perfect glass.
The reason the head'll be there will frequently be to hold the hair.
The height of the soldier will change as he consumes those greens.
These men will descend to the plain when the birds stop pecking each other.
I'll have to check some blisters!
On Tuesday they're going to be rushing the piece so that you'll hardly be able to make out the tune.
That man mentioned hanging the same way.
Will that one be there Tuesday?
Will someone try to make her cook?
The Reasonable Soldier won't settle for less than Plain Meaning.
Won't someone be exaggerating String Theory's heady consequences?

Eight strophes made by sending all of Stein's *TB* through DIASTEX5, using as seed the 202nd paragraph of the book (exclusive of titles, etc.), which begins, "Burden the cracked wet soaking sack heavily." I selected the paragraph by random-digit chance operations using

AMRD. I "mined" the program's output for words which I included in 77 sentences (each one a verse line) by changes and/or additions of suffixes, pronouns, structure words, forms of "to be," etc. Initially, in making these sentences, I placed lexical words' root morphemes near others that were near them in the raw output, but I was able to do this less and less in the course of writing the poem. The left, center, and right alignments of the typographical lines were decided by chance operations involving a die. While composing the 77 verse-line sentences, I divided them into eight strophes that successively comprise numbers of sentences corresponding to the prime-number sequence 2, 3, 5, 7, 11, 13, 17, 19.

[Precedent for the endnote: La Vita Nuova ☺*]*

New York: 12–19 September 1999

A Feather Table
Likeness of the Justice Chair

(Stein 100)

A feather table: reckless gratitude.
It is that-there that means best.

White the green grinding trimming thing!
The disgrace, like stripes.
More selection, slighter intention.

Rosewood stationing is use-journey: curious dusty empty length.
Winged cake: the cake plan that neglects to make color certain.
Time long could winter: elegant consequences monstrous.
So many guiding holders:—garments,—arrangements.
Staring then, when sudden same time is necessary, that circular same's *more*
 necessary, not actually aching.

And why special?
No straw left, the chain is missing—was winningly white and occasioned
 entirely strings.
Reason is sullenness: practices left when six into nothing narrow, resolute,
 suggested all beside that plain seam.
Pencils, mutton, asparagus: the table there.
Reddening is not to change *that* in such absurd surroundings.
Considered clearly, the large and second heat of a feather is there.
That smelly thing whistles denial, difference, surfeit-dated choices—
 everything trembling imitation.

Imitation?—imitation is a joy gurgle.
Best bent, likely disappointed.
Cake season isn't any more than most.

No cake can make a larder likely.
Not a single protection is standing—even temporarily.
Sugar and lard are suddenly shaming.
That single set comes orderly.
There the remarkable witness made no more settlement than blessing.
Increase the way steak colored coffee.
Wheatly that music half-noisy.
Reason's decline is not a little grainy.

This can mean taste where toe-washing is reasonable.
Salmon carriage?—action hanging.
Scenic bits and a nervous draught don't satisfy elevation.
There is no change.
Much was temporary behind that center—much was formerly charming.
Then the then-triumphant showed their disagreeable hidden worries.
The chair asked that the speech be repeated, supposing
attention-resemblance.
It is just summer.
Another section has a light likeness to pedestrianism.
Which is the light?
That used this there.
The chair's justice: nothing-colored mercy.
No, perhaps some is likely.

That is not a genuine bargain.
There, preparation so suits White bands' singing, and redness, that the
same sights have a simpler splendor.
No, not the same.
Wishing the same is not the same as a different arrangement.
Any measure washed is brighter than occasional string sets.
A precocious nothing discolors that extract sooner than showing it starting.
A bag place chain room winningly reasons with shining hair.
What with supposing without protection, no wound is sudden.
Coloring sullenness rushes bottom reason in gilded country.
What if it shows?
Necessarily, the whole thing there is shining.

Is that anything?
More single women are stitching tickets.
To show difference, exude reliability.
Inside that larger silver likeness, Hope tables thick coal.
Coal makes morning furnaces darker.
Joy and success are exceptions.

Four suggest a sadder surrender.
Pretense and cheaper influences are staining tender Pride there.
Sort out that little sink.
Why is the size of the baking remainder something more resembling light
than cutting?
This cheese is more calm than anything solitary.
It is still an occasion for bottom anticipation.
Reason's season cracked whatever was ripe.
Nearly all were neglected by blessing, not without nervous actions.
He's readily beginning to seed the cheese and estrange the Whites.
The celery curled its lashes at the slam.
Not-so-heated reason will little be able to satisfy another.
This was formerly used as a charming chair.
Pedestrianism showed itself triumphant and disagreeable.
Whatever was hidden worried them.
They asked that her speech be repeated.
Summer light is a likeness of justice.
Then the light is supposing attention.
That section has a resemblance to light.
Is it a likeness of the justice chair?

Eight strophes made by sending all of Stein's *TB* through DIASTEX5, using as seed the 53rd paragraph of the book (exclusive of titles, etc.), which begins, "A fact is that when any direction is just like that." I selected the paragraph by random-digit chance operations using *AMRD*. I drew words from the program's output which I included in 77 sentences (several elliptical and each one a verse line) by changes and/or additions of suffixes, pronouns, structure words, forms of "to be," etc., and changes of word order. Initially, in making these sentences, I placed lexical words' root morphemes near others that were near them in the raw output—in fact I included many phrases, and even whole verse lines, of unedited, though punctuated, output, mostly in early strophes—but I was able to do this less and less in the course of writing the poem. I divided the 77 verse lines into eight strophes whose numbers of sentences are successively the prime numbers 2, 3, 5, 7, 11, 13, 17, and 19.

New York: 20 September 1999; 14–16 May 2000

Tender Workers Gather There

(Stein 101)

Tender that blind glass!
This nickel covers differences.

Their callous hardening was a reckless change.
He wears a little yellow custom-tailored suit.
In one illustration enough of everything is standing there.

Even they were extra loud on that occasion.
They supposed it wise to show severe restraint.
Setting everything together in one place, they stubbornly complained.
It spread from the center in every direction.
Strangely but gracefully, it accentuates the coke spoons in the custard.

No exchange is necessary.
Nothing showed how lean or certain or sudden or settled they were.
That educated languor spread to their stomachs.
Stamp a tight life letter cutting a tender center.
No particular necessity!
A rhubarb mountain is no sweet reason for a working cat or a winning cake.
Open your stomachs more for the next twenty-four.

Oranges at the bottom and real rose butter!
The little that shows is all brown as it was on that evil occasion of purring succession.
That sugary shadow stream is rising in monstrous martial dreariness.
Bargaining gathers no garlands.
Melting water is more real than certain, and a likeness shows estrangement.
That awkward principal combs acres of potatoes for a wheel.
Her mounting grandeur cloaks a strange relaxing.
They pay with such a Bay tic!

Any mounted monster may certainly spread cheerfulness.
It is difficult to measure a steady whiteness.
That evil wheeler-dealer has no established occupation.
His little students show incalculable differences.

Monday shows the substance on the chair was once a snail.
None of their suggestions are openly lifelike.
Please venture to center!
Does this youth ask the Chair to consider her breast?
That is certainly settled.
Catholic weather means bread sections drowning.
The purring cats are comparing their rations.
This is very awkward.
No sound is certainly little, but many are callously loud.
The hardening youth is likely to rise from his chair and reason away in a spoony speech.
Anything is likely to settle as a symbol on a stamp.
This is, as likely as not, about to be drearily martial.
Most little illustrations make very little difference.
A stubborn likeness shows a winning necessity more than severe complaining.

Bargaining certainly suits a little yellow garland less than custard.
Languid rhubarb may be brown.
Which news?
Gather ye everything while ye may: old cake is certainly changing.
Incalculable sounds are spreading through the sodden mountains, recklessly changing the awkward customs.
One standing Grace is strange enough.
She who on the weather leans combs potatoes seeming means.
Round a way returning late, set a stream to educate.
Drown the bread in wise restraint—often things are as they ain't.
Shadowy bays estrange the Youth.
The evening is altogether no extra occasion.
This cutting shows a tender center.
Speech seems stranger.

Her central occupation is returning, difficult as it is.
A measure of settled cheerfulness is certainly timely
Please—you *must relax*!
That particular youth is so strange that he exchanges letters with certain sodden symbols.

This flowered chair estranges certain students.
Mounting the little hill she stamps on snails.
Supposing restraint is necessary, you still don't melt in water.
Sweet water is so necessary—standing in it ain't enough.
Place that sugar in the center.
That little stamp shows awkward differences on covers.
When she is working, her breasts are slowly and surely rising.
No occasion is too newsy.
The principal's acres are grander than any suggestion.
Monday shows that any substances may be compared—for a little consideration.
There's more to speech than being loud.
The Catholic Chair is venturing toward the center.
If anyone comes, they're certain to come in a cloak.
The Youth Section spreads on the hill and steadily mounts without accentuating breasts.
Certainty takes time.
It is very slow.
Beware the ticks beside the bay!
White snails are widely established on that mountain.
Wise workers gather there.

Eight strophes made by sending all of Stein's *TB* through DIASTEX5, using as seed the 50th paragraph of the book (exclusive of titles, etc.), which begins, "This is no dark custom." I selected the paragraph by random-digit chance operations using *AMRD*. I "mined" the program's output for words which I included in 77 sentences (each one a verse line) by changes and/or additions of suffixes, pronouns, structure words, forms of "to be," etc., and by changes of word order. Initially, in making these sentences, I placed lexical words' root morphemes near others that were near them in the raw output—in fact, I included many phrases, and even whole verse lines, of unedited, though punctuated, output, mostly in early strophes. However, I was able to do this less and less in the course of writing the poem. Then, while composing the series of verse-line sentences, I divided it into eight strophes that successively comprise numbers of sentences corresponding to the prime-number sequence. [Ed. Note: In March 2002, Mac Low made substantive revisions to this poem, thereby adding additional sentences to strophes five and six in contradiction to his procedural rules. Those changes result in 79 sentences in total.]

New York: 21–27 September, 4 October 1999; 12–14 March 2002

Spectacle Discolored

(Stein 102)

Spectacle with a will—clean, round, delightful, gratitudinarian.
The Reasonable means Calamity—grinding, trimming.

A red and an order—neither rudimentary—indicate a wealthy occasion.
An artichoke surrounded by ham has a strange taste.
What remains is precious and a means toward the best—kindness is it.

Why, narrower pigeon, are you claiming everything?
Please *please*: please carve a case.
Bargaining, estrangement:—nothing increases rest!
Cloudiness, cloudiness cutting opposition, ends an occasion.
Gray anticipations are declaring ice cream inside.

Act there, exercise, tenderly bestowed disappearance-conundrum!
Which is still?
No shows between, because none's folding yet in that building behind
there.
Should a single secret metal-shaded light that is hardly there be an occasion
for clinching?
Stationary means regular slippers—any and all of them wide.
More lilac than that which appeases the light, and with a wrong will, there
is some washing and polishing, more roundness, circles, and
pleasure.
I rate very low any purple that doesn't make the very best shadows.

Is that questioning green point that is dwindling again?
Very heavy: no melody makes a rose.
Let loud mean a black surface.
What is stopping this catalog from indicating choice?
Why, hardly washing the church!
That's quite a resource!

That choice of a way discolors the stone—as shown.
He seems, on this occasion, melodiously serene.
She is freely being guided away.
Supposing the widow is mean?
She's starting to be.

In *front*, not *behind*!
Staring at all that straw is not particularly graceful.
Does reason make choosing count for anything?
Learning housing is astonishing!
The object of revision is stitching.
She is selecting an artichoke!
This choice has a strangely precious taste.
It means we remain surrounded by kindness.
Estrangement is no bargain.
Lilac cloudiness is making gray anticipation disappear.
Such a piece is what would be best.
Ice cream is cutting through their opposition.
Why do they say the narrower pigeons are the best?

Please claim everything.
The case is carved from some secret light metal.
A wrong light's bestowed upon this occasion by that tender conundrum.
There's clearly ham on those dishes.
Clouds are never stationary.
Nothing increases action like resting.
Are they folding it behind?
Resting is pleasing.
This means that her slippers are regular and wide.
There's no show there because they didn't exercise enough.
When clinching, they're hardly stationary.
Does this mean that none should build there?
What they declare together is coming from inside them.
That rose discolors the black surface.
His melodies guided the widows away.
The stationary pigeons are resting together by choice.
Which is the more discolored?

Seven strophes made by sending all of Stein's *TB* through DIASTEX5, using as seed the 336th paragraph of the book, starting with the paragraph's title: "SALAD DRESSING AND AN ARTICHOKE." I selected the seed paragraph by random-digit chance operations using *AMRD*. I "mined" the program's output for words which I included in 58 sentences, each one a verse line, by changes and/or additions of suffixes, pronouns, structure words, forms of "to be," etc., and by changes of word order. Initially, in making these sentences, I placed lexical words' root morphemes near others that were near them in the raw output. In fact, I included many phrases, and even whole verse lines, of unedited, though punctuated, output, mostly in the earlier strophes—but I was able to do this less and less in the course of writing the poem. While composing the 58 verse-line sentences, I divided them into seven strophes that successively comprise numbers of sentences corresponding to the prime-number sequence.

[Precedent for the endnote: La Vita Nuova ☺*]*

New York: 24–27 September, 3 October 1999; 15–20 January 2000

Who is Showing Us
What Happened in This Corner?

(Stein 103)

Who is showing us this unordered spectacle?
They are recklessly making exchanges.

Not likely in the closet, she connects singing with a message.
He does not like to show himself singing in the closet there.
Hanging in it sooner, for no side is established there.

Suppose her cloak is spread.
A single cane is attractive.
When a white stamp stops being shown, it becomes increasingly fitting.
Housing and shows preserve their patients.
Pack some lead-colored glasses.

No stone loses the inclination to be shown.
Isn't it the same as any sign at a spectacle?
No spectacle makes a season.
She strokes wood on the spot as a charm.
Between stomachs the lightening lace is reckless and did less.
No dog needs to be wearing lace at the wrist in the summer.
Doesn't the nearest spot show?

Rounds of mutton are standard on steamers.
They do not shine as specialties.
The strange thick spaces outside the ham don't make sound like much like
kindness.
Those older goats should loosen nothing there the second week.
Like not raising blood sooner, gathering garlands increases strings.
The sooner they're tender, the sooner the opposition uses lilacs.
Symbolic stockings are not sweet.

There it's likely the shows are showing stomachers and pocketfuls of coconut.
They cloak a likely roast.
This white outline is not a likely protection because that working knife is standing.
Does this house spread open to show evenly separated handkerchiefs?

Shadows of loose change are paved with showy potatoes.
It's excellent back there.
The whole is not seen.
No reasonable cooking leaves a roast in butter.
The little cross estranged them.
They stick slender spoons in the cool trees.
Hop to it!
Oh see how they sat at the show and remain!
They remained and sat, but speaking was extra.
Oh see the show they showed!
Any stone in a line may be a little trouble with much more darkening than kneeling.
In this corner any cooking left would suggest another question and it happened that nothing smaller in it was so open.
Every clear student made a manikin and showed it, but sunshine never shows the trouble with it.

The tidiness of the package was much of it, not all, and no one sensible lives there with a stove.
Lessening a lengthening nose shows there's nothing to this.
This shows there's nothing that can lessen her lengthening nose.
He smiled at that coat in the store—more so because it was up there.
All the same, checking smiling was satisfactory, what with the sweetness of that whole thing.
Its ending up violet at that time shows that it lacks cooking.
Not enough pease in the summer season makes white buttons in moonlight a noisy choice.
Isn't it strange that a single color is pointing to the spreading of spitting there?

Sugar on a black string doesn't make for sewing but an outward show of it.
This time It is necessary to be sick this time and shown to be losing no
glass.
The lead color of the stone incline shows the house was patiently
preserved.
At the same time isn't the sign for the spectacle a spectacular treat?
The stroke season makes no spot in the wood charming.
Between their stomachs the lightening lace was reckless and did less.
Does the dog who spotted the lace worn at her wrist need to be shown the
nearest mutton?
Around the steamers standards do not shine as specialties.
The strange thick spaces between the ham and the outside of the whole
make all of that sound.
Anyway, the older little goats should have a second week of kindness.

The looseness there is nothing.
If you don't like raising blood, increase the string.
Gather ye garlands sooner.
The sooner they are tender the sooner the opposition uses lilacs.
This shows that stockings aren't sweet symbols there.
Is a pocketful of coconut stomachers likely to cloak a roast?
This white outline is not likely to be a protection.
A worker with a knife is standing there.
Does this spread show the house is even open?
Shadows paved with potatoes are seen to separate handkerchiefs and show
loose change.
There's little excellence back there—not another whole roast.
Cooking leaves in a little butter estranges no one reasonable.
Is it cool to stick a cross in a tree to see the slender spoons hop!
Oh see the show!
What they showed was extra.
Are they remaining to speak?
An extra stone sat.
There was a lot of darkening and kneeling and a not little trouble.
Would another question about cooking help suggest what happened in this
corner?

Eight strophes made by sending all of Stein's *TB* through DIASTEX5, using as seed the sentence-paragraph "A show at tick and loosen loosen it so to speak sat." This comes near the end of "FOOD," the second part of *TB*. I selected the seed paragraph by random-digit chance operations using *AMRD*. I "mined" the output of DIASTEX5 for words which I included in 77 verse-line sentences that I edited by making changes and/or additions of suffixes, pronouns, structure words, forms of "to be," etc., by alterations of word order, and by deletions. Often, but not always, I placed lexical words near others that were near words in the raw output that included their root morpheme. While composing the 77 verse-line sentences, I grouped them into eight strophes that successively comprise numbers of sentences corresponding to the prime-number sequence. [Ed. Note: Stanza seven has 18 lines, in contradiction to Mac Low's procedural rules. That results in 78 sentences in total.]

[Precedent for the endnote: La Vita Nuova. ☺*]*

New York: 5 October 1999–5 January 2000

Tender Mountain Asparagus

(Stein 104/Titles 1)

Tender that spectacle mercy can like behind imaginary strings!
Clean pieces of anything were hanging there, perfectly desperate and
 different.

Those particles may mean this and even being.
Ordinary hat-width customs the shadows preserved might have been
 custodial.
If a frightful bag on a time chain utterly misplaces plenty of places, a single
 broken showing of an orderly courteous likeness will be authorized.

This shining, and more of the same, make revision strangely stringy there.
The small and the stern remain respectable.
Saturday's difference is looseness because that's how we feel it.
Sentenced by authority, this daintiness designed her a little yesterday.
Their terror of largely safe tomatoes is curious.

Four little potatoes were easily established to be a whole breakfast.
Her persuasive tongue was scissoring his central singularity.
Ordinary mountain does are negligent.
The smell of their singular stomachs is likened to asparagus and butter.
The hangman's seconds managed to leave the white lounge.
We tasted reasonable butter widely satisfying ordinary tastes.
The middling excitement of a former time was likely.

A whole untidy piece arose.
What's a single sprightly color on those restlessly scraping springs?
The milk and water from that cake left vacancies in its package.
One is often asked to stretch her surveyance of empty writing.
The glittering buttons of mountain asparagus don't resemble change.
Give a handsome little cushion for a change.

A finer fancy takes more joy in a callous appearance than in some ordinary likable heaviness, a little gray in places.
That single paper cloak is curiously lighter.
This gray was established to measure cake, serenely washed.
The strong umbrella there was ordinarily manifold.
There was nothing difficult about that remarkable addition.

Their steadiness was seen to be a shining thing.
On Sunday the obligation to smell large feathers is simpler.
The pleasing looseness of blood is its greatness.
Are you bargaining away your liberty?
His tender freshness was not a pleasing surprise.
Is an exhibition of baked goods sadder than their hardness?
The imitation of meaning there is a present-day outrage.
They wore especially ingenious stomachers for the occasion.
The breeze between the chickens and the house was altogether singular.
That tender shadow will arise on Tuesday.
All basting of flies is ordinary, never remarkable.
The settlement is nearly solid.
The preparation of potatoes is booming.

If you hang potatoes along with a little celery, they still remain potatoes.
Meat makes the back ridiculous.
All widening of smaller silences used to be mentioned as charming.
We mentioned the comparative suddenness of his eyeglasses' blueness.
The scissors were lying in the rain at the height where one sits.
Lessening that shadowy difference in harmony has plainly come after complaints.
Despite surveyance mistakes take place.
The cream was haughty enough to be safer.
Please surprise me!
Notwithstanding the choice, sacrifice is more likely.
This chair has a strange likeness to that ordinary piece there.
Desperately different particles were hanging perfectly.
This is even being mean.
Her hat had that customary width.

Shadows preserved their custody of the ordinary.
If a frightful bag were misplaced in time, plenty of places might be utterly
broken.
He authorized those shows.

Her orderly likeness was singularly courteous.
This shining makes revision of a string more strange.
There it's more of the same.
His little sentence yesterday was largely due to terror of authority.
It was curious how the safety of those four little tomatoes was so easily
established.
Four curious tomatoes were safe.
On the whole, a breakfast of little potatoes cannot easily be established.
The center of his tongue was singular.
Her scissors persuaded them of this.
To what does that mountain have a likeness?
His ordinary negligence was secondary.
Nothing smelled then but the scrapings.
Her stomach is mountainous.
They managed to get asparagus with butter.
Why did we leave the white lounge?
Butter satisfies ordinary tastes.
In former times excitement was likely to arise from hangings rather than
from tidiness.
One is often asked whether colorful writing springs from restlessness or
from the emptiness of sprightly vacancies.
Under her surveyance milk and water cake was often packaged with
mountain asparagus.

Eight strophes made by sending all of Stein's *TB* through DIASTEX5, using as seed Stein's title *The Making of Americans: Being a History of a Family's Progress*. Stein 104 is the first poem in *Titles*, a subseries of [the Stein poems] whose making employs as seed files the titles of the works appearing in Ulla E. Dydo's *A Stein Reader* (Evanston: Northwestern UP, 1993). I corrected typos and incorporated in my file of *TB* fourteen corrections written in ink in Stein's hand, which Ulla Dydo found in Donald Sutherland's copy of the first edition, in the Special Collections of the University of Colorado, Boulder. The verse-sentences were made from the raw output of DIASTEX5 by drawing words from it as I read through it and revising and rearranging them into sentences. Revisions included changes of tense, number, case, etc., mainly through additions and subtractions of affixes. I added and deleted articles, prepositions, conjunctions, and pronouns, and forms of "to be." That is, I freely composed each sentence around root morphemes more or less near each other in the "raw" diastic output of the program, adding appropriate structure words, etc. While the production of the raw output was a comparatively rapid process, that of the composition and revision of the verse lines lasted nearly three weeks. The first drafts of the lines were grouped while I composed them into strophes successively comprising numbers of lines corresponding to the sequence of prime numbers 2, 3, 5, 7, 11, 13, 17, 19.

New York: 10–30 January 2000; 6 September 2001

Ada

(Stein 105/Titles 2)

A adventure black.

A idle spark any address really address addresses shadows and
  educated than all addition blank and education that
  a eddy chambers a add shall all edible grand and adopt
  placing.

And added chair.

Alike added ready always admitted stars a adjustment place
  and education hearing any administration quaintness
  and adventure black.

Four strophes made by sending all of Stein's *TB* through DIASTEX5, using as seed Stein's title *Ada*. Stein 105 is the second poem in *Titles*, a subseries of [the Stein poems] whose making employs as seed files the successive titles of works appearing in Ulla E. Dydo's *Stein Reader* (Evanston: Northwestern UP, 1993). I deleted the raw output of DIASTEX5 after the point where it began exactly repeating what came before (something the program does at times). Then I broke the remaining output into verse lines by placing a period at the end of each "paragraph" of the output and following it by a strophe break. I kept the typographical line breaks of the output within the two long lines.

New York: 11, 21 January 2000

Tender a Way Comes Thataway

(Stein 106/Titles 3)

Tender a way.
Shows white not.

Comes like kindness then dwindles.
Enough wagon color some made.
Taken that two shown weight.

To summer sure brown.
Then a way shows that is not complaining.
Necessary ordinarily than a way.
Shown was not come.
More making that two.

Too well?
Not famously.
Paper likeness?
The twenty-four were choosing.
Book remark games brown.
This a way room.
Why tolerable remains more clean.

They sweeter.
Cloudiness what roll?
Same more organ transfer.
Two?
Two.
Way to tomato?
Surely kindness to sweet shows.
Which more lamb?
More decent that awfulness.

Thoughtful.
Which to remedy likeness?

Likeness that.
Two.
Too wet to come orderly.
Chain there.
Twenty-four stolen when solid.
Ham cheese onions.
The owl proud.
Wood not memory.
Holey Susan.
Toys.
Sweet ploughing well so same.
Cake beginning there sweet.
Wood white?

No.
Summers have strange tastes.
Owls.
George was to come cake spoons.
Type away!
Choice was some sum.
Liver given to sweet.
Whole way not.
Remains offering.
Begin the sweet lion.
Which?
To similar none.
Arrangement?
The swelling cooking which covered same mice arrangement.
Two spoons when no memory speech.
Silence to two.
To whom not permitted were likeness.

The away slowly with no time resenting.
Piling there.

Two?
Another.
When mourning tumbler indecision's scientific.

The awkward flowered.
Which?
Not time once saving this sweetness.
Whole?
Whole soldier comes thataway.

Ten strophes made by sending all of Stein's *TB* through DIASTEX5, using as seed Stein's title *Two Women*. I deleted the raw output of DIASTEX5 where it began repeating what came before. Then I broke the remaining output into verse lines that begin with capital letters and end with periods or question marks and made a few minimal revisions. Finally, I grouped the lines into ten strophes that comprise numbers of sentences corresponding successively to the prime-number sequences 2, 3, 5, 7, 11, 13, 17, and 2, 3, 5.

New York: 11–15 January, 7 February 2000; 10 March 2002

They Arranged Their Objects in Fitting Order

(Stein 107/Titles 4)

They arranged their objects, took obligatory breaths, and then prepared the
oysters.
And there their delightfulness rated venturing gratitude, piece by piece.

Their reasonable singing was out of order, but not so strangely so.
They are designing a way to line nothing sincerely with elegant cunning.
One extreme catalogue makes a singular difference.

Their circulation is fit to wash and cool the precocious.
There's nothing strange about making free with the disease card.
Many of the elegant cracked when permitted to make ordinary distinctions.
My argument is that a better arrangement than the ordinary one may seem
artificial.
Only making wonder is of use.

The broken saucer was hurting the ribbon.
On that occasion the water was broken.
It was difficult to make even a single piece of the drawing entirely shine.
Nothing, nothing in the arrangement between the broad and trimmed
watermelons, the pennies, and the spices was gracious.
It's crazy to do your shaving leaning out.
Oh the chest of that dog shows its breed is strange!
What was lent them was an obstruction they were not to escape.

That morning they were cooking salmon with precision and slender snipe.
Often evening was overtaking whatever remained of the crust.
Between the order and the rubbing a single earnest darkening remained.
Greatness may please the old but the darker have their dinner on the tracks.
The prisoner's evening mission was principally an outrage.
I hate those strange onions!

In the present circumstances they cherish the dainty lines of the pleasanter salmon.
Nothing is pleasanter than breakfast.
They were gently soaking the chicken not from dreariness but only for ordinary reasons like protection.
There was a dog there in that old canoe.
Nothing was stolen from the pensioner's drawer but space.

Her language was questionably dirty.
The cream was steadily surging out as the butter was being prepared.
Willie remains the winner.
Why were they seeding potatoes among the oranges?
That is unquestionably a dirty case!
She sat with a stick beside the one they called "The Knealer."
That's a very orange coconut!
Lifting some truth from the press—whatever remains in it—is naturally different from cooking dinner.
She was openly relating to that wall with burning pleasure.
He earned a green outline, she an orange one.
The longer they waited the more they separated.
Holding that unmentionable dog required resignation.
We were walking on nothing that spicy evening.

The can that is wetly descending may well contain gallons of vacancy.
Is it established that the hanging did take place and did she see the hanging-place mentioned?
Their hearing is enfolded in their ordinary preoccupations.
Wasn't it strange that the door was mastered by a single placard?
Little escapes that burning looking-glass.
Which section of it is curving?
Isn't it strange that anyone is craving for nothing?
They ordered grain with different care after the hanging spectacle.
That season there no pecking—only drowning in that ocean of wrong.
That incredible spectacle showed the difference between a sinecure and hardening mercy.

Is an exchange of gratitude arrangeable or only one of washing?
Is a detainer of calamity ordinarily so green?
That single earnest piece was strangely disappointing.
Could anything be distincter?
There's no use wishing for anything out of the ordinary.
The one who was cleaning was slender and desperate.
She had handily done the wedding washing in fitting order.

Seven strophes made by sending all of Stein's *TB* through DIASTEX5, using as seed Stein's title "Orta or One Dancing." I made a series of verse-line sentences from the root morphemes of more or less neighboring lexical words in the output of DIASTEX5 by rearranging their order and adding, deleting, or otherwise changing suffixes, conjunctions, prepositions, forms of "to be," pronouns, etc., and otherwise revising the program's output. I deleted the output after the point where it began exactly repeating what came before (something the program does at times). While I composed the sentences, I inserted end marks and grouped the lines into strophes that comprise numbers of sentences corresponding successively to the prime-number sequence.

[Precedent for the endnote: La Vita Nuova. ☺*]*

New York: 20 January, 8, 14–15 February 2000

Mercy Can't Give a Girl Much Pleasure in Things

(Stein 108/Titles 5)

Mercy can't give a girl much of a costume.
She was pleased, nay, delighted to be put on the table.

Supposing some things are resolved by analyzing redness, would that make
ordinary things a little fancier?
More tables are made than are designed.
Illusion places courage where it has to be extreme.

Plainer holes are necessarily different.
More pieces make curious shows.
They cloister more washing than's set out on a string.
Is glass a necessity?
Diseases' many particles are extracted from incidents.

Dressing is necessary, because much is not particular.
Waving shuts out addresses.
Most arrangements do not have in them the necessary patience.
The necessary releases were mismanaged.
Isn't that chain handsome?
The oceans' example made saloons.
Cutlets are ministering to occasional places climate makes.

Malachite is not behind it.
Does grass consist in what it's expected to have been made into?
Ladies' colds make a necessary difference but some suppose they mean little.
Suppose you revise the mutton!
Hat sales are pleasing again.
Suppose your revisions have made many matches waver.

Dining and dressing in suggestive silence makes having a cutting period
mean success.
Why suppose a middling earner is not assiduous?
Thirst makes a difference because harmony is not satin.
Please suggest that melting more sadly together is not a medicine transfer.
Besides, clouds transfer more vagueness than authority.

Successive curly divisions make for more of the same solitude.
What makes the prices of cherries vary is not easily shown, because mixed
lectures make more calm than eating hopes for.
Much of that famous arrangement makes anticipated divisions show
necessity buttered.
A mended cake may not be plain.
It may not minister more to a cat than chaining would.
Here comes the witness whose silence is murder!
Basting doesn't necessarily make solid things untidy.
Procuring means a lapse from pleasing politeness.
Did she recollect that grain might taste better than glass?
Have you been capable of mowing a little lapse with a polite please?
The things that recollection makes!
What are necessary specs for chain-boats
Cucumbers are occasions in more ways than nuts.

Dining below the beefsteak made the waiter's action s letter-perfect.
Chinese dressing meant trouble.
That table is not a satisfying vision.
We suggest you replace it.
No decision was made about the division of the spoons.
More Chinamen were living between refusals.
Suppose we meant to make letters together for manikin shows.
Supposing the example mentioned is the same as a choice between
necessities, the suggester of silence makes a target sitting in
painstaking eclipse, because beefsteak, milk, and water—not sprightly
rooms—would be a more successful package.
Cadences in the visible always show more causes, because they're not
strings.

Necessity furnished him an example he has mastered.
Yet insistence upon dishes almost flowered more than cake or water.
Reversible saving has been arranged for more satisfactory rates.
Dedication means rights.
Mistakes mean habits.
Wet eating shows up a cleansing difference.
Fancy resolved makes redness a little ordinary.
We take pleasure in things.

Seven strophes made by sending all of Stein's *TB* through DIASTEX5, using as seed Stein's title "Matisse." I made a series of verse-line sentences from the root morphemes of more or less neighboring words in the output of DIASTEX5 by rearranging their order and adding, deleting, or otherwise changing suffixes, conjunctions, prepositions, forms of "to be," pronouns, etc., and otherwise revising the program's output. I deleted the output after the point where it began exactly repeating what came before (something the program does at times). While I composed the sentences, I inserted end marks and grouped the lines into strophes that comprise numbers of sentences corresponding successively to the prime-number sequence.

[Precedent for the endnote: La Vita Nuova. ☺*]*

New York: 9–13 February 2000

Pointing Difference Illusion Places Occasion Plate Dinner

(Stein 109/Titles 6)

Pointing difference.

Nickel breath handsome leaves question place piece reckless.
Calamity makes redness question painful pin necessity.
Cleaning illusion places occasion plate dinner.

Pack strangely glass necessity discolor permitted mixed occasional final.

Dress necessary monstrous place width such arrangement necessary.
Necessary occasion piece oil occasion occasion makes.
Places decision peace light necessarily because.

Roses curves addition pearls little lace treading.

Please necessary revision pounding midnight nice strange steps

Suppose artichoke pinching linen exchange entangled shows suggestion.
Occasion pealing distinguish because clearly means.
Earnest assiduous purple single second remains.

Thirstiness because division principal.

Light recollection tomato makes suggestion exterior potatoes.
Dispute succeed pleasanter hopes famous vacation.
Place silent pocketful pliable makes necessity disappointed.
Perfect singular sack strange makes necessarily.
Decision place singularly luck separation crossing.
Witness question poison wide receptacle soda.

Pheasant loaves occasion purred cider succession.

Salad beefsteak suppose question.

Please with faces.

Salad dressing.

Suppose question placing lighter accomplishing relating shows.

Chinese erection please with mice because satisfy suggest.
Question perfect time decision separation division.
Spoons position plain hill much always lives necessary.
Everybody passed little success vacancies shows.
Varnish question place visible face always trees.
Causes decision pre-occupation discloses much strange.
Shows furnished ponderous plainer single section.
Vacant shows dishes location principle with occasion.
Arranged lacks rights occasion place wideness occasion pleases.

Please cleansing question place piece reckless calamity makes.
Redness question painful pin necessity cleaning.
Illusion places occasion plate dinner.

Sixteen strophes made by sending all of Stein's *TB* through DIASTEX5, using as seed "Picasso." I modified the output of DIASTEX5 minimally, deleting the last part of it soon after the point where it began exactly repeating what came before (something the program often does). The output lines were already grouped into "paragraphs," each beginning with a capital letter, with indentations before lines after the first (if there were such). I attached a few single-word lines to the lines before them, deleted the indentations so that each line began at the left margin, and made each line a sentence by capitalizing its first letter, if it was not already capitalized, and by inserting a period after each line. The 16 strophes comprise numbers of verse-line sentences corresponding successively to the number sequence 1, 3, 1, 3, 1, 1, 3, 1, 6, 1, 1, 1, 1, 1, 9, 3.

[Precedent for the endnote: La Vita Nuova. ☺*]*

New York: 20 February 2000

Nothing Could Make That Costume Reasonable

(Stein 110/Titles 7)

Nothing has an interpretation.
Surely her costume is reasonable.
Don't question that earnest red.

Customs are more desperately different than doubly necessary.

A lax indication may lead to a sure result.
Some customs are necessary, stubbornly necessary.
The addition to her bag was utterly remarkable.

The nurses had ways of reserving the watermelons for themselves.
Revisions only make midnight holes in shallow circumstances.
He's reasonably excellent but neither earnest nor ripe.

It was done in purple distemper.

The difference is that on Saturday it wasn't dated.
She's a little careful about what she consumes.
In the Liberty Circle we tremble necessarily but don't wail.
Mathematics and nausea simultaneous? Not in every circumstance.
I like the middle specimen.
No language goes unrepeated on that mountain.
Customary language isn't necessary during a sudden vacation.
Her nearly silent winsome gurgle makes decisions necessary.
My cat is making a sample stream to prepare for your questions.

There's no question that his green little bottom tastes of oatmeal.

Is it a salad?

It is pale and regular.

With Chinese glasses on, they're indifferent if it's small.
I suppose a cape is necessary at a sentimental resignation.
They penetrated her cape no less in midstream.
On paper that little statement seems singularly questionable.
Surveying a single circumstance can never vacate time.
Not all mountain habits are resolved by the same system.

Is it likely that cleaning it could make that costume reasonable?

Nine strophes made by sending all of Stein's *TB* through DIASTEX5, using as seed Stein's title "Nadelman." I first modified the output of DIASTEX5 by deleting the last part of it after the point where it began exactly repeating a series of lines that came before (something the program often does). The output lines were already grouped into "paragraphs," each beginning with a capital letter, with indentations before lines after the first (if there were such). I eliminated the indentations and transformed each line of the output into a normative sentence and verse line by rearranging its words and by changes, deletions, and additions of suffixes, prepositions, and other structure words, and of pronouns and forms of "to be"; by capitalizing its first letter, if it was not already capitalized; and by inserting an end mark after it. A few output lines each became a verse line occupying more than one typographical line, which is indicated by indentations. I retained the breaks after output paragraphs, which became strophe breaks. The strophes comprise numbers of verse-line sentences corresponding successively to the number sequence 3, 1, 3, 3, 1, 9, 1, 1, 1, 6, 1.

[Precedent for the endnote: La Vita Nuova. ☺*]*

New York: 20–21 February 2000; 14–19 March 2002

Pointing
All Glazed Elephant Seasoning

(Stein 111/Titles 8)

Pointing all glazed very program.

Clean that very place pleasure place very purple closet black.
Very places.

Elegant charm gray plainer closed that gray pieces cloister.
Spark only plan.
Plan change many particles slender.

Black very present place.
Place only pink place that.
Away particular all scarcely very particularly blaming.
Practice only place all that very placed alley places
rosy pine.

Climb practices tiny purr plate that many
peeled.
Black.
Black.
Very plain.
All that praying place!

Place feathers away pigeon!
Claiming claiming bury Pole blinder.
Read they pink glass what?
Very present gliding mean they pain blazing meal
many.

Pleasanter all means gray pocketful all than
tray.

Perfect plain reason many plan cloaking
really very.
Piercing all weather only protection all place
easy.
Precisely all chaining only place all orange
very.
Pint closed change.

Very procured alone boat tiny post.
Placed plaster holy path all meadows.
They pet slam.
Nearly play puff please near.
Very particular glees chalk play
pudding slender.
That they pee all leave only.

Please please away!
They piece play that they place black meant very
place all that.
Very pleasure all chair they put all that they plain.
Plain that very pink plentiful chance away
penetrated.
Cleaned that they place place chair very plates floor.
Plainer relying placard climate that tray place
slanting slanting.
Very pen clergyman chamber very principle cloud
change very.

Place all than only pecking elephant
seasoning very.
Program clean that very place pleasure place
very.
Purple closet black very places
Elegant charm gray.
Plainer closed that.
Gray pieces cloister.

Spark only plan.
Plan change.

Many particles slender
Black very present.
Plan change.
Place place.
Only pink place that.
Away particular!
All scarcely very particularly blaming

Practice only place.
All that very placed alley
places rosy pine.
Climb practices tiny purr.
Plate that many?
Peeled.
Black.
Black.
Very plain.

All that praying!
Place feathers away
pigeon!
Place claiming.
Claiming bury Pole.
Blinder read.
They pink glass what?
Very present gliding
mean they
pain?
Blazing meal?
Many pleasanter.

All means gray pocketful.
All than tray perfect.

Plain reason!
Many plan cloaking.
Really very piercing!
All weather only protection.
All place easy precisely.
All chaining only place.

All orange?
Very!
Pint closed change.
Very procured alone boat!
Tiny post!
Placed plaster holy path all meadows.
They pet slam.

Nearly play puff.
Please near!
Very particular glees.
Chalk play pudding.
Slender that they pee.
All leave only.

Please please!
Away they piece play that they place.
Black meant very place.
All that?
Very pleasure!

All chair they put.
All that they plain.
Plain that very pink.
Plentiful chance away!

Penetrated cleaned that they place.
Place chair very plates.
Floor plainer relying placard climate that tray place slanting.

Slanting very pen clergyman chamber.
Very principle cloud change very place.

All than only pecking elephant seasoning.

Twenty-one strophes made by sending all of Stein's *TB* through DIASTEX5, using as seed Stein's title "Play." I kept the order and forms of all the words in the output (though Americanizing spelling—which did not interfere with the diastic sequence), and I retained repeated word strings as given, but I improvised sentence and strophe breaks, end marks, and strophe placements. (Seeming inconsistencies in sizes of left indentations are intentional. Some were partly determined by the lengths of the longest lines in strophes.) The numbers of verse-line "sentences" in succeeding strophes came to follow the sequence 1, 2, 3, 4, 5, 4, 5, 6, 7, 8, 7, 8, 9, 8, 7, 6, 5, 4, 3, 2, 1, which developed as I wrote the poem.

New York: 23–24 February 2000; 10 March 2003

Perhaps You Can Be Analyzed Dirty

(Stein 112/Titles 9)

Perhaps you can place a single-little red-and-white match on my button,
Cousin.

What could be anything slighter or simpler or sounder?
That blight isn't *dangerous*?
It's more a case for concentration.

Which merciful feeling clashes more with her slenderness?
And which is lighter, black or white?
Her seltzer bottles are manifoldly handled.
Which one is very black or serenely white?

Width distinguishes red from black.
He could care less about regular bedding.
It's certainly no longer practiced, in the main.
It is frightfully mounted!
What is leaving?
What is *that*?
Besides, what made that bud become so regularly centered on the cloth?

Is there anything between those careless places?
In the water-meadow season they bought that handkerchief and a bolster.
"More single" means he can make more of anything that shudders a little.
What few spats get thicker and thicker the farther they go?
Bidding nothing for the candy means the table has more places.
Which blackening of white is real?
That shutting laugh!
That little bank manager in the beautiful leather coat is wavering: it doesn't
match the color of his earpieces.
The peas of the past were the best.

Let a muncher touch a muncher . . .
A breakfast of potatoes is dinner in the morning.

Which of you have curtains that'll wholly settle all discrimination?
Since it'll certainly be her birthday, will she be slenderer rather than stouter?
Besides, does mutual kindness narrow them more?
Which kitchen is *the* kitchen when we feel that *neither* space is anything like
    a blanket or a pleasure?
His beef will be a consideration.
That sink makes us gather and bury chicken feathers.
What repose!
A melting measure only soothes the ordinary.
Besides, no one murmurs at merciful hardness.
Anything successive goes.
Is darkening the way to see that little youths' misdeeds are cheaper because
    so final?
Anything for more calm places!
With a bent for *that*, can there be *anything between* them?
How can that slight, singularly ordinary butler not be single?
That place is more of a cage than a mouth.
His glasses were worsted by whatever kept shaming him.
Little beside that monster blisters the tune of our cow very much.
I lack more than a slight piece of height.

The shadow of your little white belt has the color of blighted plaster.
I mostly say, "Not corn," at lunch.
Her clothes were sticky from the candle.
They neglected their wheatly meadows.
A little bought politeness.
That other being cannot have met any day-stream Crackers—in wet weather
    or *any* weather.
Leave the grain in the coach's little chambers.
Measure your land in cocups!
Neither, *neither*, made more pieces.
After whist, is real butter with real width any lighter in the center?
If he burnt more lines, it means he now has a morning piece that changes.

Which one might be a simpler means to height?
You've frequently had to hinder an*other* be*fore* now.
They made more of them on Monday.
When—for certain—will it be ready?
There was a small change in her discharge but none in her mended hangings.
You'll have to sacrifice that mirror at whose center the sun is always shining!
What is your measure of length?
Is that weather brushing another blue connection?
A bather mentioned a mixture.
To what height did the scraper clean?
Which one of them was resenting that the blotters were certainly shorter?
Another line would certainly mean a space.
What did color-selection mean to that little Southern tumbler?
The ponderous master marked the back of the placard.
Is there anything in the center?
"Why, certainly," the monster shouted, "It'll lead to a little witch!"
But no nonsense!—more cake!
It was very exactly purchased.

Would you rather be single than captured?

Another careless venture!
Be something.
Each curving dance means weather and weather may be mean.

Why secure tears?
The haughty Center pleases every Cracker.
Be continuous!
Many a Sunday hat is far more special.

What likeness does red weaken?
That feather circle is our pleasure before venturing to the top!
She makes a fancy for matches or anything white with stripes be analyzed dirty.

Eleven strophes whose numbers of verse lines successively correspond to the Lucas-number sequences 1, 3, 4, 7, 11, 18, 29 and 1, 3, 4, 3 (turning back on itself at the end). They were written by sending all of Stein's *TB* through DIASTEX5, using as seed Stein's title "Bon Marche Weather" and revising its output. First, I deleted words from the second half of the output, starting right after it began to repeat itself exactly. Then I composed sentences from neighboring words, sometimes changing suffixes, word order, and line breaks and inserting structure words, pronouns, and forms of "to be." I amalgamated some words by inserting hyphens and substituted a homonym for an output word. Some lines became two lines and sometimes two became one. Punctuation was inserted in accordance with sound, sense, and syntax. The lines became verse-line sentences by initial capitalization and insertion of end marks. As I grouped the verse lines while composing the poem, in strophes whose numbers of lines corresponded successively to Lucas sequences, the number of those sequences and the total number of lines and strophes in the poem mutually influenced each other.

24 February–7 April 2000; 12 October 2001

What Monday?

(Stein 113/Titles 10)

What?
That slightly concentrated clash was carelessly white, not bolster-colored.

Discrimination settles out as misdeeds.
Some places slight other places.
Her glasses worsted that little monster who blisters plaster.

Has that blight bought another height now?
It's Monday but for the length of a tumbler.
What a ponderous placard!
Anything for the monster?
In no case does that mostly-white bottle say, "Candle-day weather."

Would that neither piece change now!
Which color did you select for the Center?
Her little Cracker cousin shouted as she purchased whatever she pleased.
Their regular bedding is lighter than seltzer bubbles.
Which is the cloth that laughs?
It doesn't slight leather any more than every little-one lacks her lunch.
Has that simple candle-cracker measured weather more than anything else?
Why will the smaller continuous hangings dance in the Center on Monday?

Four strophes comprising successively 2, 3, 5, and 8 verse-line sentences. They were made by running the raw output produced to make "Stein 112/Titles 9" through DIASTEX5, using as seed the 41st line of that output. The number 41 was found by random-digit chance operations involving *AMRD*. "Stein 113: What Monday?" is the tenth poem in *Titles*, a subseries of the Stein poems, whose making utilizes as seed texts titles of Stein works published in *ASR* or, as in this case, partially made by a procedure using as source texts other poems in the *Stein/Titles* series. In making this poem, I made verse-line sentences with words from the output of DIASTEX5 by keeping neighboring words' root phonemes near each other but modifying word order and sometimes adding, deleting, or otherwise changing suffixes and adding structure words, pronouns, and/or forms of the verbs "to be," to do," and the like as well as a few other words. These modifications changed the tense, mood, number, case, etc., of many output words. I chose the line and strophe breaks, capitalization (or lower-casing), and end marks as well as the sequence of numbers of verse-line sentences in successive strophes.

New York: 24 February–3 March 2000

A Likely Not Genuine Bargain

(Stein 114/Titles 11)

A likely not genuine bargain, gratitude same.

Any be some clóset silk, a lining too sincerely.
Elegant gate: earnest-any-bóx, sometimes stopped-síck and lengthened soóner.
Wing'd, wing'd, gather, cause any breák.

Bottle around dark line: monstrous, mónstrous-length garments.
Has anything blaming no showing?
Pick a left, not long.
Grace makes, say,-bróken; do shows' mark and lie?

No single single grass, dark crystal best.
Couple whole pink, a little-hot-cándy virgin glásses, ladies' ways by post.
Brown, reckless, a-likely-more mónkey - laugh gets sáles, any-boók.
Book, book, báck again: little-to-rings king-goód.
Sáturday-day be nót should turkey-a-líning-roll tender, large.
Glass, water, anything bóne, not stockings, cork, or lamb.
Soaking and likely not single, single green sample trying.

Be cold, choking lack and laid.
Could pensions single goods, lárge-way boat colored-loóse?
So final language gray makes jóy breeze more anóther.
Luck and light, not lunch.
Single grand candle, any-by-nó-wood báck?
A long knot can hang green washing.
Wáy-bed rows, cooking back and loaves cool.
Dinnerweight grand mán: any bay so coól ticks and loosens, loosens . . .
Since hanging greater tables, any-be-doúbt, cooking alike.
Littler-alíke, not hinder single glåss was way by mótion.
Two sack and loss, not hangings.

Single green makes ány-bell whole.

Choke a lying, so renewing a heíght-gallon;
looking,   looking,   constipátion-disgrace.
Gláss-back any blísters.

No   shows   looking glass and lárger,   so sín-emigration.
Grain   taxes-any brídge - location, cloud lacks and lilac.
Not center,   haughty gáme has wáy: be continuous moón.
Nickel a likely not genuine bargain.

Eight strophes in which the numbers of verse-line sentences successively correspond to the Lucas-number sequences 1, 3, 4, 7, 11 and 1, 3, 4. They were written by sending all of Stein's *TB* through DIASTEX5, using as seed Stein's title "A Long Gay Book" and minimally revising its output. First, I deleted words from the second half of the output, starting with the sixth word after it began to repeat itself exactly. Subsequently, I changed a few suffixes and some word order[s] and line breaks. I amalgamated some words by inserting hyphens or deleting word spaces, and I substituted homonyms for a few output words. Some lines became two lines and sometimes two became one. Punctuation and enlarged spaces between words, indicating pauses or prolongations, were inserted in accordance with sound, sense, and syntax. The lines became verse-line sentences by initial capitalization and insertion of end marks. While I was composing the poem and grouping the verse lines in strophes whose numbers of lines corresponded successively to Lucas-sequence numbers, the number of those sequences and the total number of lines and strophes in the poem mutually influenced each other. Reverting to my practice in "154 Forties," spaces within lines indicate half-beat and full-beat pauses. [Ed. Note: Mac Low's *154 Forties* was posthumously edited and published by Anne Tardos (Denver: Counterpath Press, 2012).] Hyphenated compounds are spoken a little more quickly than other words, while spaced hyphens [-] signify "slowed-down" compounds. Acute accents mark stressed syllables, and stressed diphthongs have accents over their second vowels.

New York: 15–30 March 2000

Mercy Makes Sensible Silence

(Stein 115/Titles 12)

Mercy giving cushion present.

Feather much more joy.
Board and in and makes mistake.
Best closet string: sky-gray coke, brown muncher.

Muncher kill fish.
Sausages feeling curtains circle.
Hurry all and meantime restraint.
Considering, settle skate there.

Towel onions' coffee mass.
Single oyster sense.
Fold puff dirty there.

And another made a display cause stretch.

Skip the receptacle.
Chain-boats little make violet-less chess.
Fled burst stretches.

Purred in a cider mass.
Simple was loosen so sky there.
Were likeness little, made single disorder.
Does certainly put there from a disposition.

And disposition makes sensible silence.

Eight strophes in line-number sequence 1, 3, 4, 3, 1, 3, 4, (3), 1 (var. of Lucas sequence). Penultimate five-line space (silence) takes the place of missing three-line strophe and strophe breaks.]All of Stein's *TB* was run through DIASTEX5 (method by JML; program by C. O. Hartman); seed text: Stein's title "Miss Furr and Miss Skeen." Revisions of output: punctuation, line and strophe breaks, strophe placement, and a few word-order changes.

New York: 30–31 March 2000

Pointing, Not Spreading, Glitter Covers Tyrannical Doubling

(Stein 116/Titles 13)

Pointing, not spreading, glitter covers breakages, polishing interesting oysters.

Cardboard kindly questions light increases.
Grinding substances distincter, furniture blights 'em.
That indicates, then, that the cloister plates have been measured for wealthy parties.

Colored plates were constantly selected by the most severe, but ordinarily not when too long a chance was missed.
Mounted, several, choosing tyrannically, authorized four places.
That stitch is enough.
Suppose cranberries were potatoes, a-cookin' in the mornin', then any recurrence of standards would be an exudation.

Circumstances occasion cuts.
Colors lengthen the outside crust, overtaking four uncertain resonances and strengthening all of them.
There, anything is music.
Together they buttered it as necessary.
Perféct no more that separation.
Ordinary determinate explanations of crestfallen teasing monsters are not fine.
Tuesday, crossing handkerchiefs in laughable folds pleased the sweet little principal.

That draught relieves peculiar pains.
Soup with an acre of butter in the center occupied a spreading description of lingering coming coming.

This greater exaltation is blending substances authorized for sleeping when
that directs the lengths of them be measured together.
Put no more that freer, separate attention of yours on penetrating a cake,
lengthening this question more than's agreeable.
Anything is satisfactory in principle if all then venture to object to speech
mistakes.
A stranger pussy is so much more than just a safer spectacle.
Some declarations of overbearing care are tender fountains.
Glass spectacles may ordinarily be charming.
Substances like vegetables and feathers place them.
What selection of something could be analyzed?
The splendor of a piece of coffee is dirtier the distincter its color is.

Relaxation is something like restitution.

If a catalog of boxes is handy, their substances may sometimes indicate
tyrannical doubling.

Five strophes whose numbers of lines successively correspond to the Lucas sequence 1, 3, 4, 7, 11, followed by two one-line codas. In composing the poem, I ran all of Stein's *TB* through DIASTEX5, using as seed Stein's title "Portrait of Constance Fletcher." I usually retained the word order of the program's output, but sometimes changed, added, or deleted suffixes, structure words, pronouns, and forms of "to be." I made line and strophe breaks and inserted initial capitals and end marks in the lines while writing the poem.

New York: 31 March–7 April 2000

What Change That Hour Had Hope Prepared By Hardening It?

(Stein 117/Titles 14)

What change that hour had Hope prepared by genuinely hardening her
costume?
Resolved and fine, the little ones have been scattering greens again.

Cotton: perfect for a flattering shape!
This means restitution replaces the wagon.
I suppose recognition is different there.

What a splendid address for a flower!
Their Sign covers necessity altogether.
The actual settlement was in its present place.
There are only whites in that place who have particularly hopeful
complexions that got there by rubbing.
Release the educated, and four or six or seven of them will have no
occasion for outrage.

A praying particle was placed on her plate.
Why should that have gates?
I hope your copper is collecting harmony.

Sincerely, it's a standard feather I'm simply saving till I have an occasion for
it.
His bottom was more than a pocketful.

All of that chicken was on that tray.
The separation of the hurt cake dipped as its outline withered.
She selected five fine tunes not accepted there at present.

A very old chain worked a change.

He was bitten while hanging the hanging.
An apple on the carpet was shaking the floor.
It bestowed a sprain on an acquaintance with a perfectly charming little
 head.
They are somewhat alike but this wooden one is smaller.

They deplored the stupefication they were earning there.
After the silence was repeated, we heard five movements made up of
 anything.
The scenery was not always put away that way, which showed the five
 cadences were separate.

They were simply fastened.
One lover mastered and measured the current as the other lover visibly
 flowered.

All occasions are not for all places.
The whole thing was one continuous hat.
Why was the vacation asparagus prepared by hardening it?

Ten strophes in which the numbers of verse lines in successive ones followed the prime-number pattern: 2, 3, 5, 3, 2, 3, 5, 3, 2, 3. In composing the poem, I ran all of Stein's *TB* through DIASTEX5, using as seed Stein's title "What Happened / A Five Act Play." I retained the word order of the program's output as often as feasible, but sometimes changed it and/or added, or deleted suffixes, structure words, pronouns, and forms of "to be." I made line and strophe breaks and inserted initial capitals and end marks in the lines while writing the poem.

New York: 7–15 April 2000

Objects in Spectacle Color More Willow Vacation Sacrifice

(Stein 118/Titles 15)

Objects in spectacle color has surely will very handsome convincing.
        Very vegetable exchange much question before covering.
                One and the could case bargain seal.

Very may sincerely very needle occasional machinery waist.
        Serene argument of and even.

Coat particular for veil very particularly longer very left.
        Much exchange plenty besides choosing of and eyesight.

Cold makes strange sullenness virgin made single volumes relaxed.
        Lace tight sight thicker widening out in the could.
                Jam more.

Table valuable papered many.

Veal.

Vegetable.

Cucumber nothing re escape surrounding oftener and the circle.
        Same circumstances pealing vapor darkening tenderness.
                Valor medicine sacrifice mathematics something.
                        Sparse certainty of and does cutting water parts ceiling.
                                Variety vary bone vacation means occasion
                                        much together.
                        Single certainly of and steady cake cake perfect real.
                Very dainty single very necessarily decision tightly.
        Worsted little crossing ordinary.

One one cow gas very collection very large pint very best eucalyptus.
With plaster little explain old and the.

Cold mass surging neglected vegetable saddle went.

Veal.

Very receptacle with relet slender widening.

Only only the cocups lay ear bell voice was rental very center.
Nice higher doubt please blending of in when change.
Was surprise.

Replacing very made hinder very center much such something.
Middle anything of any there closer bather scraper.
Bell very target window vacancies very accounts righteous.
Equator another evasion of in the causes tables string.
Whole very back ponderous vacant center ancient gathered.
Together change coloring once and where change cake.
Very negligence very capture can very certainly lacks.

Catholic debate righteous abundant of in does cooking same.
More willow vacation sacrifice.

Tender very.

Certainly.

Exchange much question before covering one and the.
Could case bargain seal?

Very may sincerely very needle occasional machinery waist.
Serene argument of and even.

Coat particular for veil very particularly longer very left.
Much exchange plenty besides choosing of and eyesight.

Cold makes strange sullenness virgin made single volumes relaxed.
Lace tight sight thicker widening out in the could.
Jam more.

Table valuable papered many.

Veal.

Vegetable.

Cucumber nothing re escape surrounding oftener and the circle.
Same circumstances pealing vapor darkening tenderness.
Valor medicine sacrifice mathematics something.
Sparse certainty of and does cutting water parts ceiling.
Variety vary bone vacation means occasion much together.
Single certainly of and steady cake cake perfect real.
Very dainty single very necessarily decision tightly.
Worsted little crossing ordinary.

One one cow gas very collection very large pint very best eucalyptus.
With plaster little explain old and the.

Cold mass surging neglected vegetable saddle went.

Veal.

Very receptacle with relet slender widening.

Only only the cocups lay ear bell voice was rental very center.
Nice higher doubt please blending of in when change.
Was surprise.

Replacing very made hinder very center much such something.
Middle anything of any there closer bather scraper.
Bell very target window vacancies very accounts righteous.
Equator another evasion of in the causes tables string.

Whole very back ponderous vacant center ancient gathered.
Together change coloring once and where change cake.
Very negligence very capture can very certainly lacks.

Catholic debate righteous abundant of in does cooking same.
More willow vacation sacrifice.

Thirty-two strophes made by running all of Stein's *TB* through DIASTEX5, using as seed Stein's title "One / Carl Van Vechten." I retained the order and forms of all the words in the program's output and in each of the lines except for the two lines in the middle of the poem. Changes were made only in capitalization, punctuation, and placement "on the paper" of the strophes and the indentations of lines within strophes. Placements and indentations were cued by features of the output such as its repetitions. The division into strophes corresponds to the division into "paragraphs" of the program's output, except for the two one-line paragraphs in the middle of the poem, which were broken from the lines immediately above and below them because they are not repeated later. They are centered, as are the other one-line strophes. All other strophes are iterated twice. The multi-line strophes are left-justified in their first iterations and right-justified in their second. All lines *within* strophes are indented, in the first section at the left, and in the second, at the right, both in relation to the margins and to each other. In all lines the words and their order are exactly those of the computer program's output.

New York: 15, 19 April 2000

That Arrangement Could Never Be Selecting Dwindling Heaviness

(Stein 119/Titles 16)

That arrangement could never be an ordinary search.
Can a tassel believe in gratitude?

With ordinary selection dwindled heaviness.
And are not inside.
They indicate established measures are fitting.

The cloistered selectees were trembling strangely.
Those freely not coming selected actuality's supposition.
August presented no ordinary selections with establishment measurements.
What a treat!
Actually aching chance!

Umbrella foliage graces a few little ministers.
A malachite umbrella would be strange.
He has a frantic bottom, habitually articulate.
Her pencil is precise.
How are they aiders of breakfast potatoes?
Were they dining on artichokes?
A usefully crusty surface—might be antisocial.

I reduced their excellence to splinters and trunks.
They search between regions with mutual whistles.
Away!
Aren't choices choices?
Tremblingly sincere, all their greatness sat in their rising choices.
Stumblingly composed, the principal hates solid music and establishers of
its specimens.
After a breakfast of potatoes—and loverly cups of tea, they were pliable.
Is her silence original?
Between the articles piercing that crumbling minister, they arranged no
chain of searches for the signals he would have accepted.

Cranberry chains aren't chance singularities, either procured or precocious.
Bite me again!

Searching wheatly, recollection aches.
Preparing butter and grain could be his principal capability.
Potatoes and cress!
Are potatoes on a chain-boat too ridiculous to mentally shoulder?
That set that dines on artichokes—it's the one that wouldn't bestow a press on us, but rented us a chair—a choice that troubles us.
This arrangement is greater than a vision exercise, but it's startlingly disagreeable.
Organized and betrothed, their livingways were indicated by symbols and examples.
Green without solid delicacy, they funneled together.
Not choice—but speech—established their package alright!
Often a stairway selection, for example, may be mastered by a creature who sets seeing music as an ordeal.
Her canister—and a practical little copied chance detail—captured a principle with plain but choosy appeal.
And are they together for nothing but aiming at lilacs—translating mistakes into cravings—but not habits?
Attaching a nickel difference——behind a chancy tassel—he was not prepared to believe that ordinary gratitude would never be selecting dwindling heaviness.

Six strophes comprising numbers of verse-line sentences corresponding to the prime-number sequence. The poem was made by running all of Stein's *TB* through DIASTEX5, using as seed Stein's title "Article." In making the poem, I brought the lexical words into the poem in the order in which they appeared in the program's output—with very few exceptions, if any—but I freely substituted function words, forms of "to be," pronouns, and inflections and other suffixes (or the lack of them) for each other, deleted them, or inserted them as well as auxiliaries.

New York: 15 April–5 May 2000

Glass Coconuts

(Stein 120/Titles 17)

Glass, hurting pointedly, is likely to accustom one to vegetable gratitude.
Desperate adventure, double up two tables on occasion.
Breaking complications distinguishes particulars.
Establishments green just Whites—yellow equals disgrace.

Gracious arrangement's arrangement *and.*

Spreading shown explanations samples practical mounting sectionally.
Outstanding altogether: handkerchiefs' golden eucalyptus.

This.

Coconut tails develop natural cuddling.

Vegetables slant shoes up, peculiarly chalking Charlotte.

Chicken's, beefsteak's preparation-temperature resembles.

Given surroundings which could little agree—incalculable!
Bedroom principles—and opportunity's another spelling.
Regular exercises count on resemblance declarations.
Rudiments resembling gates surround this feeling.
Catalogued substances: particular arrangements' arrangements.
Always spectacles choose wholly complex occasions.
Choose!

Surely umbrellas cultivate nonchalant glasses necessarily!
Outstandingly quite ceilings arranged the little coconuts.

Nine strophes made by running all of Stein's *TB* through DIASTEX5, using as seed Stein's title "Guillaume Apollinaire" and minimally revising the program's output. I brought words into the poem from the program's output in the order in which they appear in it, inserting none except a few contractions of "is." I freely substituted some suffixes for each other, inserted them, or deleted them. Some lines cheerfully violate the inversion taboo. I retained the output's line breaks and line groupings, letting left-marginal lines and interlinear spaces cue strophe breaks and their sizes. Punctuation and capital letters were inserted where appropriate. When words in the output began to repeat themselves exactly, I didn't bring any more into the poem.

New York: 5–26 May 2000; 10 November 2001

Milk Places Joy
Down There a Piece

(Stein 121/Titles 18)

Milk places joy in difference.
Resonant cultures may be altogether oily.

Dogs so widen our linen that their place in the kitchen is saving our journeys
from any bitterness toward recklessness.
No widthwise signal makes a saving.
Any joint song says paper is pink.

A jet of oil is ordinarily likely to be dark.
What a splendid color!
A turkey may resemble more places than it makes.
Does choosing anything lengthen the means of recollecting making a journey?
Pigeon linen signals a sinecure.

They nearly mended their onions.
That kind of depot is perfect for cocoa just around lunchtime.
Dear Bill, well, many may be saying there's joy in jerking, but for a nickel
more . . .
Behind the mending they make a width that doesn't join learning to many
spools with pins.
We do well to judge the intentions of any of those monstrous cleaners.
Really!—so the turkey dog is a mixture!
To nearly strengthen the splendid sky makes silver ways remarkable.

Joining makes soaking altogether silver.
All peeled relaxing is altogether shunning more repose.
Color is altogether a joy! a joy! a joy!
The meadowed are learning remarkable lilacs' languor.
The spool is broken and the pink post makes darkness necessary.

Make a perfectly nonchalant culture by relaxing and choosing very resonant
pieces.
So choose that your collar becomes a little more gilded sooner—not just
soaked in lilac.
Point to the kinds of places recollecting prudence more than luck.
Are the ways of silk milk milk's ordinary ways?
The joy of onions is prudence the way gilded pennies are joyful.
Who peeled the kitchen's monstrous repose?

Anything can be the length of anything it resembles.
Pack colors around your pay.
Darkness makes us strong.
Pin it on Jack!
No judges make the colors that make it pedestrian.
Do you pay more jack for your milk?
Those seven joys just make the mixture a means to shun tenderness more.
That muncher widened so much more the joint was wondering.
His color was real singular.
Choose the color necessary for lunch.
Post a little broken time.
We wondered sooner at his dark pedestrianism.
Seven of the packs were bitter again.

The *Post* says color is recognized by silk.
Can any post get tall the muncher's way?
Again that song!
Just a collar and pennies don't paper the way, justly says the cleaner.
She was more reckless than a jet pet!
All joy to the more reckless pigeons!
Anything joyful is more likely for the lucky nonchalant.
It was a tall calamity when they recognized more time for their sky pet.
In a cocoa languor Bill was singularly jerking on the meadow.
Where is the medicine depot?
Down there a piece.

Seven strophes comprising numbers of verse lines that form the prime-number sequence. I made them by running all of Stein's *TB* through DIASTEX5, using as seed Stein's title "Pink Melon Joy." I randomized the words of the program's output with the help of the program GEN, written by {a friend of the poet Henry Taylor}, which had randomized the numbers from 1 through 9999, and Microsoft Excel. Finally, I made sentences from groups of words in the randomized output, often changing suffixes and word order within each group, inserting function words, pronouns, etc., and I grouped the series of verse-line sentences in the seven strophes as I went along.

New York: 8–26 May 2000

Pointing Out Your Silvery Song

(Stein 122/Titles 19)

Pointing out your differences with a sinecurist recklessly makes for a very
calamity.

Color's in its journey intends to say paper's silver song.
Packing more color around you anyplace is being just monstrous.
The width of a pin may be more dark than learning to choose ordinarily well.

Just so!
Any oily piece?
Wondering, broken, at a more-mended culture, he's choosing the strength of
his joints.
Does she say that the place's bitter length makes the darkness remarkable?

The gilded color seven judged so many ways was posting little pennies.
"Reckless" means "dear" when the tall depot-cleaner joins the dog sky.
Peeling Bill the Muncher makes Jack be meadowed.
Milk?
Enjoy your cocoa on linen.
If anything, be joyful that the pigeon in the kitchen isn't a kind of turkey.
Make resonance collar repose, saving jerking sooner.

The way of prudence is the nonchalance of lilacs, more pink than
resemblance.
Splendid recollections may be shunning joy more than anything.
It's perfectly singular how many soaking mixtures are real relaxing!
That altogether widened jet was to pay for the pet's signal languor.
Milk makes it necessary.
All recognition is again joy or no joy by post time.
Lunch!
Luck nearly makes a silk spool of onions just one more pedestrian way.

She's likely to be tender.
Nickel mercy medicine's a color, the color behind a journey to say "paper."
That silvery song!

Five strophes comprising numbers of verse-line sentences corresponding to the Lucas-number sequence 1, 3, 4, 7, 11. I made them by running all of Stein's *TB* through DIASTEX5, using as seed Stein's title "Pink Melon Joy." I made a verse-line sentence from the words in each line of the program's output (except for one output line that I divided into two verse-line sentences), inserting a minimum of function words, pronouns, etc.; inserting, deleting, or changing some suffixes; and sometimes changing word order. I divided the series of verse lines into the five Lucas-number strophes as I composed the lines.

New York: 8–29 May 2000

Not Taken

(Stein 123/Titles 20)

Not bloody likely!

How callously chairs are places and things not very much matching this closet.
Redness comes to question strangely.

A dirty message was certainly contained in the rosewood cause of the thing.
The curves of desperate lilies are plainer and more necessary there.
For very long, this, presented as a necessary current, has been unjust.

Dark and quite awkward, he's just been standing there, regularly standing there.
No longer left a suitably housed patient, he was taken away chained.
In that joint they were showing the oceans and other places in their very colors.
Where does culture place the cutlet?

Supposing more than that . . .
The climate decided it.
Were they coloring reason?
Her waist was gliding o'er the grass before she left the country.
Eat and articulate there in the places where the Virgin is shining so that space is different.

The nurses were cleaning custards of sorts.
That little stream was pounding and really blackening whomever the nearest whites had been doing.
And little on that pillar matches.
Will you be dining?
The sauce suggested the vapors of poisonous chickens, which made the uneven chairs clatter.
On Sunday a surfeit of suction was outlasting a roasting and spilling rush.

Bargaining for spices was raising and gathering the collars and linings of the sadder after the recital.

The larger clouds have the vagueness of no prized juice.
There, successive certainties curl those very denting rhubarb stockings.
This salve is real outstanding!
That abusive clamorer was loving many and eating respect in his famous
vacation.
Not leisure but a succession of surrenderings was certainly a necessity.
I suspect she was hurt, hurt by mistake while mounting, but was
cloaking it by relaxing.

Water!
This winsome one dipped and withered—likely, martial riding caused it.
Necessarily, very many more scissors were placed in the house than
necessary.
What color?
Sugar and lard, that privately mounted chaining remedies, have blisters!
This uglier murder's a little large, and again, whole plates.
That vegetable's not noisy which mussed a foolish cloud.
Your custard of narrowly little preparation was, no question, enlivening
and radiant!

It's capable, this grass, of leaving butter.
Loaves call and ridiculous white cocups voice no "which" piece.
There there.
The Chinese chair's suggestion is to corner those who replaced her
questionable acquaintances.
The room table, this one, showed the copper lesson fast.
And who's living sullen?
Suppose no very being, which is on the whole supposing Curly, is
more dusty.
That!
Releasing pleasing renewing, her refusal was painstakingly like what
the State does.

The cellar line's the same.
Did that visible place always be so very much more?
It's a climate of which there are fifteen plates.

The currents—the currents of air—mastered their surface indecision by
 counting.
The one that remains is larger and whitening.
This is quite awkward!—and little has any design or secret shoals.
That very lover, this exact piece, is supposing chance purchased currency!
Certainly exchange's principle movements may rain.
This nausea flowers as flowers the lilac.
Dance and choice were yesterday useless, violent cooking-slippers.

The place centers on cleansing.
Certainly!
Substance is very little prepared to question covering the rate case.
The thing that is reasonable there is a little calm, ordinary preparation.
That string's whole redness!
Very not fainting, the mercy table places covers surrounding certainty.
Restitution's exchange is sometimes doubling, red, and washed.
Brighter does neater but clever is losing the mark and coming.
A stone necessity very long, this which is present is necessary.
The current is just dark and quite awkward where you are standing and
 standing!
The Regular has suitably housed the patient longer than the Left has taken.

Eleven strophes comprising numbers of verse lines corresponding to the series of cardinal numbers from one through eleven. All but one of the lexical words come from root morphemes of words derived from running all of Stein's *TB* through DIASTEX5, using as seed the title of Stein's very short play "Ladies Voices / Curtain Raiser." Listening carefully to what each "raw" line of the program's output seemed to be saying, I turned each line into a verse-line sentence by making small changes, including insertion, deletion, or changes of suffixes, changes of word order, insertion or deletion of a few function words, etc. After the output began repeating itself, I deleted the remainder of it. Each line is indented a number of letter spaces equal to the number of lines in its strophe. The only line of the first strophe is indented one letter space . . . the eleven lines of the eleventh strophe are each indented eleven letter spaces.

New York: 30 May–1 June 2000

Can Mercy, Perhaps, Borrow All Substances Necessary?

(Stein 124/Titles 21)

Can Mercy, perhaps, borrow fancy and not bed with little white
mentionables?

Coffee, a thing more clean than designed, is not enough for relaxation.
If more gates make it at all necessary, some substances may be necessary.

More closed pieces are indicated.
An *and* might be clever.
More packs are collected whole, strangely marking every starting lately.

No, Red, not more of those particular careless garments!
More learning is not always necessary, nor is that blaming.
Between me and anyone else it would be done more easily.
Enough, enough elegance makes all sides the same.

It'll show well, if at all.
Those ministers are careless and so, I suppose, are the pieces they're
showing.
Cold makes Malachite sullen.
The stomach is a more nearly fairylike means.
Nearly ten, he makes little mention of anything but leather or candy.

More of them there are crazy.
They're nearly leading within their needing.
Blackening a plate?
Directly again.
An orange?
Artichoke-resumption means that some will have some, and this will make
our spaces stranger.

The length of a stronger social success would be more obtrusive than any
snipe.
Comb a large silver smell in a mutually narrow moreness.
Not every dirty never-beef is a little nothing blanket.
It was carved with much wailing.
He's searching hurriedly, not for medicine, but a little pretentious mission.
And do it with calmness!
All recognition of perfect baking is a delight.

That student was merciful.
Hate makes us have a stream of strange resemblances, and still more solitude.
The prices of undertakers there make a case for silence.
It influences reality more than language and more early there.
No cups of tea and no eating at *that* wedding—being single meant more
capital.
The arrangement there's an annoyance, yet really necessary.
That soaking rescue was altogether very ordinary!
Thoughtful searches of more collections make for more ease.

Utterly harmful to the stomach again was the state of those plates.
And in the end, they say it is cold.
That stick is cold yellow.
It might be a candle, more nearly hoary, nearly the best.
Utter that caution, for the blanket met the daystream narrowly.
Mercy!—Hurry!—A little new butter!
He's cutting that little plank a little more.
They're dining in a draft!
The artichoke occupation makes time for hangings—and what of it?

They were needing more spreading behind that stone.
All the Chinese can end the wall of silence—or are they making it swell more?
The surprise there was that every little birthday was not mentioned.
That more has been burning between them there is Curly's delusion
necessarily.
Not that wetting in the middle is anything, but it *is* a blue and circular
diminisher.

Her every lying breath is stating more of a distaste for milk, water, cake, and
any spice.
Yet the sprightly chairs are successes, alright—and *what* successes!
The varnished curtain is all real, but the stairway was certainly mean.
That name is always there because there's little hint of folding another.
For mourning ears the very years are empty, but not yet—not *that* negligence.

Between a turtle and a clergyman, is currency a satisfactory bridge?
Clinching a dedication means that each one makes a steady object.
Showing more liking yesterday is useless there.
Is cooking all the willows more naughty then scratching them?
No ingredient of their mercy was even a little bit genuine yesterday—not one!
They have very many interests there.
That little white one mentioned coffee.
Is a thing's clean design enough?
Take more relaxation.
That gate makes it necessary.
Are all substances necessary?

Endnotes

Source Text: All of Stein's *TB*.
Seed Text: Stein's title "Marry Nettie/Alright Make It a Series and Call It Marry Nettie."
Method: I ran the source and seed texts through DIASTEX5 and then modified every output line by changes of word order and "helping words" until near the end, when I made verse-line sentences from parts of lines up to the point in the output where lines began repeating exactly.
Form: Eleven strophes in which the number of lines follows the integer series 1, 2, 3, 4, 5, 6, 7, 8, 9, 10, 11.

New York: 4–15 June, 28 July 2000; 1 October 2001

Fanciful Smells

(Stein 125/Titles 22)

Fanciful Mercy can't borrow a bed, perhaps?

Our little nothing blanket met the daystream narrowly.
Hurry, Mercy, you new little pretended missionary!

They calmly recognize all perfect baking as delight.
Student, be merciful!
Hate makes some streams narrow.

Hurry, Mercy, those little Whites are mentioning nothing new.
The blanket met the daystream and, strangely, space.
Malachite sullenness is the stomach being harmed again.
They say those yellow plates will coldly state the end and it'll be cold.

Is a nearly mighty candlestick about to lead more of us within?
Does this need blackening?
That orange plate is again an artichoke.
Its resumption means that *having* makes necessity real.
Yet that soaking rescue was altogether very ordinary.

Thoughtfully, we searched the collection more easily.
Enough, enough of elegance!—make some of the streams less narrow!
Hurry, newly merciful little Whitie—mention nothing!
Lately his blanket met the daystream strangely marked, starting evermore.
No, Red, not *that* particular care!
Fewer garments are not always necessary for more learning.

They more than indicate closure.
The pieces are clever.
More of them pack the collection easily enough.
Enough elegance makes some streams strangely resemble solitude.

There the prices are the undertakers'—the case makes silence more real.
Does it influence cooking anymore?
Does it make more willows?

Is it that the language there is more crazy, though nearly the best?
All the willows uttered that caution.
How did the blanket meet the daystream?
Narrowly.
Hurry, Mercy, mention new little leathery candy more.
Nothing more there that early.
No teacups or eating at *that* wedding!
A single means made the capital arrangement there annoying.

Is it all necessary—is *that* substance really necessary?
Her recognition soaked him in delight.
The student was having mercy on them.
Hate makes us have a narrow stream.
Hurry on, Mercy, with no or little pretence of a new mission.
Perfect calmness rescues all baking.
They are altogether very ordinary!
Though a thoughtful search collected the whole, it was strangely marked.
Lately, more were starting every day.

No, Red, not *that* particular!
More careless garments, more learning always.
If it's not necessary, it's not medicine.
Mention *nothing* a little.
The blanket narrowly met the stream.
Hurry: Mercy, the little White mentioned new coffee!
A clean, more designed thing: more relaxation.
More gates make some strange resemblance to more solitude.
There the prices of the undertakers make a case for one side.
If it all shows well, comb in a large silver smell.

More of them are mutually narrowing.
Not every dirty little White never mentions beef.

Not white *leather*, a little more *candy!*
More were there early.
Nothing at that wedding—no teacups and no eating at that wedding.
There "capital" meant a single arrangement.
Is that annoyance necessary?
Are all those substances really necessary?
Yet that soaking recognition delights our merciful students.
Hate makes necessity, not medicine.
There was little or nothing in that blanket.

Was there much wailing when they got carved?
Search—hurry—not for medicine, but for a little mention.
No more leather candy!
Nothing leather!
Most of them were nearly crazy there.
Nearly ten little fairies were mentioned.
Coffee is not a clean thing.
They were designed for more relaxation.
More gates make streams narrower.
Hurry!—mercy!—a little new butter!
Cut more of those little planks.
Why are you dining in that draught?

What is the occupation of an artichoke?
Hanging takes time.
Does it?
All the Chinese could really end that wall of silence.
Perhaps its ingredients influence more naughty things than scratching.
Can't Mercy borrow a little fancy butter?
Not a little bed and butter?
Let's cut one more little plank!
How can you dine on artichokes during a resumption of the draft?
This means that those who have make more.
Uttering, stomachs *mean* more.
Stomachs are doing more harm than uttering does.
In the end, their plates and states are cold.

They say the yellow stick is cold.
A candle was nearly leading within that needing.
Blacken a plate?
Let the oranges and artichokes resume what's really necessary.
Yet that soaking rescue! . . .
That wasn't very ordinary.
Search for more thoughts, collect them whole.
Is the stream narrowing?
Hurry new mercy.
The pretence of the little mission was calmness, and all that perfect baking rescued it, and altogether it was a very ordinary thoughtful search through a collection more at ease in making silences than in swelling.
Is it more so in making any and all cooking the same?
Is it more so than the willow's earlier language?
No teacups?
He was eating at that wedding because his capital was singularly mean.

What an arrangement!
Did they make any more?
There, *annoyance* was necessary, not *medicine*.
Any cooking of willows is the same.
Is it more?
Make it more.
There was more early language there, but no teacups.
They were eating their capital at that wedding.
Not a single arrangement there was an annoyance.
Medicine was not necessary.
They were making no pretence of having a mission.
There was little calm and all.
Cooking's perfect recognition is delight.
Hate makes some students more merciful.
The stomach's means of utterance is making more than ten of them.

He and his stomach were utterly mean.
This means they were making more utterances.

She was nearly a merciful fairy.
He recognized her delight.
Nearly ten of them made no pretence to having a mission.
She was baking in perfect calmness.
Hate might be more harmful to the stomach than to plates.
The students were delighted at our mercy.
In the end, they said they were cold in that state.
Those yellow candlesticks were cold—nearly hoary.
You might say they were more nearly hoary than any nearby fairy.
Near ten, there was little mention—nothing—about a blanket.
Much *wailing* carved the hurried searchers, not any of their *medicines*.
There was little mention of Nothing when the blanket met the daystream.
The little white ones mentioned nothing about a blanket.
Her little mercy was hurried and narrow.

How much wailing carved it?
Search in a hurry, not for medicine.
The arrangements there make annoyance necessary.
Hurry new mercy, little candy, much more leather.
More there are crazy, nearly all the best.
Is it more naughty to be scratching?
Silence is a real influence.
What are its ingredients?
Utter that caution.
Cold yellow candles are sticky.
Search for more garments.
Let's make a case for silence.
Mention nothing narrower than strange resemblances.
Sullen undertakers make the case for silence.
How can you enlarge a large silver comb?
Some oranges are yellow.
How can you comb a smell?

Source: The raw output that had been revised into Stein 124.
Method: I sent the raw output made for Stein 124 through TRAVESTY, asking for an order-9 output (or "travesty") of 9,390 characters. I revised successive word strings of the output (often pseudo-sentences) into normative sentences which were grouped into strophes whose numbers of verse-line sentences followed the integer sequence 1, 2, 3, 4, 5, 6, 7, 8, 9, 10, 11, 12, 13, 14, 15, 16, 17. Then I stopped, because the output was too repetitious to further hold my interest enough to motivate my converting the rest of it into normative verse-line sentences. (This is the 22nd poem of "Stein" subseries "Titles.")

New York: 5–18 June 2000

Scattering Accustoms Us To Having More Joy Than Scattering

(Stein 126/Titles 23)

Scattering accustoms us to having successful lining in everything.

If all results of arrangements indicate journeys, let them be red.
Measuring does nothing necessary or remarkable for the precocious.
What beautiful cranberries!

Their tails are cream and orange and absurdly longer.
Clearly an active suction is dated.
Clean everything in succession, and in the case of the blanket, the greatness of that choice is soothing and really perfectly practiced.
Their reason for the remainder in mathematics is singularly lamentable.

Her astonishment at that original tray was slight.
The suspect mended lightly and actually not necessarily more than arranged for.
The glasses are almost beside the separate delicacies.
Yellow cranberries at rest mean moist shadows spraining eggplants.
Measure butterflies in a reasonable receptacle.
The longer they are bewildered there the more they satisfy another acquaintance.
Much was made of her essential reception of exercise.

His disagreeable speeches were alike in their changing resemblance to stars.
I question the symbol: nothing but resignation is reversible.
An incredible difference!
Her breath and the charming program she chose were showing us more joy than scattering.

Source text: All of Stein's *TB*.
Seed text: Stein's title "Accents in Alsace: A Reasonable Tragedy."
Method: I ran the source and seed texts through DIASTEX5. Then I made sentences from word strings in the output. I retained all lexical words but sometimes changed their order as well as changing, inserting, or deleting suffixes and helping words (articles, prepositions, personal, possessive, and relative pronouns, etc.). I inserted capital letters and punctuation marks where appropriate and grouped the successive lines in Lucas-sequence strophes as below.
Form: Five stanzas, having numbers of verse-line sentences corresponding to the Lucas-number sequence 1, 3, 4, 7, 4 (turning back on itself at the end).

New York: 6–23 June 2000

A Longer Orange May Come

(Stein 127/Titles 24)

A longer orange would be absurd since clearly length is socially active.
I suppose an ancient thing is much ageder than most.

Does nothing of the pleasure and surprise, the color and the harmony, of
 any occasion continue?
An ingenious pocketful can make for an almost astonishing inclination.
All the results of a shuttered relaxation may be pierced by all who ride.

Temporary explanations may be more necessary than scissors.
Remarkably, they presupposed a remarkable tree.
Would you be breaking your skates behind that single, neglected, readily
 shaded scene?
A bland white ocean may make the cuts of solemn lashes seem reasonable.
A succession of stretches may come to occasion a nervous occasion.

Will eating old roses at successive elevations please us?
Temporarily, an artichoke may please a reader less than a red leaf.
Hanging may or may not be an action.
Their differences—incredibly—are reversible.
Her program's was charming, but she showed more joy on seeing us scatter.
The shape of the thing was fuller in the morning.
Mildred's method supposed a curious increase.
An increase on any occasion might be occasional.
The selection of a string may be careless.
It might be selected anyplace.
The customary arrangement is away from the direction between rubbing
 and releasing.

The lesson of the purse is nothing remarkable—but it's reasonable.
Rectangular everywhere, the carved chairs are bigger there.

Liberty spices are accounted green and slender till they're raised to melting.
Cutting them for a salad, the prison authorities surrounded them with
circumstances.
And the remainder makes an occasional pocketful ingenious.
They're almost inclined to astonishment when all results in relaxation.
Your scissors are piercing our shutter!
They're all riding more than necessary.
It was remarkable that a presupposed tree could break a single neglected
skate.
Behind the readily shaded scene, whiteness makes the ocean bland.
The reasonable are cut with solemn lashes in nervous succession.
That occasion stretches into a succession of old roses.
When eating is more elevated, a pleasing occasion may come.

Source: All of Stein's *TB*.

Seed: Stein's full title of her play "Accents in Alsace / A Reasonable Tragedy / Scene Mulhouse"

Method: Running source and seed through DIASTEX5, using words in each output line [beginning with the 8th line since previous ones are identical up to that point to the output for Stein 126] to make normative sentences by changing word order and/or changing or adding suffixes and helping words. Dividing resultant sentence sequence into six strophes comprising successively numbers of verse-line sentences corresponding to the prime-number sequence. [Ed. Note: But skipping 7 in the sequence of primes.]

New York: 6 June–21 July 2000

Tender Cousin More Because of the Mountain?

(Stein 128/Titles 25)

Tender Cousin Hour.

There sometime surely obligation prepared that soft you there.
Question before?
Rhubarb, beefsteak, and deliberation determine their horticulture.

Circumstance and suffering.
A student, two thoroughly shiny onions of.
This does show that prices are gliding because of mountains.
Which lamb more?

This is no abuse.
There vacation gently.
Of crusts that could not.
Altogether extraordinary solitude!
Yesterday's recollection: rhubarb.
Chain-boats' satisfactory circumstances sweetened it whole.
Everything there, even that-there game cracker.

Wretched occasion of light!
What was more—the torch or the fountain unordered?
Glitter is surely an obligation.
You prepared that soft question there before.

Does rhubarb or beefsteak deliberately determine horticulture's
circumstances?
These two shining onions show the student thoroughly suffering.
How prices are gliding!

Which lamb is more because of the mountain?

Endnotes

Source text: All of Stein's *TB*.
Seed text: Gertrude Stein's title "Tourty or Tourtebattre: A Story of the Great War."
Method: I ran the source and the seed through DIASTEX5 and modified the output by minimal revisions of word-order, suffix changes, and additions of "helping words." I divided the resulting sequence of lines (as I composed it) into stanzas successively comprising numbers of lines corresponding to the rising and falling Lucas-number sequence 1, 3, 4, 7, 4, 3, 1.

New York: 22–23 July 2000

A Carafe Is a Kind of Perfect Flattering Shape Where Small Places Clash

(Stein 129/Titles 26)

A carafe is a kind of strange mercy costume together with a reasonable tassel.

A painful place for an image.
Very.
And places.

What an elegant charm is gray's, and its catalogue time is three, which is
doubling.
A pounded increase and a cloister dinner string are precocious.
Because an establishment is necessary, is its place necessary?
Anything else than only a place away that's very in cut with it.

More placed careless.
And a Japanese likeness.
The cold size of a strange peace because of a pencil.
A breakfast of cranberries, potatoes, and oranges is very clear and plain.
All that praying inside and a comb of ripe purple, which should clatter.
Choices and choices' differences are hardly as thick as accounted.
Singularity withdrew consideration.

They had pride and also a plate of pink glass.
What is a very kindness in a can?
Warmer prices little mingle circumstance with a cake of silence.
More mischief and influences are singularly necessary together.
For a perfectly plain reason many a plan is really very cloaking.
Crumbling and mixed in that very place they sampled surpassing glasses.
All comes tightly worsted in a sauce of languor, orderly and remarkable.
A necessary pint closed the very change they procured alone.
A tiny boat comes into the light with a nervous bunch in singular clothes.
Meadows and cup size, more which is singular, a capable receptacle.
Peculiar.

Potatoes blew in the shade as we played with a pudding so slender we ate it
on a chest.
A nice, bursting piece bundled bundles in succession in a cake bin.
Since her disturbance, we consider her birthday trouble.
A pleasant place for a feat, they're putting out all they can.
Its only commensurate likeness is in a mirror which is likely in the center.
Tidy and cut, signed Curly: a special mixture, circular and penetrated.
Disorder plumbs sleep that they are in a place, a place with a chair.
Very is a color, fifteen.
Currents single out darkness and administration centers.
Singularity, singularity, politeness all that tray.
A slanting place, a slanting.
Any center's a very distractor, more exactly a turtle, chance-purchased.
And a clergyman's single currency.
Checking circumstances, details, surveyance of strangers, pussy, and all.
Then only a pecking elephant is very seasoning.
Cleansing is giving that very place a circle of chance and nonsense.
A could.
A light purple fancy mixture dwindled necessarily, concentrating a perfect
flattering shape where small places clash.

Source: All of Stein's *TB*.

Seed: Stein's title "A Circular Play, A Play in Circles."

Method: Running source and seed through DIASTEX5; minimally revising the output, sometimes changing word order or changing or adding suffixes or helping words, even punning once; dividing the resulting sequence of lines (as I composed it) into six strophes successively comprising numbers of lines corresponding to the Lucas-number sequence.

New York: 23–27 July 2000

Pointing That Season

(Stein 130/Titles 27)

Pointing is this unordered.

Glittery borrowing is giving regularity a resemblance to preoccupation.
The tablecloth's a pond and all that tray and the flowered visible.
Lover, lover, not all occasions are in this place.

Enough that season was strange, not ordinary like yesterday's preoccupation.
The tablecloth's a pond and all that tray and the flowered visible.
Lover, lover, not all occasions are in this place.
Enough of that season!

Source: All of Stein's *TB*. Seed: Stein's title "Photograph, A Play in Five Acts." Method: Sending source and seed through DIASTEX5, adding or changing a few helping words and word orders in the output and adding a letter, and dividing the result into three strophes whose successive numbers of verse-line sentences follow the Lucas-number sequence 1, 3, 4.

New York: 30 July 2000

Resembling Red Is Surely a Simple Occasion

(Stein 131/Titles 28)

Resembling red is surely unwelcome.

It certainly showed, and showed little feathers in circles of pleasure.
In a place of pleasure what could be very much dearer than purple?
The closet was black.

Very sincerely it spread, and the wagon ribbon's a desperate success.
One curious establishment was sick and dusty in winter.
Washed then to a brighter result.
Soon an actual aching bloomed in animosity.

An umbrella's lesson was rightly spreading more exchange.
Any more.
A cloth that anything is between.
A tumbler places all tiny places there to blacken that real, purring plate.
Many sisters peeled it, aided by ink.
Crusty yellow cocoa, no longer cumbersome, often overtakes success.
Not it.

What birthday inside that lighted room best remains active and smelly?
That exhibition was largely recognized by reason of its resemblance.
Part of the rhubarb is more tender than intended.
The mutton was spoken for.

Anything can shelter another for any reason more perfectly plain than many.
Most beware wet plans cloaking what's really very much there and what's
caused it.
Are a knife's and a colored shadow's tender likenesses ordinary?

A round of hurts is outstanding, with nice absent nothing.

That solid blister's recognition made a sudden scene.
Was that dirty meal capable of putting aches into reasonable rows?
That's an extra heated case.

Any moon that another churner bolsters may have purred on all elevations.
That only too bended part may play at having been bended as they showed it
the place.
Any enclosure that ends on the floor surprises the sister with an ordinary
growth of much nothing.
That its wood was singular was right.

Better no reason than an in-between one.
A startling scene behind an almost yellow singularity remains.
The bedroom's larger size was certainly needed.
It shoals up the little purchase of a single chamber.
The powder cloud changed so very much that no dedication at all took place.
Only the ingredients were incredible.
The callous oyster's gratitude was not ordinary.

In her sight the sash disgraced his white suit.
The redness of the box is not the same.
The singular custom of scattering recognition is exhausting.
Be sure to place considerable paper around the red china.

On the whole, that which is ordinarily serene is in a place far away.
That colored pin held the button in place.
It won't be standing very much longer.

Custody ended in a bloom of animosity.

I was wondering which of the objects was the broken one.
Suppose it were entirely so.
The difficult disgrace of water rushing to the bottom is best left.

That's a simple occasion.

Source: All of Stein's *TB*.
Seed: Stein's title "Reread Another, A Play, To Be Played Indoors or Out, I Wish to Be a School."
Method: Running source and seed through DIASTEX5; minimally revising the output, sometimes changing word order or changing or adding or deleting suffixes or helping words. Dividing the resulting sequence of verse lines into fifteen strophes successively comprising numbers of verse lines corresponding to the alternately rising and falling Lucas-number sequence 1, 3, 4, 7, 4, 3, 1, 3, 4, 7, 4, 3, 1, 3, 1.

New York: 31 July–2 August 2000

Mercy Changes the Stitches

(Stein 132/Titles 29)

Mercy, giving color a hardening interest, changed the mustard dangerously.
Then, sooner than illusion, that thing's enough for relaxation.

By a single established means, all need for paper and lighter's impounded.
Particles around this are of altogether assured lengths.
Scarlet and careless in more than direction all bend color.

They were mounted and colored.
Enthusiastically, that thing alone resumed a realistic stitching.
That suggests you mean a some kind of lead-colored pole.
The custard is colored.
The asparagus is on the table.

This shows how absurdly changing length suggests a precious means.
On her birthday all of us tenderly resumed revering chickens.
There looseness shadows choice around designs.
Something perfect in its superposition's mathematics withered solids.
They shaded the water's little solitude and stockings.
This show shows liquor's resignation together with scissors' retraction.
Make mistakes all lard.

Our water glasses worsted the trees, but the sherry was loosely natural.
Being plowed her blanket.
Potatoes make a solemn sight.
Cold and clear the crescents labored, showing what they'd accomplished.
Natural change and thought's exaltation are confused when mentioned.
The window's silver silence enthralled and changed the descender.
Suddenly, then, there's another adjustment.
Their distaste for lying breath was established by more signs than unfolding
colors.
Simple disgrace can show one the quaintness of solitude.

The more they shouted together, the sweeter their recitation.
The sizes of all the center's chairs were clearer than yesterday's windows.

Other than violence what could secure that wretched collection?
Notwithstanding, they're withstanding cultivation more.
What tender color disordered yesterday's roundness?
Violent, refusing things connect together carelessly.
Mustard-like selection singles out a harder cover.
Mildred sometimes stopped them—a result of their *thing* together.
The colors of argument awkwardly address the showing of the actual.

Enough—enough uttermost elegance!
More ministering balloons!
His broader readiness there entirely resumed its blessings.
That shows volumes.
It changes the stitches.

Source: All of Stein's *TB*.

Seed: Stein's title "Mildred's Thoughts."

Method: Running source and seed through DIASTEX5; minimally revising the output, sometimes changing word order or changing or adding or deleting suffixes or helping words. Dividing the resulting sequence of verse lines into seven strophes successively comprising numbers of verse lines corresponding to the rising and falling prime-number sequence: 2, 3, 5, 7, 11, 7, 5.

New York: 1–4, 21–22 August 2000

Is Adventure Feeling That Occasioned It?

(Stein 133/Titles 30)

Is adventure feeling?

They stamp some substances and make others—very melodiously.
Everything was selected necessarily with serene restraint.

The arrangement of facts is no more sudden than the straw's there.
That handsome occasion educated her more than has been indicated.
Does education add different colors to a place?

The stern symmetry of that earnest comb ripened its valor and large calm.
Nothing springs from simultaneous sacrifice resulting from division.
The four have no more safety there than this.
There below the section where a question was bestowed came a chair.

To the suggestion of an erection a question is added, but by whom?
The sky can symbolize more by coming to be very solid.
Tidiness adjusts the attention of gamboling fish-diminishers.
So they've decided to hear straw mentioned no more?
An indecisive quarrel fastened on the location of the dishes that occasioned it.

Source: All of Stein's *TB*.
Seed: Stein's title "Idem the Same/A Valentine to Sherwood Anderson."
Method: Running source and seed through DIASTEX5; minimally revising the output, sometimes changing word order or changing or adding or deleting suffixes or helping words. Dividing the resulting sequence of verse lines into five strophes successively comprising numbers of verse lines corresponding to the integer sequence: 1, 2, 3, 4, 5.

New York: 22–23 August 2000

Substance Writing

(Stein 134/Titles 31)

Substance.

Callous being.
Change light redness.

And an order, something.
Pin fine singly mentioned detainers.
Wish a place, blue flat lily.

Surfaces have this thing's spectacle cleansing *and*.
Indications made six fires, sending songs considerably cooling.
Nothing: a place clashes small grey sides, cases things.
Standing light, necessary *a* and *and*: same eight singular weights.

Wedding wetting evening; a plan: plans change grey shows washed brighter.
Than substituted, necessary, and only and scarlet lines: line lengths
particular, external.
Nothing actual practiced slender than only shown last white; winning joints
equal *and*.
Inside so kind center-length nothing, raining calling a perfectly old (that very
sectional) way.
Onion thing roast beef necessity, any *and* and some difference, kind lengths
leaning: reasonable nothing.

A poisonous all weak praying spread earnest chickens; things whistled *chairs*
and *in* and said *ministered*.
Single bigger staring bedding blaming a purr, claiming, claiming burying
slender, raising blinder dinner together: clouds and . . .
And ordinary sentence violence: none long sacrifice recognition, denting,
and pink glass (what?); they so make quivering pain.
Potatoes necessary and an *and*-sample, single language gurgle inclines original
talking arrangement, perfect plain reason; many seasons take fright.

Plan solitude; necessarily a knife and scissors mistake singularly slight
teasing, choking, rushing, a period old chain very so bad.
This cunning potato plates *and* and cuddles sprain-time lunches, gauging
surging, cocoanuts seeding asparagus pitting glass, reading very,
soup's particular principle.

Principal questions leave *and*, and *and* supposes little dinner-weights remain,
leading, winning all peculiar old oranges only since salad scissors
tunny-sweet Chinese.
All ending suggestions differ; longer heights, cooking nothing, wait and
pleasure all: chairs, they suppose, can fail mean questions; supposing
arises, and suddenness.
Summer dispositions mention single, sensible, lessening evenings; a paper
sleeps that they so cadence quiet than meant *always* and *in*, and
strings disgrace none.
Bright furnished currents, reliable and placardly climates, that tray strangely
has writing change, slanting shoals are, and order saving pieces
considers single smiling nothing exchange.
And plain, plain that—very; some has this rain; something's right and,—
and,—and,—and,—and surely windows can haughty hanging seasons
peck and pedestrianism please.
Chairs, very sugary callous beings, change light redness and an order;
something pins fine, single, mentioned detainers wishing a place;
blue flat lily surface has this thing.
Spectacle cleansed and indication made six fires send songs considerably
cooling nothing, a place clashing small gray sides, case things
standing light, necessary *a*'s and *and*s: same eight.

Singular weighty wedding wet evening, a plan; plans change, grey shows
washed brighter than substituted necessary and only and scarlet line,
line lengths particular, external, nothing actually practiced.
Slender than only shown last, white winning joints equal, and inside so
kind center length, nothing raining calls a perfectly old,—that very
sectional way,—onion thing roast beef necessity.
Any and some difference, kind lengths, lean, reasonable nothing: a
poisonous all, weak praying spreading, earnest chickens' things
whistling chairs in and saying, Minister single bigger staring,
bedding blaming a purr.

Claiming, claiming, bury slender raises, blinder dinners together, clouds,
ordinary sentence violence, no long sacrifice recognition, denting,
and pink glass: what they so make quiver, pain potatoes necessary
and sample single languages.
Gurgles incline original talking, arranging perfectly plain reasons many
seasons, taking fright, planning solitude's necessity; a knife and
scissors mistake singularly slight teasing, choking, rushing a period
old chain; very so bad this.
Cunning potato plates and *and* cuddle sprains; timed lunches gauge surging
cocoanuts seeding asparagus pits; glass reads very soupy particular
principals, principally questioning leaves; *and* and *and* suppose little
dinner weight remaining, leading, winning.
All peculiar old oranges, only since salad, scissored tunny sweet, Chinese
all, and ended suggestions' different longer heights, cooking
nothing; waiting and pleasuring all chairs, they supposed cans'
failing meant questions supposed arising—and suddenly.
Summer dispositions mention single sensible lessening evenings; a paper
sleeps that they so cadence quiet than meant *always*, and *in* and
string disgrace none; bright furnished currents rely and placard
climates; those trays, strangely, have writing.

Source text: All of Stein's *TB*, which I half-heartedly scrambled to make this poem.
Seed text: Stein's title "Saints and Singing: A Play"
Method: I first ran the source and seed texts through DIASTEX5. Despite the program's repeating itself exactly after a certain point, I kept all the words in the output except the last 38 (which were not retained because of the number patterns described below) and a few *ands*. I revised some words by changing or adding suffixes, but I never changed the word order. During composition I divided the resulting word sequence into verse lines that comprise, successively, numbers of words following the integer sequence 1 through 36, punctuating, italicizing, etc., as seemed appropriate, and dividing the sequence of verse lines into eight strophes successively comprising numbers of verse lines corresponding to the integer sequence 1 through 8.

New York: 23–25 August 2000; 31 August, 5 September 2001

A Likely Difference
Is a Little Like Wisdom

(Stein 135/Titles 32)

A likely difference is a little like mustard.

That's a little like the kindness of the latest research on cattle.
Dirt cushions that appearance.

A likely circle's tassel of gratitude was losing to a desperate little system and a lily.
Lilies distance dust a little.
A large will is likely to mistake that little bit for the best.

What a letter nicely loses are the little roses.
Mildred's restitution is a likely little case.
It likely mingles custom and cotton.
Let that lining have a ribbon.

A large time ago they were last wetting any lamp that circulated signs of disease.
Be assured that they were left dusty and empty and discolored by lead.
With the best away, the middle was long.
Just its length and width distinguish that from custom.
What a long, circular line!

What else would have lifted that and left it just as it had last left it?
Long missing is like all leaving.
That was the right little lesson.
The best piece is in the center.
A bitter likeness is best.
Is anything astonishing?

Lying about her size is disgraceful.
A spot was left.
This time her sister simply resumed the footpath with her sister.

Anything for the ladies but mild custard?
The feather was a little light.
He was a little reserved.
That's a little absurd.

They are learning that life is better when leaning farther.
Bidding has hurt them a little.
She was picked because of her little laugh.
His lip was white.
Of all those little rings on it, that one was the best.
It's likely he was a little past letting goat milk aid him.
She is certainly discriminating about her asparagus, fish, and custard as well as her linen!
The longer the resumption of dirty singing the lengthier the birthday.

Inside they are large and silver.
All that distemper makes little difference.
That one was just a little like the last one.
Leave the one in the middle that has that laugh.
What a little case!
A little liberty was rising like a feather.
Yesterday the sentence was withdrawn.
The long lilacs disturbed that section of the lining.
Her letter largely withers where it rests.

That one has a light resemblance to the little dirty one in the middle.
That lamentable line of music is a little astonishing.
His resignation restrained the louder mischief altogether.
What was that little lamb's instruction?
Anyone loving fish mushes that language witness's basting best and a little pint best bitten and again a little mill basting best and a little pint best bitten again and a little mill basting best and a little pint best bitten again and a little mill best bent on being likely disappointed has that mixture lightly rescued.
No single dusting is a likely unstrangeness.
A mind rises to that lucky seat.
A little fine likeness beside the best likeness has that little gas next and a lack.

Was that white bird rushing a little?
Is it likely that little wine is the best?

That piece was messed up in the post a loud time west.
She likes to aim at a little less meat.
A little is best with oysters.
A laughable little fish cautioned another.
A long, mussy display may result from a large wine and a likely little custard
    if the custard makes one ache.
That little hill has better asparagus.
Her sight rested on the butter as she tasted the wide loaf.
He mostly tasted little particular bits.
The mussel was a little wide and dirty, alas.
Loaves of Western pastry are a little less violet than the rest.
Did he have a little fit when they said "niggers"?

Yes.
What did a little piece of that land cost?
The best all cost the least.
Leave the rest of that cider mass in the bin.
He labored beside an oyster.
Neither was loosened.
Rose butter is all they've lacked since that lighter time.
Her letter bestowed less than a fast little piece.
All that lifting disturbed his liver.
She adopted all the leaves.
Their distribution was an instance of lingering bestowal.
At that time her sister left her mister.

That little sign did littler than their absence.
They left a lesson in the window.
Was that a living silence?
It was less of a feat than the letter.
Was the loss of likeness fitting or a disaster?
What else was likely?
A little disorder containing a little tidiness.
The hill certainly destroyed its descender.

Since he signed his resignation he's lived a dimmer mixture of resistance
and lying.
His life had lost its filter.
Her giving had been lessening since the distance of their lives had passed a
little line.
All he was looking for was a little light rest.
It's like simple fastenings that mastered winter and led to a single
resemblance to quite awkward sin dishes.

Little that's visible rests on that.
It has as little light as any lover or distractor has white.
A location that size is assuring.
It has a lap sign that all the others lack.
Liking a line in the center the cases' resemblance is just a lilac light.
Was that liking like white light's resolution to lilac light?
That's not likely.
It's appearance cushions the circle of what's best away.
It's light with a mistake.
In that case a little singing would be no disgrace.
Let the cattle mingle.
Distant wingèd silver dust is no restitution for loss.
Losing that little disease assured his rest.
What a long line distinguishes the customary length and width from what
lifts the widow's learning to wisdom!

Source: All of Stein's *TB*, scrambled to make "Stein 134/Titles 31" and rescrambled to make this poem.

Seed: Stein's title "A List."

Method: Running source and seed through DIASTEX5 and then making sentences from the lexical words that are relatively near each other in the program's output and most of the helping words, but freely adding, deleting, or changing suffixes and helping words as well as changing the words' order from that in the output.

Form: Fourteen strophes that successively include numbers of verse lines corresponding to the integer sequence 1–14.

New York: 26–28 August 2000

The Cushiony Band Top Is Chancy

(Stein 136/Titles 33)

The cushiony band top rapidly questions the substances though their resemblances are clean, for they're the same.
Their copper chairs spit at obligation's natural sweetness.

That carafe has no hope that indications make the cracking of the indicated particles doubtful.
Suppose that the incident substituted a constant but scarcely the darkness of a chance bag.
The cup's entire length was a crystal disgrace.

Instead of "change" say "separation."
In addition, regular ladies are direct.
Needless to care, man.
That's an expression of reliability.
How's your chest?

Asparagus entirely curtains their deliberations about reparations.
At length their overtaking whistles seemed to resemble courage.
On Saturday the cup minister counted separation as a fact suitable to be complained about.
Supposing the mountainous ladies at the recital are beautiful, they're still certainly vague.
The calmness of their delight in superposition resembled something like nausea.
Cutting the water, they repeated that they loved the vacation despite its regulation.
Those with capital pensions could again have the constant sight of the basting cup.

Though talking about the cup, the article roasted that special cheese instead.
Intent on cloaking its likeness to water, they ordinarily didn't dip it up.
Dainty and solitary, nothing martial caused Cage's explanation.

It was natural that they chained up the cut potatoes tightly on Tuesday.
That makes the supply of stripes a bit questionable.
This is one way vegetables are capable of being unequal.
Suppose the chain-boats *were* relet and excreated, what can be accomplished by establishing that?
The wall was replaced to satisfy ordinary questions as formerly.
The change made the copper snail resemble a doubtful substance.
Did their eyeglasses come to be separated from their upper beginning positions?
Its resemblance to an apple can be plainly seen at length though its delicacy is special.

Her changing pallor could not be established.,
They chose to penetrate her separately.
Carefully she removed the curved cake.
They carefully separated the entire elastic without quarreling over the separation.
Having carefully copied the darkness in its center, that made the monster recite.
Asparagus had accumulated in the center as they danced.
The sight disgraced the painful roundness of the circle.
He's such a card!
The Japanese were polishing a substance that increasingly resembled a cover.
I hope this is an indication of the presence of the particles.
Currently all the indications are darkly doubtful.
They easily hoped for a special spectacle.
Their umbrella is chancy.

Source: All of Stein's *TB*, scrambled to make Stein 134 and rescrambled to make this poem.
Seed: Stein's title "Capital Capitals."
Method: Running source and seed texts through DIASTEX5 and then making verse-line sentences from the lexical words that are relatively near each other in the program's output and most of the helping words, but freely adding, deleting, or changing suffixes and helping words as well as changing the words' order from that in the output.
Form: Six strophes that successively include numbers of verse lines corresponding to the prime-number sequence.

New York: 29–31 August 2000

What Center Was Singing Dark Messages?

(Stein 137)

what center was singing there?

notwithstanding negligence, did resemblance attract the present success?
natural exchanges are desperate
some feel plain success

when were holes' calamities welcome?
cleansing the whole, that nice cut shows gratitude's illustrative
everything established discrimination's complications
obstruction disappointed discrimination

notwithstanding many extraordinary hats
many tables, perhaps more differences
desperate resignation
recognition prepared the restitutions simultaneously
notwithstanding more streams, more cutting was curious
music makes no bones, not ever easily
beer means not not not showing

pensions' anticipation is exceptional
notwithstanding the institutions
churchianity, stripes and rudeness
and then, strangely placed, slighter rounder answers
a color to color feeling
success, attractive at present
resembling relaxation does not cover indication
nothing shows gratitude
illustration established everything
the complications of discrimination disappointed the obstructors
extraordinary discrimination notwithstanding

the choice being to celebrate cultivation
some climb with desperate resignation
recognition of preparatory arrangements
don't surroundings have ways?
and she finally substituted standing
division restrained and sided with whomever else had ever been shining
no complexion dirtier than necessary
a frightful purse
the chain purse
chance decent'rings open chains
cake results are hardly occasions
just a little white winning
no round reason was shining
enthusiastically showing shaving
cutlet, not eyesight
likenesses are difficult
discrimination is obstruction
disappointed extraordinarily, discrimination notwithstanding

Europe's resolution and little stripes
little whistles differ exceptionally, institutions notwithstanding
even cutting rudeness is white
disappointingly analyzed but not red
new slighter, sounder obligations of precocious courage are established
circulating suggestions is not necessarily diminishing
not exchanged after slender, necessary concentration
the seen never shows nothing
almost eyesight likeness
difficult discrimination obstructed disappointment
and preparation and even elephants even
supposing which asparagus abundant
rudimentarily analyzed?
and again a single red was furnishing the chairman with a stranger medicine
occasional adventures
sugar makes certain questions venture nonsense
enough everything when connections weigh cigarettes

establishing each excess cloister, supposed it necessary
stretching accentuation is exaggerating resignation
no mean spread is ever revered
comb every open purple
silver heat remains
could not but be relieved by egg plant preparation
and made very occasional preparations likely
preparation of occasions and an *and*
so time spread needed standing and this temporary lifting
returning? darkening? expecting? no, not yet established
open when single
little right doubt triumphant showed

everything showed that even silence organized frequent brushing
and with the living not very enthralled there, when?
there the scene is always shown between scissor raindrops
no lying eclipse is little enough
careful separation was disturbing
no quarreling because of defiance of paper vacancies
the water changes and every little organization changes
correction was not more righteous because of the sweetness of that location
sizing makes careless occasions
exercise any wide slippers a and an
an extraordinary discrimination notwithstanding
in any case an elephant drowning
clouds not abundant
but not even things added and white pins
not even the sight
a negative sore hanging there is doubtfully something tyrannical
tardy separation and much unprecedented peaceful shining
reliability and resonance strengthen ordinary prisons

and besides, no divisions resulted in a solitary suggestion
circumstances' regulations accomplish obligingness notwithstanding
pedestrianism supposes appearance there
for it was done

and which justice?
asparagus painful?
round be resemblance's color
callous present resembling is an indication of relaxation, not cover
nothing elegant
when connections have more covers
laxer corners, lighter cakes

everything than be colored
seltzer particles are occasionally slender needles
melodiously august standing there on the surface
tender central
this reliability is nothing valuable
the plate and the roast beef
dinner incidents are certainly occasions

recognition makes centers entire
which way restraint?
distinguish not
it has been shown that cutting desertion is not everything

notwithstanding more sacrifices
notwithstanding the care flowers save
no round cooking-height stomachs notwithstanding

only dark messages

Source: All of Stein's *TB*, scrambled a few times to make Stein 134–36 and rescrambled to make this poem.

Seed: A long sentence from the last paragraph of *TB*: "The sensible decision was that notwithstanding many declarations and more music, not even notwithstanding the choice and a torch and a collection, notwithstanding the celebrating hat and a vacation and even more noise than cutting, notwithstanding Europe and Asia and being overbearing, not even notwithstanding an elephant and a strict occasion, not even withstanding more cultivation and some seasoning, not even with drowning and with the ocean being encircling, not even with more likeness and any cloud, not even with terrific sacrifice of pedestrianism and a special resolution, not even more likely to be pleasing."

Method: Running source and seed texts through DIASTEX5 and then making verse line from the words in the program's output, but freely adding, deleting, or changing suffixes and helping words as well as changing the words' order placements of word strings throughout from those in the output.

Form: Thirteen strophes that successively include numbers of verse lines corresponding to the rising and falling Lucas-number sequence 1, 3, 4, 7, 11, 18, 29, 18, 11, 7, 4, 3, 1. The strophes' relative placements on the pages were determined by a method involving die throws in which repetitions were disregarded.

New York: 29 August–4 September 2000

Carafe Resembling Chair Centre

(Stein 138/Titles 34)

carafe resembling size strangely losing wetting disease coffee

seltzer size strange behind sullenness educated consists
been sizes strange cleaner returned

suppose chance beside size remains

kindness uneven whistles courage best size remainder learning

student
interleaved certainty very puzzle separate chain sudden silence
chart see size sugar behind beginning recollection

custard be razor strange eaten remain relieve cut belows size
separating likeness reason disorder coats mean size
metal making design flowered change needed sizing
organization moment curving example chair centre
size strangely losing wetting disease coffee
seltzer size strange behind sullenness educated consists
been sizes strange cleaner returned
suppose chance beside size remains
kindness uneven whistles courage best size remainder learning

student
interleaved certainty very puzzle separate chain sudden silence
chart see size sugar behind beginning recollection

custard be razor strange eaten remain relieve cut belows size
separating likeness reason disorder coats mean size
metal making design flowered change needed sizing
organization moment curving example chair centre

Source: All of Stein's *TB*. Seed: Stein's title "Cezanne." Method: Sending source and seed through DIASTEX5, replacing uppercase letters by lowercase, eliminating left-hand indentations, and centering everything. All words and their order and spelling and repetitions, as well as all line and strophe breaks, from the program's output. Form: Eight strophes of 1, 2, 1, 1, 3, 9, 3, and 4 lines, respectively.

New York: 4–5 September 2000

And Even You Elephants?

(Stein 139/Titles 35)

And even a place?
A sounder one.

Whose hanging showed a desperate resignation?
Recognition and restitution prepare extreme pleasure.
Amusing concentrated heaviness can be splendid.

Circulating cigarettes distinguish resignation.
Exuding recognition won't enlarge all circumstances.
Consider an entirely reasonable description.
Would such a description coagulate recognition?
And what would it express?

Glass.
Four sincerely intentional gliders resigned.
Instruct us to recognize persecution.
Can't all eyes recognize it?
All could.
Nothing's enclosing space, necessity's originary institution.
Which choking explanation is even a sauce for the crestfallen?

We seconded singular eucalyptus preparations.
What preparations?
Isn't that strangely prepared asparagus soup too glassy?
Merciful heating is necessary for cooking.
Have straight descriptions of preparation disappeared?
Can glass establish erections?
Frequently astonishing cooking restores resignation to birthdays.
Resignation and brushing can be especially wetting conundrums.
Lengthening daylight and preparing for penetration are examples of alleviation.

Would counting plates and burning placards distract a mercenary opportunist?
Can Justice's splendid declarations withstand even you elephants?

Source: All of Stein's *TB*. Seed: Stein's title "An Elucidation." Method: Sending source and seed through DIASTEX5, and revising the output into sentences by changes of word order, affixes, and "helping words." Form: Five strophes comprising numbers of verse-line sentences corresponding to the prime-number sequence.

New York: 28 September–7 November 2000; 22 December 2001

Those Tender Arrangement Hours Will Turn White

(Stein 140)

Those tender arrangement hours will exchange extreme mercy for
monstrous cunning.

They're at the top.
I believe the reckless are suggesting disappointing things.
Stationary ways shatter and scatter where everyone is scattering.

Ways and uses of shape changing are doubtful but not too slender.
The success of all lilies resulted from one lily's having stopped.
Time enabled us to diminish that large dusty weight.
They speeded the handling of seltzer.

We made that hat there and wave it very well.
Pick a binding.
It was all broken but they mended it.
They exchanged rubbings.
That extra element is drawing more astonishment than expected.
Don't press anything between these mounted spats.
I say this tiny green and white bare spot is not a thing leading to closure.

What a beautiful little turkey!
There was much beautiful wailing.
The error of the whole exhibition is sacrificing certainty for quantity.
That division is something shunning anything to present youths' early
exclamations.
That exceptional separation of juice is not necessarily eating.
Staggered sprinkling wet these glasses.
Surpassing suffering is a way of continuing.
When countering orange moisture on steady little plates be open and kind.
With a seat that cuddles cheese make more loud white breakage in time.

That dark display had met another polite widening.
Remain leading where bland clothes mean dressing this-a-way.

That hat and that pudding and horse were mean.
Were they earning exchanges of apples?
Why was that hill ready?
They organized useless brushing and bought exercises.
What were they cooking for the wedding?
Neither eggs nor dressing.
Cutting in to lay his sold neck on the table, he was neither winning nor quarreling.
Whist! whist!, woodling—is it extra?
This silver center was where this tender change was done.
Burnt behind the question, the sister suggested an entrance thing, Mister!
Exercise diminished excitement.
The chair mentioned starving discrimination through doubt.
Education is supposing beautiful expression.
Why is there anything?
Why is the ordeal there more sound than stubbly chance?
Is it likely that sound is reversible?
Another lacks fifty objects.
The Chair complained that the season's overbearing clouds were mistakes.

Sacrifice all haughty slippers to the weather.
Safe weather is best.
The callous will even sing of reckless gratitude.
What makes them reasonable?
Greatly exaggerating fainting can sometimes cause doubling.
Suppose it was showing up as wet weather with breaking joy and obligation everywhere.
Suppose the nearest piece precise.
Expression may have manifold consequences.
That white break is silver in the middle.
Black and yellow holders aren't quite so much guided as exchanged.
Many are kindly.
Is it an even exchange?

Many of them are making plenty of occasions for counting and choosing them.
Are they expected to be as courteous as they're tall and tardy?
The nearest oranges' exudations smell good.
Everything's settled and understood.
What is equal to sound?
Their kitchen discriminates between likenesses.
A little kindly looseness, please!
Tin makes wailing there simpler.
Another who succeeded had been sadder yesterday.
She really sacrificed really solidly!
What splendid nausea!
Tender darkness was gliding behind like an undertaker,
Whole feathers vary.
All blazing corks have the resignation of language instructors.
If a piece is precise must it be sound?
What a little seedling!
What makes a little section exceptional?

Was early fright piercing her solitude?
White unstrangeness is working by standing there.
This shows the easy shady sauce that has a slight cold shadow.
What does?
Nine blazing questions curled the searching principal.
Chain-boats widened the woodling section.
Every copper exercise was perfect there.
Dressing in leaves would truly resemble every oyster's using sunshine.
May strongly fainting cover a cunning black gate?
It was quite red.
Shall we relet that confusing chamber?
They were connecting the smaller and separating the others.
Any organised succession is lengthening a distance.
So brushing has breadth?
Because of a little bottle's barometer lines the lake was monstrous.
The life in the lake lacked sectional curving.
They were trimming and trimming that white thing.

What if anything make all books mention hanging and pecking?
A cup of hair sudden places astonishing clouds amid separation lightning.
Nothing narrow was aiming to turn.
Cut a white white stone even excessively if necessary.
One incident was substituted for the really dirty exchange.
Does it say *pole house* there?
Are you grinding reasonable things together?
Cranberries suggest languid distress.
The salad was singularly better in the center.
I hope that the whole thing is settled.
Harder!—very much harder!
At length it was like a birthday.
What ancient hands exchanged those blackened things?
What was eloping compared to touching coal?
They were learning to preserve what they'd exchanged for housing.
It was sadder yesterday when they really had to sacrifice.
Is it even that even?
Which if any were standing there?
Please have a splendid resignation!
Her standards have tender piercing unstrangeness.
She was standing in the cold exceptional shadows.
Fright pierced her shady solitude.
Their chamber lacked even one solid connection.
His early language was ablaze.
What nausea?
Does any oyster leave a blaze?
All corks instruct us to narrow our undertakings.
What is a woodling chain-boat?
He is seeding the darkness with questions.
The books mention nothing about their aiming to turn white.

Source text: All of Stein's *TB*.

Seed text: A fragment (found on a note I made of Anne Tardos's Paris hotel room's telephone number 9/6–9/00) from the penultimate strophe of Stein 30 (7/19/98), an early poem in

the "Stein" series: "truly expressing what any one is sounds a little like what another has heard. Walking and talking is existing. What they said can be quite exciting."
Method: Sending source and seed texts through DIASTEX5, and then making verse-line sentences from words gathered from various parts of the output. Modifications were made in the lexical words' affixes, word order, etc., and some "helping words" (structure words, pronouns, forms of "to be," etc.) were modified, inserted, or deleted. Composition was stopped when I had nearly exhausted the output of DIASTEX5, using at least once each of the root morphemes of the output's lexical words (including the partial repetition of the output word string that takes place when this program is utilized), and I had made enough verse-line sentences to fill all the strophes in the following form.
Form: Eight strophes comprising successively numbers of verse-line sentences corresponding to the Lucas-number sequence.

New York: 7–10 September 2000; 6 September 2001

Are Pens Replacing Yesterday?

(Stein 141/Titles 36)

Are pens replacing tears with negative sight?

Prepared elastic is furnished to flat objects.
It's plain that desperate methods may be handy.

Present your changing fancies together.
Orderly occasions may be collapsed by someone pointing to them.
Convincingly pointing collapses occasions of order.

Planned empty places surround our venturesome journeys.
Does circulation lengthen a spectacle or crack it?
What's the ordinary practice?
If only that green chain were a lesson!

Wondering at country practices, I ordered plates to match them.
Are those mountings habitual?
Crusty chance exchanges obstructions for occasions.
That supposes tender orderly pigeons practicing staring.
Practice can shut down pretences of practice.

Are all your sentences in place?
Either variety of pain can thoroughly melt her.
Breakfast changes practice.
Shelter can be delicious when practically neglected.
Ordinary oranges may change to white shadows.
She procures a wheatly path through the proud meadows.

Why don't they experiment on bunches of vegetables instead?
Our little sister, for instance, may press for a mean enclosure instantly.
The pleasure of harmony is that of a chair.
Startling starving tendencies are only indicated on that green plain.

That disturber will destroy whatever peace arises from without.
That special something defies and changes distance.
Often a tree space hints at the harmony of ribbon preparation.

That pond is practical.
Those haughty distractors are mercenary monsters.
Slant!
Who cares if they purchased that bridge?
Their small captures differed narrowly.
They pleased the crackers that season.
Which decision about light did the research mention?
Bright elastic buttons are so yesterday!

Source text: All of Stein's *TB*. Seed text: Stein's title "Practice of Oratory." Method: Running source and seed through DIASTEX5; various revisions of output including changes of word order; insertions and deletions of affixes and "helping words" (structure words, pronouns, forms of "to be," etc.) to make sentences retaining the root morphemes of lexical words. Form: Eight strophes successively comprised of numbers of verse-line sentences corresponding to the cardinal-number sequence 1 through 8. The poem's title indicates that that this is the 141st poem in my series "Stein" (begun April 1998), made by drawing words from works by Gertrude Stein, mostly by the diastic method, and revising the output to various extents; it is also the 36th poem in the subseries "Titles," in making which I use as "seed texts" for diastic text selection titles of works by Stein collected in *ASR*.

New York: 17–27 September, 29 October 2000

Hurt Stranger

(Stein 142/Titles 37)

Hurt resembling "A" in red.

The Change.

There very handsome mercy, some giving behind string shallow beefsteak,
necessity having certainly an in.
And thick?
Thin.
The praying hold revered comb obligation,
clean rising sparrows.
Practical?
Certainly has rests and in and that.
This even?
Very.
Has.
Be something!
Splendor?
Stranger.

Source text: All of Stein's *TB*. Seed text: Stein's title "He and They, Hemingway." Method: Running source and seed through DIASTEX5; minimal revision of output: line breaks, capitalization, punctuation, one added "n."

New York: 27 September 2000

A Blind Cousin? No.

(Stein 143/Titles 38)

A blind cousin was unordered.

At the nickel cover hour a sinecure for mercy was unlikely.
Callous mustard suggested disappointing stationing.

That's the way silk and cotton are light.
And are the wagon signs different?
Three are the same.

The last is curious.
How is it a loss?
No giving freely was shown.
The other shows were starting to resume—every one.

No shows pick chance to grace their little, habitual separations long.
Lightening and blackening, the white sign gets to be such.
A wedding piece is different.
More have the taste of ham than a chance.
To powder the bone that is left, have more sweets.

It shows there.
Early hopes are choices.
A pocketful of cheese does it gently.
A chicken result of solitude widened ordinary excitement.
Surpassing worsted, little sets are much more.
Are a witness's widening suffering nose holes bad or best of all?

The climbing cows develop likely colors.
Sausages cross them and hurry to mercy in bed rows.
Cooking is back.
Chicken's a word.
At dinner a piece was bundled with the conclusion.

The husband's suggestion had a consequence.
Separating which?

It was fitting, yet nothing.
When is it a little different?
A green hill makes a disturber,
Color's not always alive.
No.
Giving a likely seduction, the stream will slowly empty.
A bottle is no store for a cook, a cook no hanging place for little creatures.
Solitude disturbing obligingness and everything, why is there a time rate?

They were Catholic.
Their suffering was big.
All the same, to be haughty and safe is best.
No cracker was unwelcome or liked not covering like.
Supposing it's violent there!
I fancy a closet would be best.
Silk cleaning to concentrating, their sincerely single.
Surrounding Mildred's attractive selection, everything had its width.
The piano didn't show the widow is wise or the sofa necessary.

Hope has a chance.
They were new but weren't for long.
They had the same stomach, and more.
The flower was nearly a fairy.
Bidding nothing for the whole, they're looking for a choice.
Where's a hole for a little resolute monkey?
They paper over discrimination, exudation—everything—but distinguish nothing.
What is weak and has a different size?
The older ones have gates.
It's a case of a clear collection.

Powder the left one.
Have more sweet bone.

It shows there early.
Hopes are chosen by the pocketful.
Cheese does it gently to chickens.
Solitude does not ordinarily widen excitement.
Its result may surpass it.
The little sets were widened and worsted by witnesses.
It was so their nose holes suffered.
Best of all was to climb up to the cows.
That someone would develop multicolored sausages was more than likely.

Mercy crossed the bed rows in a hurry.
What is a word for cooking the back of a chicken?
The conclusion of the dinner was a bundle of pieces.
Was the husband's suggestion a consequence of their separation?
Which one was fitting, yet nothing?
When is a green hill a little different?
When its color's a disturber?
Not always.
Doesn't it live for giving?
No.
Their seduction was likely.
The stream slowly emptied there.

The cook was a cook.

He didn't store any bottles.
No little creatures were hanging in that place.

Solitude is disturbing.
Is obligingness everything?
Why?

What is it?
What's her rate?
Is she Catholic?
Is she big on suffering?

Some of them are haughty.
Are they safe?
The best of them are.
Are they crackers?
No.

Source text: All of Stein's *TB* rearranged by chance operations. Seed text: Stein's title "A Book Concluding with As a Wife Has a Cow: A Love Story." Method: Running source and seed through DIASTEX5 and revising the output by changing some affixes, word order, and helping words. Form: Seventeen strophes, comprising numbers of lines corresponding to two cardinal-number sequences: 1 through 12 and 1 through 5.

New York: 8, 28 October 2000

Victory's Saving Bent Was Kind of Green And Very Rudimentary

(Stein 144/Titles 39)

Victory's saving bent is toward a swan spectacle.

Pointing at glitter, it's surely been yellow.
Four were not necessarily made of color altogether.
The selection of colors in the sack was astonishing.

A splendid plan was compressed on a card whose color'd increased.
They were trembling from an incident whose consequence is current.
Yellow and very darkly monstrous they weren't left with much to exchange.
Plenty besides anything virgin were made single or trimmed.

They trimmed two pieces of shiny tomato—surely yellow.
The hurry at that very station clearly makes cuts a social certainty.
That vapor is excellent for splinters.
Praying does spread feathers around, a tolerable obligation.
The thirst of those authorities was an outrage.
Their certainty has nothing more than curliness.
That very same tender variety of exclamation is a temptation.

Authorities can practically succeed.
This means they make remarkable exchanges of utterly bitten colors for
stolen ones altogether mended till perfect again.
Not more separation than ordinary!
Suppose an explanation of a crestfallen sauce neglected a furnace.
Her very lack of languor meant she was necessarily less a vegetable.
Another caution: wash the dinner veal!
Oxen are only pie to owls.
It was an election anyway.

Yet that mean chair there does not mean something's a diversion.
Permission to shine the enclosure floor is an arrangement intended to make
    the room pleasurable.
The substance of a little memory is frequently startling.

A way of earning can come to be very sullen.
It couldn't contain that very seduction because nothing had lengthened.
A little curtain there tasted of varnish.
Can two trees be in line?
There are plenty of lights there, yet the religions quarrel.
The little cover's coloring shows.
The metal service once had color and size.

Indeed, his principles were narrow though he was quite cheerful.
They complained of the card more than of the tassel.
The willow vacation sacrifice left much of the center's victory.
The cattle sash in question was kind of green and very rudimentary.

Source text: All of Stein's *TB*. Seed text: Stein's title "Van or Twenty Years After, A Second Portrait of Carl Van Vechten." Method: Running source and seed through DIASTEX5 and revising the output by changing some affixes, word order, and helping words to make a series of verse-line sentences. Form: Seven strophes in which the number of lines follows a Lucas-number sequence which turns back on itself in the 6th strophe: 1, 3, 4, 7, 11, 7, 4.

New York: 8–26 October 2000

Is of in Obligation Exchange

(Stein 145/Titles 40)

Is of in,
that hour will handsome hardening will.

Come any cotton,
not come purple,
likely little connect disgrace;
mentioned piece,
coffee dirtier distincter color;
relaxation something restitution.

Of.

If plainer time,
necessary cigarettes,
shows pieces occasion is of.

If the song colored kind hearty disease,
time assured could border;
summer suppose settlement,
settlement substituted;
stretched preserved practical,
not more particularly;
color misplaced spreading eyesight of *of*.

Petticoat light necessarily because.

Roses curves,
addition is of it,
tall post,
all loud head life lime;
a.

Count,
count jam.

Elephant,
little reckless realistic resolute entangled particular.

Considering circumstances,
that reparation
restraint education;
description obligation.

If pigeon kitchen,
because separating shows
spoons division;
is of,
is that,
not splendid,
tender,
have kindness lamentable.

All cherries to temptation,
temptation little mingle character;
cherished neglected place,
not persecution that restraint;
relaxation determined explanation on,
of precisely;
piece sectionally,
separate grass spaces question;
instant of in this combing,
pull wedding heated with;
time acres chest,
how remain,
leap bundle,
bundle draught;
excreate respected place,
contradiction morning;

that floor,
similar established acquaintance,
ordinary;
of pleasure single reception,
clear means confusing;
position.

Is of,
is the collection,
silent mind have different come.

A construction,
not name supposing regulation weather connection mentioned,
mentioned preoccupation,
mourning ears;
southern color separation,
scientific administration;
of,
of practical little,
once shoals satisfactory,
reversible;
occasion it if in that,
no,
all cold had disappointment;
obligation exchange.

Source text: All of Stein's *TB*. Seed text: Stein's title "If I Told Him, A Completed Portrait of Picasso." Method: Running source and seed texts through DIASTEX5. I deleted the output where it began to repeat exactly (due to a glitch in the program) and revised the remaining output by breaking lines at chosen places, inserting punctuation marks at most line endings and inserting one- or two-line strophe breaks where there are similar paragraph breaks in the program's output. Form: Fourteen strophes made up of differing numbers of lines of various lengths.

New York: 25–28 October 2000

Glass Resembling Yesterday

(Stein 146/Titles 41)

Glass resembling program bargains
increases principles strengthening yesterday.

Glass tendered two suggestive
exteriorly special teacup astonishments.

Necessary gliding mended cloaking
single unstrange mountainous presuppositions.

Astonishing certainly gliding receivers
show single disorder miserable.

Constipation altogether certainly gathers
mercenary flowered emigration water.

Distracters principally researched strangely
green and red shows.

Hanging color relaxation
principally strengthened yesterday.

Source text: All of Stein's *TB*. Seed text: Stein's title "Geography." Method and Form: Running source and seed texts through DIASTEX5. I deleted the output a bit after it began to repeat exactly and it had "spelled out" the seed word seven times, and I divided the remaining output into seven couplets: six of four-word lines and a final couplet of three-word lines. As I did so, I retained the order of root morphemes, changed many suffixes, replaced one word with its homophone, and added an "and." I capitalized the first letter of each couplet and ended each one with a period. Finally, I modernized the spelling and centered the poem, title, and note.

New York: 9 November 2000

A Different Red Resigning

(Stein 147/Titles 42)

A different red has a mercy program principally spitting descriptions.
The descriptions coagulate simultaneous recognitions.
What are they of or who are they of?

Like likenesses of solitary water, none presents more delicious surrendering.
Astonishment does best between the sticks one never mounts.
Presupposed eucalyptus preparations are being prepared.
The obligingness of preparation is the obligingness of a looking glass.
The size of a little cover is coloring a recitation on emigration.
A righteous distemper is everywhere the denial of a weak case.
It's a coloring trick.

Bargaining is principally a certain exclamation of resignation.
Their instruction was on the unstrangeness of fine little sets.
Each remedy colors a separate present.

The asparagus extractor is reasonably dirty.

Mean Western specs and razors widen descriptions of astonishing
 acquaintances.
Resign to be resigning.

Source text: All of Stein's *TB*.
Seed text: Stein's title "Descriptions of Literature."

Method: Running source and seed texts through DIASTEX5. I deleted the output after it began to repeat exactly and mostly retained but sometimes changed the order of root morphemes, changed several suffixes, replaced one word with its homophone, and inserted several "helping words."

Form: Sixteen verse lines divided into five strophes. Line breaks were cued by those in the program's output and strophe breaks by its "paragraph" endings.

New York: 12 November 2000

Not a Single Spectacle in That Show Was Quite Visible

(Stein 148/Titles 43)

Not a single spectacle in that show was showing a tassel in painful earnest.

This silver system's adventure was an extreme success.
There singular silver particles were extracted in outward time.
The awkward holder of that suitable establishment was educated elsewhere.

This little one bought six.
The fire was not between the pencils.
Between what then?
Your entirely mistaken standards for linen were shown not to be singular
there.

Every particle of that education of yours was shown in this birthday.
The size of the snipe was betwixt and between.
Anyway her ageder trembling at the recital was little strengthened by not
chewing.
Its shape had largely a resemblance to an eye.
It had little weight in that white eddy.
The soup was nice but the nuts drew shame.
Their rental was accomplishing a standing for them.

Time had not shown the trouble condensed in that possible entrance.
He added that this which was so silver did not show the force of the trouble.
The special suddenness of her disposition was shown there in her
gamboling.
Was that eclipse of her education sensible?

It showed the entire show was another disgrace.
That was just another of fifteen singularities.
That single tablecloth was sound but a little awkward.

The accumulation was even quite visible.

Source text: All of Stein's *TB*.

Seed text: Stein's title "Sitwell Edith Sitwell."

Method: Running source and seed texts through DIASTEX5. I deleted the output after it began to repeat exactly and often retained but sometimes changed the order of root morphemes, changed many suffixes, and inserted a number of "helping words."

Form: Twenty-three verse lines divided into seven strophes in which the numbers of verse lines correspond to the waxing and waning Lucas-number sequence 1, 3, 4, 7, 4, 3, 1.

New York: 12 November 2000

Ordinary Buttons Hurt the Plates

(Stein 149/Titles 44)

Ordinary buttons hurt their clean, glittering systems.

Japanese roundness is in.
When they believed the rates,—what gratitude!
That custom was an illusion from some adventure catalog.

This box of the substance resulted in an indicated journey.
Cigarettes increased.
A certain compression of the incline broke it into many many colors.
Custom permitted occasions when they could be together.

He was altogether behind.
Their sullen rush was habitually tyrannical.
The collapse resumed.
Their outline is a blank.
He makes a delay by leaning on that watermelon.
The cranberries and vegetable bed at summer's resumption entangled us in
a distressing choice of circumstances.
But in taste, all sections remained distempered by the necessary divisions.

Resonance buried the surround.
It rested on the choice of a string design.
Vagueness soothes.
And besides, the volume way up disturbed us.
The sacrifice under those exterior circumstances influenced the intender.
Because of the authorities' instructions, they were loving brown coffee.
The persuasion by scissors in the bidding for sauce was not at all well done.
The stream in question was singularly teasing.
The cut vegetable was radiant.
Those little bolsters on the chain-boats might have been needless.
It was in and will be below.

What section of the bottom was questioned by the stranger?
An artichoke bended the sum bestowed.
The action given in the center remains established.
Can any be made for holding the fact retained?
Their tidiness is and has been all due to filtering a special stream for
    everybody.
Together they were altogether bright.
His insistence mastered the supper.
There are blisters in the administration's scientific darkness.
All that burning circumstance was beautiful but vacant.
Their locations were together.
This translated into much of the case being active.
Silence pleases.
Notwithstanding our surprise, they were breathing.
They took care of all the buttons.
To my cousin, the system was altogether unwelcome, but the furniture was
    substantial.
The message is in the design of the lining.
They're exaggerating success established in the washing.
Those who weren't idle were washing the plates.

Source text: All of Stein's *TB*. Seed text: Stein's title "Business in Baltimore." Method: Running source and seed texts through DIASTEX5. I deleted the output after it began to repeat exactly and often retained but sometimes changed the order of root morphemes, changed many affixes, and inserted a number of "helping words." Form: Forty-four verse-line sentences divided into six strophes in which the numbers of verse lines correspond to the Lucas-number sequence.

New York: 13 November 2000; 31 October, 11 November 2001

likely difference grinding suggesting

(Stein 150/Titles 45)

likely difference
Supposing place matches grinding suggesting

<u>Source text</u>: All of Stein's *TB*.
<u>Seed text</u>: Stein's title "Lipchitz."
<u>Method</u>: Running source and seed texts through DIASTEX5. This is the unedited output. It ends after the seventh word because no word or name in *TB* has a "z" in the 8th place from the left.
<u>Form</u>: Two verse lines, one of two words, the other of five.

New York: 13 November 2000

What Torches?

(Stein 151/Titles 46)

What a carafe!

My cousin comes prepared.
Suppose the preparation surrounding restitution is resignation.
What callous leaves!

And is that an example of excess?
Suppose one could make an actual, elegant, necessary argument by complaining.
Would you resign?
She recognized the curtains around that simple summer.

Succor and restraint are necessities, considering those specialties.
Need a description of an exhibition be an exaggeration or can it be a description?
Does she superpose a smell on every certainty?
His curliness went unrepeated.
He exclaimed that he was astonished that he was instructed to resign.
She changed potatoes with the same respect for customary succession and restraint.
The necessity of the institution was explained to the crestfallen.

Prepare the eucalyptus after preparing for its preparation.
Is it clean?
No.
That summer soup is reasonable.
He left after selecting a straight preparation.
Is this a description of his disappearance?
If an established exaltation were replaced, would that replace what happened?
Her birthday was frequently an astonishing resignation to resignation.

His chance will come when she commences to have the necessary
disposition.
What disposition would that be?
Toward a painstaking reduction of penetration.

What preparation would alleviate it?

An elastic example of separation might build a surface outline of it.
Her singularity was a distracting opportunity for a declaration.
Notwithstanding, some chose to prepare torches.

Source text: All of Stein's *TB*.

Seed text: Stein's title "Composition as Explanation."

Method: Running source and seed texts through DIASTEX5. I deleted the output after it began to repeat exactly and often retained but sometimes changed the order of root morphemes, changed many affixes, and inserted a number of "helping words."

Form: Thirty verse-line sentences divided into seven strophes in which the numbers of verse lines correspond to the two successive Lucas-number sequences 1, 3, 4, 7, 11 and 1, 3.

New York: 13–14 November 2000

Scatter the Occasion

(Stein 152/Titles 47)

Scatter an absurd liquid in a stream, pounding particular blackening
cultivars.

Consider the circumstances of horticulture, which wither us with outrage.
Light, denting the very resemblance of space to water, is shunning our
teacups.
Coconut persecution is an institution with no explanation.

An accepted acquaintance was as triumphant as her husband was organized.
She's frequently indifferent to pleasant stupefication.
Circumstances disappointed "white rights" authorities.
Exchanging now seemed safer in black cases.

It was a surprise that the principal description was a description of
coagulation and not a recognition of the occasion.

Source text: All of Stein's *TB*.

Seed text: Stein's title "An Acquaintance with Description."

Method: Running source and seed texts through DIASTEX5. I deleted the output after it began to repeat exactly and often retained but sometimes changed the order of root morphemes, changed many affixes, and inserted a number of "helping words." I also retained Stein's favored form "stupefication" (which the OED calls rare and obsolete) rather than modernizing it to "stupefaction," because diastic consistency demands retaining it. [Ed. Note: This spelling also occurs in Stein 96 and Stein 117.]

Form: Nine verse-line sentences divided into four strophes in which the successive numbers of verse lines correspond to the Lucas-number sequence 1, 3, 4, followed by a one-line coda.

New York: 14–15 November 2000; 27 May 2002

That Tender Spectacle Is Bitter

(Stein 153/Titles 48)

That tender spectacle's likely difference is the difference between a vegetable
and an oyster.

The journeys of the curious wealthy, open and gray, are brighter.
Does this thing–the losing of a little excess coffee–discolor a certain state
which is only black?
If just that sudden green sign graces the white reason that long filled a
difficulty there, does this make those shining curves be judged as
real?

Gracious, gracious, the white show arises!
She sits a little differently.
The ladies in the depot placed wet white matches there.
What were their sizes?

If only the joy of a successful tea is turning its good order into a consuming
thing, is this everything?
Like sight suffering something, joy gurgles more than gently.
Does that article frighten you?
This smell is likely to come as a single awfulness.
And is that dog on a separate chain?
The height of the settlement was the old joy of cuddles.
That town was nearly green with the grand being that cuts.

They needed laughable little puffs.
This same ocean in just the summer season may be more wrong and white
than tenderly green.
That spectacle is likely to be different.
The differences of vegetables are interesting.
There was a delightfulness in venturing to get a place in the matches.
The curious got wealthy out of the journey
The open grays are brighter.

Does the thing they were loosing exceed a little coffee?
Just quite that even guided those who were housed.
When, like time, the sofa was necessary, it ended in darkness.
Was that necessarily frightful?

Only just as much as reason's plentiful grace was shining.

Those glasses make your likeness bitter.

Source text: All of Stein's *TB*.
Seed text: Stein's title "The Life of Juan Gris/The Life and Death of Juan Gris."
Method: Running source and seed texts through DIASTEX5. I deleted the output after it began to repeat exactly and often retained but sometimes changed the order of root morphemes, changed many affixes, and inserted a number of "helping words."
Form: Twenty-eight verse-line sentences divided into seven strophes in which the successive numbers of verse lines correspond to the Lucas-number sequence 1, 3, 4, 7, 11, followed by two one-line codas.

New York: 15 November 2000

Groan, Redwood Pressed Together

(Stein 154/Titles 49)

Gróan, redwood!—téars!: that thing's stripes húrt!

Óut with suggesting earnest places slighter than the glass showing its
rédness there!
Her obligation to change was due to her heavy success.
That líght change there was expécted.

Let enough extra delíghtfulness in!
Before they quite had light, they were largely given to fainting because of
their weight.
The wétting show is stárting.
It's been altogether compressed.

Summer cigarettes are sooner gone.
In wingèd cloisters they gathered 'round, extracting incidents together.
That hat is quite an argument!
Even there, green selections were seen and shown.
Óne of the umbrellas was enóugh.
Besides, they were hurting the buds.
They suddenly went blind together.

The climate guided them to remarkable woolens with nearly nothing
between them.
His hats and curls were enlightening things.
That green flower is a ticket to be whów* there? *[pron. "how"]
Thin pigeons have curtains, entirely resigned.
Spaces for desertion are good choices this week.
There was a single change.
Hair supposing pigeons is a bigger thing than the direction they go.
It means a spot is nearly a blackening thing.
Suppose we neglect a mountainous turkey.

Its weight might have gathered feathers.
Another íncrease in desígn choices might hurry the authorities.

Lighter than the subject of receptacles, gliding means to be showing béing there.
Coffee holes are guessed at sight.
The height of the grass there is cunning.
Altogether by chance, we saw holes there.
We guessed at that sight.
An altogether cunning pocketful, almost gently bent, showed retraction.
Widen the house!
Sugar the furnace tightly!
A tender, accepted, golden pet nearly got loose.
Being the handle of a hoary cup, its green was more neglected than its shade was sought.
Don't become estranged although the whole lounge is between you.
Hanging curled, the vegetable goes into the china butter receptacle.
This means it's cool there.
George's draft surprised her.
I suppose the tunny is a regular secret!
Your expecting a greater height of cóoking there is the thing to chánge.
What happened was much bigger.
Changing the bigger glass will never be shown to be essential.

Their startling, agreeable, worrying hairs quietly changed together.

There they admitted that gliding while receiving was a showy sacrifice.
The single thing they've signed off on is that sunshine is plentiful there.
After that necessary closer adjustment, they were gamboling there.

Lying there that evening, restless at that height, the sugary committees were surrounded.
I guess being the cook there changed him.
The curtain hinted at a change in their regret.
China insisted that mercenaries gathered and flowered there where little had changed.

Sugar or the chánce of sugar there made that moment of grace necessarily sickening.
Being overbéaring húrt whoever suggested places for themselves too earnestly.
The glass they showed there was ever-so-slightly red.
Her obligation to change was heavy.
As we'd expected, the light at the gate had successfully let enough extra delíghtfulness in.
Before the light had fainted quite, they were given a large weight.
Because the show had started, they were wetly pressed altogether.

Makingway and Delivery Endnote

Source text: All of Stein's *TB*. However, the order of its paragraphs had been scrambled by random-number chance-operations before it was utilized as a source text.

Seed text: Stein's title "George Hugnet."

Method: Running source and seed texts through DIASTEX5. I deleted the output after it began to repeat exactly and I often retained but sometimes changed the order of root morphemes, changing or adding several affixes and inflectional endings, and I inserted several "helping words." "Whow," pronounced and meaning "how" [OED], occurs repeatedly just before the end of part 1 of *TB*. I've retained it because it was obviously important to Stein as such and substituting "how" for "whow" would violate the output's diastic consistency. (One only modernizes word forms when doing so would not do that.) I allowed the use of the output as source text to continue for a few lines after it began to repeat exactly.

Form: Fifty-nine verse-line sentences divided into ten strophes in which the successive numbers of verse lines correspond to the two successive Lucas-number sequences 1, 3, 4, 7, 11, 18 and 1, 3, 4, 7.

Delivery: An acute accent indicates a stressed syllable. A four-letter space [   ] indicates a silence or phoneme prolongation as long as an unstressed syllable; an eight-letter space indicates a silence or phoneme prolongation as long as one stressed syllable, or beat.

New York: 15–16 November 2000; 26 February, 13–14 March 2001

Even Kindness Can Be Distant Noise

(Stein 155/Titles 50)

Even kindness can be red.
Its negative detainer is even distincter.

Every elastic thing could be quite a bit harder.
They feel the spectacle is desperate.
Unordered but even expected there, *this* kind's getting complicated.

Is increase ever an even thing?
That lead and silver spectacle is elegant.
Was it ever easily practiced?
The binding was shining there from being rubbed.
Their exchanges were handsome but misplaced.

Which of the houses were cold—even theirs?
Exchanging everything leaning on obstructions was not easy.
They tended to distinguish there the practical from the suitable.
Everything this one read made his eyes redder.
That remains a pretense for a sentence!
Even these evenings are misdeeds.
The mouse and the salmon had language instruction before their white
wedding.

Was *it* ever *early!*
Nothing practical was neglected for an instant of ease.
Every instance of seeding this white land has been an exchange.
Which of the houses were cold—even theirs?
This was the middle where every husband tended to indicate he was
enthralled.
Even sudden rain commences wetting without defiance.

They evaded the distant establishment by folding themselves up.
That hearing disgraced the separatists entirely.
Even these ponderous currents express a *practical* current.
Every excellent price is golden.
How can even pieces of wood be ingredients of a gold currency?

What's that distant noise?

Makingway Endnote

Source text: All of Stein's *TB*.
Seed text: Stein's title "Evidence."
Method: Sending source and seed texts through DIASTEX5, and revising its output. I deleted the output at the point where it began to repeat itself exactly, and by changes of word forms and order and some insertion of "helping words" not in the output, I turned each output line into one or two verse-line sentences. The whole series was divided into strophes.
Form: Five strophes whose numbers of verse-line sentences correspond to the prime-number sequence 2, 3, 5, 7, 11, followed by a one-line tailpiece.

New York: 18–22 November 2000

Mercy No More

(Stein 156/Titles 51)

Mercy—no, perhaps some giving—prepared them for this ordinary calamity.
The dirtier furniture was torn.

Fewer were contained on that side.
There reason and distance made for too long a time.
That trembling gray argument is regularly overtaken by fact.

Bend and rub that measure no more.
Would it be the same if I didn't?
You're misplaced and more handsome than graceful.
My crystalline charm is exemplary.
Those four tumblers were bought for any spread.

Send that winning letter—*send* it!
So does an obstruction of exchange have more meaning than good order?
There were more shadows than harmony in that gloomy recital.
Ordinarily there were four and no more.
In the safety of recollection they were sincere about anything seeding space.
After more instruction in the language they cooked more.
There were more gray breezes than solemnity in that room.

I was so nervous that I had constantly flaking blisters.
That dinner was real as a spool.
For instance, that coffee set me surging!
Her permission did not cover a very much greater erection.
He had more charm than substance.
It wasn't certain that all five would be discharged.
The hangings that season were a little smaller.
There some students' "delicacy" suddenly resembled circularity.

Giving breadth to the shadowed plums made the barometer more agreeable
at the equator.
For more color, none of the curtain strings was fastened.
Current practices are expressions of monsters, not of strange grains of time.
The youth flower together more and venture something like dedication
where the curving spectacle doesn't surprise the green morning.

They celebrate the wrong Chair no more.

Makingway Endnote

Source: All of Stein's *TB*.
Seed: Stein's title "More Grammar for a Sentence."
Method: Sending source and seed texts through DIASTEX5, and revising its output. I deleted the output at the point where it began to repeat itself exactly, and by changes of word forms and order and some insertion of "helping words" not in the output, I turned each output line into one or two verse-line sentences, whose series was divided into strophes.
Form: Five strophes whose respective numbers of verse lines correspond to the prime-number sequence 2, 3, 5, 7, 11, followed by two one-line codas.

New York: 20–21 November 2000; 18 June 2001

Hurting Colors Pleasing Crackers

(Stein 157/Titles 52)

Hurting colors are unwelcome there.

Sewing can sometimes be as convincing as breath.
She comes rapidly.
Then she's round and has red ones.

One blight is more than enough.
Those that clash are slender, but the plainer ones have holes.
How soon can that be at bowline speed?
The color holders were holding dirt and showing how frightful it was.

They were mounting a regular hurting, so the news was showing shudders.
They had boils there, not blue bows on, though they'd not been bare in the
stream.
His wrist was closing upon that laugh.
In his little leather hat and coat he was surrounded by the cows.
There—that's better!
Considering that powder, what makes us ask and hope for delicious
certainty?
Beer is their choice.

Anything white between you and another may hurt, so beware!
They were soaking that so the best color wouldn't get mixed there with a
cow tune.
The holes are real work.
The best are procured from that which is colored.
The plaster is more holy than the town.
Skate there!
That town makes mostly beads.
Some narrow clouds have to be better prepared for.
There's a butter boom on!

Why are her cocups so white?
How come she's so steady?

Her acre of butter is really come.
She's dressing the part, too.
The width in the center is lighter and has no separation now.
There there!
When between they always asked but added nothing.
No one has been burning the two that are smaller and more symmetrical.
Have his constructions always something there that's blue?
Where?
His connections were always mixed.
He built that room to be habitable.
Her religion's surface was blistered.
That looking glass was an ordeal.
Which monster in what chamber has more hands?
Powder the whole soldier!
Some monotony may be abundant now and then.
It's not his habit to wet more books.
Are the shows in the center haughty?
She has no pleasing crackers!

<u>Source</u>: All of Stein's *TB*.
<u>Seed</u>: Stein's title "How She Bowed to Her Brother."
<u>Method</u>: Sending source and seed texts through DIASTEX5, and revising its output. I deleted the output at the point where it began to repeat itself exactly, and by changes of word forms and order and some insertion of "helping words" not in the output, I turned each output line into one or two verse-line sentences, whose series was divided into strophes.
<u>Form</u>: Six strophes whose successive numbers of verse-line sentences correspond to the Lucas-number sequence.

New York: 17–25 November 2000

Is Has Breakfast The

(Stein 158)

Is? Has. Have green not to, but has red. That there roundness flat.

Cloak. Climb. Has silver. Some box purple. Not this the preparation.
Very and is. Makes mercy to spread. More is.

If wagon sign, extra light.
A flower, only way that white pieces brighter there than ever.
Many makes lead certainly more manifold. Substituted which?
Kindly? Not much.

A is width selection. Holder yellow is.
If is it is, is no complexion. Not away and open just.
Wondering.
Saucer? Saucer.
Objects.
If well, the blind places anything. The.
The. The rosy make remarkable reason.

This measured difference reserves head veil, has fairy, has in.
And received dear whole.
Asparagus.
Oranges.
Roast beef entangled it. And which tending thing length birthday?
Splinter besides.
Eyes lace worn case, satin rising, saving to sweeter.
Cloudiness, not sadder. Same more little, really the why.
The they no nausea, same resemblance, and is more surely receptacle.
Authority of, of not same eating that than ever very.
And present age of absent belt relieved change little.

> Painted a is, is it?
> It is be eyelets that check.
> There enlivened clear.
> What was?
> Way.
> Lay.
> Vegetable left shut makes hop more never the shatter that when?
> The shall. The easy can.
> Eating ting a, adopt.
> And accomplishing acquaintance make when?
> Harmony window enthralled exchange, contained containing.
> Disturbance color, so name, name.
> Why ring not such there there? Were pale mentioned circular?
> Scissor surround lessening.
> The which that that? That. That there breadth. They.
> Did.
> Looking a it not straw selection. Enough the.
> The. The tray. Little visible cake water no measure. Price what?

Which careless another be dedication? Cases rest big.
Oyster.
The which there trimming? A. All not color. Obligation change attractive.
Altogether vegetable, altogether filling to circulating.
Winter that white. Pieces brighter if it is. Is not to.
Very middle, very settlement, because argument for.
So stretched!
Coat languid external surface and altogether all, ordinarily.
Rubbing turned.
Purse open. And? And occasion. Occasion stool? Measured virgin.
Perfectly there shining are addition reserves' prints.
Whole little. Little tight that shadows are blanket.
Nearly best. Farther of. Of a. Ale balloon mistake laugh.
And directly it. It bank realistic itself and no does.
Soap means kind.
Chest piece of string. Exhibition superposition.
Interleaved this shade. Than.

Change express expresses recollection, either exclamation.
Salmon rinsing language. Breakfast by water than white.
Place. Height. The shawl steady, very closed, bad.
Could present there murder?
See the color there then.
Climbing when chicken. That that. The shows cake remedy take intently.
And fright mixture kind, separating, smelling, crumbling.
Tightly and slight, which staggering? Which carpet?
Necessity mountain searching wheatly that blessing.
Nearly crane.
They? They need play. Makes? Makes day. Has narrowly. Have development.
A? It old and question to with pump. Wide mow have and receptacle.

Is it blew west?
Pastry.
Cutting fit not more to that, the example occasion, square accomplishing.
Obtrusive, obtrusive tenderness is inside the that.
The besides revered best remains exhibition remainder.
Simultaneous merciful, largely very.
Interleaved makes certainty than.
This, this shunning. Stockings were receptacle.
All exclamation outstanding. Of and grass are seen remarkable.
Moist.
Milk pan constant very bad.
Guessing utter needles to not exchange, excuse cup nearly sudden.
Without increase.
Two awfulness thoughtful sets to, is it? It is jet. Much ease white.
Nice belt! Which boat?
Lunch plaster.
Another was this day there, the green.
Very little wide cake receptacle, is it? Blew west.
Necessary.
Cream measure express example in it is. Is be by the—the steady.
Salmon.
It in a is tick, oh knealer, only leaf liver make offering.
There, the there play done, not needed. Not. Not so settlement there.

From door, morning was shape. Which? Which? Which that?
There? There very room was refusal. Trouble comes little.
Not has name. Name makes a. Arises not choice, speech established.
Package blotters would the. . . . This place which tied there.
One very lights. Air? Lake. Lake a. And? And of and ancient.
Resemblance that should are tray, has not supposing.
Urgent hands more capture reversible. And? Indeed, and!
Has come.
Supposing change care center, but red, and is not pen tears.
What little likely kind in!
Cloak outward behind there. There present ordinary cover cleansing.
Is and does selection. Relaxation inside? Change something!
Upright of gray ribbon, rate extreme. Light shape sincerely.
May?
May.
May to which when only not cover, not even ever the church it of.
Supposing the choose than whole green just there, reason almost.
Occasion? Anything.
Coloring is in white charm.
Waist piece match to the. . . . Then many her.
Was severest. More always sleeve. All means table way balloon.
Wedding green black.
Cooking there hurry. Measure have any, because certainly make.
Taste joy besides. Remains good places, broken hair.

Dirty fact no more, not sofa action. A . . . is little. Say middle.
Real soldier mutton nothing, makes harmony morning.
Bargaining accounted slender feather, recreation horticulture.
Interleaved.
Cranberries' old eucalyptus out is.
It is, is break. West? Best. Mostly that mountain keep and cross blew.
Tree there specs ridiculous. Never shatter they that.
Where there just dust, dusty dirt weight.
The any there that the only justice fountain white grinding.
White splendor furniture no strange. Which?
The blight place which to the, the many kind in spectacle will.

Glittering.
Tumbler shining there.
They cover gate cunning. Come rate, believe whole the things dearer.
Best thing then? Then.
Very which necessary. Large time four to corners. Last circulating.
Fitting necessary incident surrounded the the. The.
Only mismanaged was way besides best.
An of little several colored, is it? Is. Is all.
Glasses color glide. Single severest more widening and two-space.
Very.
There rhubarb there.
Very measure! Have any having ham?
Lovely! Excellent in stouter is inside middle ribbon.
Kindness revered. And, and, and sets room is at. In is at best. Remains.
Not.
What there difference?
Cranberries' that plate-counting direction. Little that to closing.
To compliments, case what? Little estrangement, right?
What?
The chinking tracks' nonchalance. The?
This.
There they kindness, and shows show the. . . .
What the loving color mushes the hopes undip and . . . and color goods.
Recognition between little meaning bitten golfing.
In utter be be date settlement. There murder means solid.
More nose.
Two, the nearly open of, and exchange made altogether all moist.
Milk white for does hurt.
What than fright? Which? Which four? Four work dusting singularly.
Violent selected fine has five.
Choose colored plates—means meadows is.
It is, is that. Which? There dinner say any wood. That.
They seen wild neglect result. Yellow number stretch solemn.
Cucumber!
Shoulder bewildered to owls, George was relieve the away choice.
Reed, reed some wide. accomplishing possible replace.

Daughter that two spoons there, two. Two whom that two?
And green the there, the being than which that shows.
A arises. Question freer pale, not why single bather.
Nothing guess all another. There always the moon—two!
Which tied with much, this awkward flowered. Which visible?
Bridge, which another it has, lacks invitations' cases.
To church show regular being attaching violent the.
Sweetness the morning light!
Sunday fountain makes trimming over in of. Is not same comes rudeness?
Not earnest same. Same occasion is, if is not natural.
Some likely not sad game green makes. Which silver outward?
Light the change there, stem in hearty card, waving none. Not. Not.
Oftener.
Hope resemblance, else easily spectacle. Special protection.
Exchanged. Misplaced that.
Mounted and is making an little piece, makes more equals really.
Black.
Black.
Took.
Black blank of of, which there prints spices. Which the than sleeve.
Very a precise.
Dress.
Aider, stop! Let there, outside, resemble particularly authority.
Sacrifice recognized is. And and? And all. All shade, very.
Recollection liquor restrains practice present.
Intently and is not, does not. Of in solitude very with.
That trying be puzzle.
Wet. And blisters has second wet. This then pierce between the.
Choose the very much lack way. No! No, with bake ready, use and. . . .

Luck, explain nervous, nervous painted experiment enlivened.
Just dust dusty dirt. A is you. Very costume. That worse.
Wood certainly likely to them.
There very color makes color feeling plainer. Reason. That present.
Bed red change means.
Glass.

A in and resembling has—was—sample. Established slender pleasure.
Necessary circulating substituted specialties.
Strange. Strange, certainly! Clearly below's possible.
Replace, daughter, commensurate construction, temperature.
Obligingness. Obligingness practical. The awkward.
Flowered, this shown the very fingernails.
To purchased single currency moment, when be all spelling all?
And dedication?
Catholic that class being. Being circle is attaching anything.
Is and lilac care. Just white they—they that best that.
Which?
Please! Only continuous! Not you, useless, abundant lilac sight!
Makes sweet and all selection then. The. . . . That white to. . . .
The.
The only elastic? Every precocious courage, genuine being not.
And is mistake. Fancy kind very four was. Send mercy.
Nothing single nonsense. Fewer more certain. Was that thing sincerely?
Which taken, that the only hearty card waving none. As. . . .
Is awkwardly.
Hope ended necessary, not only, and use, missing, misplaced right.
Nothing about and an. . . .
Any occasion.
An elegant bud. Center well the readiness best to the—the rosy.
Left.
Time coke wheel broad. Big delay. Life depot returned needless.
Jack?
Mutton.
Fish.
Custard morning have why to shin. The easy cutting does cumbersome.
More than more, because certainly no control alteration.
Of in colors praying. Feathers' large distemper that.
There uneven whistles' standard increase string soon there.
Sooner clouds' really prized baking section surrounding.
This two-liquor little includes breakfast, decent jelly.
Just—just—just white showing nearly little that the seen vary.
Little mill makes more the. The blisters closed middle.

Bad way into and up. In climb guess bottom heating all.
Pliable silence original.
Suspect buttered of—of cracked climate. Choices shouter mixed.
Caused not timely. Make house singularly, not tightly.
Sauce—tender, neglected—nearly blisters that teeth.
Staggering, ordinary and nine comes.
Apple.
Apple plates' corners a . . . and cuddles with time kite, with a path.
Coconut being, being polite choice, painted particular.
Necessary razor less rest. Rest white.
Shoulder.
Dining.
Dining west, leap bundle. Bundle peculiar scissors temperature.
Target!
Why between? Because gallons sleep. That folding tied together.
Being necessity evening, disgrace entire much fifteen.
Ponderous, incalculable in the—the—the—the behind quarreling.
Religion? Religion answer administration obligingness.
Harmony whitening.
Excellent borrowing, that charity. Really, what tax chamber!
Checking very . . . has—has invitations' cases to church.
This nausea place all than even if resolution be aiming makes.
Trimming resemblance, slighter splendor, winter red.
Color table was yesterday polishing precocious.
Pieces hardly than colored be.
Seltzer.
Bottle particles neglect silver.
The this black state, this—this even consequence, was only. . . .
Yellow and blue color.
Hat dark, waving, none better. Red the even kinds and clouded
show.
Likeness is entirely nothing, half same size.
An' is charm.
Waist sullenness—woolen the them.
Please many!
Was simple calling whole curves, ladies' mild curls—this, the thing.

Least delay makes ways of, and there few. No more are always.
Cold in kind and two whow in it.
Cups.
Cake.
Dinner bed yellow sand. The station hurry there absurd because. . . .
Symmetry—the turning, the measuring—assiduous, tolerable.
Orderly goats'—gates'—determination without there.
Measurement.
Suppose standard A. And old garland bake settle nothing darker.
Redder together, composed youth reason? Music?
A—all silence, which the spoken cheaper so. Same hopes water single.
Colored.
Could witness silence yellow smelled?
Climbing solid remarkable, made of—are—cup.
Cooking remarkable made there solid blisters' recognition.
Closed so, almost more than room. Bent declare certainly.
Does remedy urging intently strange?
The, when that dusting is in, and altogether, and widened so really.
The shutter weather dreariness excitement. All the. . . .
Singularly privately bidding separation laughable.
Necessary neat, so not went wine. Little sight reason.
Nervous draught!
Eating and rejoining—also fitting nothing. Sack season, the torn.
This, the sacrifice there, the when there.
There whole which white, green there—there tender.
The eyes there whole. It is name—no, signed. That chance there filter?
Scene: the . . . that whole regulation weather-wetting blue.
Mentioned to the circular resemblance, "There is wind."
Not conundrum shadowed there difference. No! No! Always!
It hint, causes having time, no politeness. Little has.
Rests place, borrowing sound fingernails' bridge.
Cloud seem habit, circle same black. Such active!
The—that cream lily, and is likeness more to care green. Is of worse.
Nothing sight a . . . all selection white.
The slighter, which blight tender that there mercy medicine.
Perhaps, polishing substance. What will interest?
Light and is what red will yellow in, of, into.

It is—is no loud extra A, and of cunning kind place, one if wear.
Then dwindled, concentrating, which taken that the. . . .
Only measure length than cause, because better surface.
Hope resemblance has—has easily in and accident there. There!
Special, besides disgrace, preserved is, and window.
Nearer fairy.
Cough! Cough ticket! Belt symmetry! Large room distemper obligation.
Japanese strength, that twenty-four-spoonful, not makes compliments.
Case, stall memory there! What the bury not darker remain?

Together, A is melting, cutting recital authority outrage.

Of not stream, strange that . . . that the they at.

Breakfast. The. . . .

Makingway Endnote

Source text: All of Stein's *TB*.
Seed text: All of Stanza VI of Stein's SiM.
Method: I sent seed and source texts through DIASTEX5. Then I deleted the output after it began repeating itself exactly and, after making each output line a verse line, I inserted punctuation marks, capitalized the beginnings of "sentences," divided the series of verse lines into strophes and codas, and left-indented each strophe and coda differently than the one before it. The word "whow," a variant spelling of "how" [OED], occurs in the next-to-last paragraph (beginning the subsection "This is the Dress, Aider") of "Objects," part 1 of *TB*.
Form: Ten strophes whose numbers of verse lines correspond successively to the Lucas sequence 1, 3, 4, 7, 11, 18, 29, 47, 76, 123, followed by three one-line codas.

New York: 17–30 November 2000

For Anne with love on the eve of her 57th birthday

That Orange

(Stein 159/Titles 53)

That spectacle is strange.
It's glazed and changed.

They're constantly careless with the seltzer.
If they only had more learning and were patient!
The practice of protecting the spectacle indicates unprecedented separation.

Their satin stomachs were especially astonishing things, at least, in that breeze.
I used a plain mounting instead of mending it since I was not inclined to mend it.
Ordinarily, separation protects unstrangeness.
There was a single place to stand, but even the freezing was musical.
"Peanuts" is no more.

Besides, it meant displaying a blanket.
Was it an upslanting succession?
It was a simple succession.

What?
An orange?

Makingway Endnote

Source: All of Stein's *TB*.
Seed: Stein's title "Stanzas in Meditation."
Method: Sending source and seed texts through DIASTEX5, and revising its output. I deleted the output at the point where it began to repeat itself exactly, and by changes of

word order and affixes and some insertions of "helping words" not in the output, I turned each output line into one or two verse-line sentences, whose succession was divided into strophes.

Form: Five strophes whose numbers of verse-line sentences correspond to the waxing and waning prime-number sequence 2, 3, 5, 3, 2.

New York: 17–18 November 2000

Is Adventure Feeling Being Connected with Others?

(Stein 160/Titles 54)

Is adventure feeling being?

A strong light may indicate calamity.
Where do the parts connect?
Neglecting altogether how scarce the stems are, they cracked them idly.

I have no particular animosity toward even *them*.
Even if they'd been indirectly educated there, their shiny additions might
have made their garments incoherent.
Don't put any does in there again!
'Twas summer!

That principal seemed earnest, but how long was he educated?
What places does "that element" go to on Saturdays?
It eddies.
Drafts of ordinary "slenderizing creams" occasionally shatter perfection.
So where there were formerly instances of added means, doubt may now
discriminate between them.
A suggestive tendency's absence is never as pleasant as sleeping.
To whom?

It's admitted that they were seen questioning certainty's being connected
with delicacy.
So, did plenty of adjustments commence right there?
By dinnertime we'd penetrated to certain distasteful stairways.
The *administration's* the place to look for and see examples of *that!*

When doubting anything, hesitation may be legal—but pricey.
In their golden chambers some of the clergymen ventured to feel their being.

What light could indicate calamity so strongly?

Every part is connected with others.

Makingway Endnote

Source Text: All of Stein's *TB*.
Seed Text: Stein's title "Identity a Poem."
Method: (1) I sent the source and seed texts through DIASTEX5.
(2) I deleted the output a few lines after it began to repeat itself exactly.
(3) I transformed each remaining output line into a verse-line sentence by changing its word order and some affixes and sometimes inserting a few "helping words" that do not appear in the output lines. I retained all of the lexical root morphemes and most of the "helping words" that appear in each output line.
(4) I divided the sequence of verse-line sentences into strophes.
Form: Seven strophes whose numbers of verse-line sentences correspond to the waxing and waning Lucas-number sequence 1, 3, 4, 7, 4, 3, 1.

New York: 1 January, 20 November–23 December 2000; 25 February, 26 June 2001; 29 April 2002

For undeniably dear Anne Tardos,
with undiminished love and admiration,
just after the Winter Solstice, 2000

Disappointing Not Sweet Redness

(Stein 161/Titles 55)

Disappointing not occasional southern buttons yesterday flat.
Particular courage this substance.
Callous interest.
Light together with nothing pointing to cleansing.
Tumblers shíne there letter-nícely.
Sugar.
Nothing doubtful places delightfulness,   no reckless gratitude.

Supposing numbered ways,   four hearty-glásses surrounded áccents.
Left like right,   nothing about the ocean's *that*.
The long   fill together.   Such lengths   replace decisions.
Coloring much that season, different flowers made mountains.
News.   Prints.   Resolute.
Little darkness,   little.
Vegetably nothing about necessity there.   That-there length? A birthday.
Regional light   tóast.   Chairs' denial, not   dirty súction.

Suppose a bigger fact: same-hour closing shutting off pléasure-surprise.
Lines withdrawing organ-authority.
Something lilacs the why.
The letter withers.
Light,   light!   Safety prices due to exclamations, little sálmon.
Liquor final language soup.   These vacation solitudes!
Little-fine-glásses neglected much outstanding plate.

This that cheese-loud tíme: light with móuntain-hearts dirty.
Bóre-recollection's narrowly white,   better for makers.
Lounge.
Sausages question nervous succession, little-Víolet.
Eggs with chests expressed to white   land with eggs supposing right.

Dressing, hot faces part.
Supposing folders, fólders, waiter, true quéstions adopt conclusions.
Exercise léssons,   windows together. Admit exchanges.
Suggest that the . . .
The líkeness-disaster signed too múch together, supposing darkness.
Such weather commences disposing temperatures.
Freer pale-blue sénsibles   penetrated gallons surrounded.
Lengthening dístance-sign: the righteous equator always.
The . . . the . . . the little hint together with light dishes.
Design not once that borrowing measure fíngernails.
Taxes would exercise méasle-location-accumulation.
Liking líne-sight light,   líght.
Clearly supposing changing likeness, aim at sight,   síght, sweet Redness.

Makingway and Delivery Endnote

Source Text: All of Stein's *TB*.

Seed Text: The title of Stein's play "Doctor Faustus Lights the Lights" (written in 1938).

Method: (1) I sent the source and seed texts through DIASTEX5. These are deterministic reading-through methods—not chance operations—though their results are unpredictable.

(2) I deleted the output of the program where it began to repeat itself exactly.

(3) I minimally revised the remaining output lines without modifying their order but changed word order within some lines, inserted a few helping words, capital letters, punctuation marks, and stress accents, enlarged a few word spaces, inserted or deleted some final *s*'s and suffixes, etc.

(4) All but the last of the line- and strophe breaks in the program's output were retained.

Form: Forty lines divided into five strophes, respectively comprising 7, 8, 7, 5, and 13 verse lines.

Pauses: Four letter spaces between words [   ] indicate a pause as long as an unaccented syllable; eight letter spaces [   ] indicate a pause as long as one accented syllable or "beat." Strophe breaks indicate pauses of two to three beats.

New York: 1 January, 23–25 December 2000; 25 February, 24–26 June 2001

For undeniably dear Anne Tardos,

with undiminished love and admiration,
before & on Christmas Day, 2000

Mary Pickford and Harry Truman!*

XXXXXXXXXXXXXXXXXXXXXXXXXXXXXXXXXXXXXXXXXXXXXXXXX

*happy happy new year & century & millennium

jml

Editing the Stein Poems

Michael O'Driscoll

Editing Jackson Mac Low's Stein poems was at times vexing in a way that has now become commonplace for posthumous editions of twenty-first-century authors: digital files can provide an unwieldy and sometimes unstable supplement to print copies of an author's manuscript and typescript archival documents. Because I had access to both Mac Low's computer files (as carefully retained by Anne Tardos) and print copies of the files created by Mac Low and preserved at the UCSD Special Collections, I was confronted by both opportunity and challenge. In almost every case of these 161 poems, Mac Low produced variants in both digital and print media, and in many cases those documents are inexact replications of each other. At times, print versions are extant for which there are no digital equivalents, and certainly the reverse is also true. One might offer some conjecture on the conditions that could have produced such an archive: working on a personal computer, an author is prone to print a copy of a particular file, and then overwrite the original digital content. Similarly, an author might make holographic corrections to a typescript, but then never enter or preserve them in digital form. The result can be a confounding and conflicting set of potential copytexts whose priority can be resolved only through careful genealogical analysis and an awareness of the complexities of determining authorial intention. Deducing the order and priority of the textual variants in the Stein poems corpus has proven a major task in producing this volume.

The fact that any digital file is timestamped with minute-by-minute precision in the act of saving the most recent Word document version does provide some opportunities for determining the time and sequence of a given poem—that is, understanding the succession of documents and their relationships to each other can be made easier by the affordances of computer technologies. But not always. At times, without determinate evidence of authorial intention, I've had to revert to trusting Mac Low's entry of an ostensibly authoritative version into a folder on his hard drive labeled "stein series all" that was created as part of Mac Low's process of producing these poems. But those versions are by no means the only available, and they're not always the last produced, and often there are variants that challenge the authority of that potentially "official" version. Stein 6, "The Big Stay Away," is a case in point. While the only two extant digital files seem consistent with Mac Low's practices, a search of the UCSD archive revealed a printed version that not only was never preserved as a digital file, but seems to interpose itself between those available (Mac Low's dating practices provide sufficient evidence to draw that conclusion). He seems to have made several corrections in producing that print version, corrections that arguably improved several lines in a manner in keeping with his typical practices. For example, the convoluted "There the house is more than those that come there more" becomes "The house there is more than comes there"; or, "Last time there rhubarb mattered like the little green way" becomes "Last time there green rhubarb mattered like the little way." In these instances, Mac Low's alterations often move toward a consistent prosody and a more intuitive meaning that might be discerned in the sentence; after working with the poems over several years, I have found these tendencies recognizable as such, at least to me. The problem, however, is that because this *perhaps* "improved" version was not transposed to the computer records and not saved as a digital file between May 10, 1998, and May 29, 1999, the authorized, final version on the hard drive does not take these revisions into account. My best guess is that Mac Low, having not saved or having erased the revised version, accidentally reverted to the unedited original. What to do? It was tempting to intercede, but my decision was to respect the authority of the final version, even though it might, just might, have been unintentionally inferior.

When I do intervene, as an editor, in the versioning of these poems, it is to do one of several reasonably straightforward things. There are minor typographic errors in the poems and in the makingways notes that accompany them. When these accidentals appear in typescript, they are almost always self-evident, and my tendency has been to correct them silently. I've also tried to ensure the accuracy of Mac Low's dating of the poem's production and revision. Mac Low concludes each poem with a series of dates, or date ranges, that document that poem's creation. However, on many occasions he would revise without documenting any intervention, or would neglect to include additional dates. When the timestamped digital files or his own dating practices in hard copy make this evident, I've altered the dates to reflect the true history of the poem's creation. One further alteration in this area: each poem concludes with that date range, the place of composition (always New York City), and Jackson Mac Low's full name. Given the redundancy of the poet's name in a collected volume such as this, I've dropped his name from the end of each poem, in confidence that the author's identity is obvious. This was the practice, similarly, of any publishers fortunate enough to print one of the Stein poems during Mac Low's lifetime. I noted instances of previous publication, and other substantive editorial decisions, in the notes below, in order to provide a record of my decision-making process.

Throughout the editing of the *Complete Stein Poems*, and with that kind of judicious reserve always at the forefront, I have sought not only to ensure the accuracy of the resulting versions presented here, but also to maintain the visual prosody of the poems. Mac Low's decisions about line breaks, spacing, margins, justification, and the visual blocking of text have been respected as carefully as possible. In those instances in which he oversaw the printing of these poems, Mac Low was demanding of publishers about such matters, as he understood such formal properties to be essential to the meaning making of the poems on the page and usefully directive for their vocal performance. At no point, however, did Mac Low insist on matters of typographic font, and that's important. In producing the typescript versions of these poems for his own use, Mac Low would often deploy various, and seemingly inexplicable, type fonts before printing or saving them. I'm not sure why he did so; I'd presume it was for his own amusement because whenever the poems were issued for publication, he standardized the fonts, eschewing the use of lurid gothic or exuberant comic sans types, for example. With that in mind, I've narrowed the range of type fonts to reflect Mac Low's own most commonplace choices when producing the poems: the sober (if not also modern and digital) sans serif Arial type for titling and dating, and the serif Goudy Old Style (a modernist revival of a classic aesthetic) for the body of the poems and the makingways notes.

On the advice of the book's reviewers, I have sought to reduce the length and density of the makingways notes. Mac Low often repeated the same pieces of bibliographic or contextual information verbatim from one note to the next, cutting and pasting those text strings with the expectation that some of the poems would be published or performed independent of the others. Their appearance as a whole in this volume makes that unnecessary. However, I did want to maintain the idiosyncrasies of voice and shifts in form of the notes as the volume progressed, and so rather than making them conform to a particular format or phrasing, I have tried to reflect their individual uniqueness as much as possible. I also followed some basic principles in doing so. I edited for readability and economy by avoiding redundancies and employing abbreviations, while maintaining key pieces of information that detail the singular production of each poem and maintaining any new details or context when it is first introduced (but not thereafter). My hope is that this makes the notes more accessible and signals more clearly the value and meaning they offer.

Notes and Acknowledgments

The following entries attempt to capture editorial decision making when that proved necessary, and also provide what I hope is a complete record of the appearance of these poems in earlier publications. When a Stein poem is not noted below, nothing more than minor silent corrections have been made to the final copytext, and, to the best of my knowledge, there has been no prior publication.

Stein 1

One initial hardcopy draft dated 27–28 April 1998, followed by five digital versions over next four years. Final digital version omitted a makingways note, so that has been transposed from the penultimate version while retaining final authorized emendations. Producing a final version without the note was an occasional practice by Mac Low. In some cases, Mac Low created versions without the makingways note for performance or publishing purposes. Previously published in *Thing of Beauty: New and Selected Works*, ed. Anne Tardos (Berkeley: U California P, 2008), 377–78.

Stein 3

As with Stein 1, final version is 29 April 2002, with addition of makingways note from previous version.

Stein 9

Note that there is a performance version produced in February 1999 that introduces variants not reflected in the final corrected version from January 2001. Mac Low produced the performance version (with lines attributed to him and Anne Tardos), but then didn't incorporate those changes into his final, authorized version for print purposes. This is a common occurrence throughout the archive.

Stein 11

This poem presents an interesting conundrum. All versions up to and including 27 May 1999 conclude the final line with "the eaten very loudly." This corresponds with the title of the poem, "And Sing More Very Loudly," as Mac Low characteristically titles the Stein poems with a juxtaposition of their beginning and final words. However, on 28 May 1999, Mac Low saved a digital version of the poem with the final words "the eaten very loudly follow necessity" and maintained that ending through subsequent versions. This change has the virtue of completing the diastic writing through of the name "Tardos"—Anne's full name was used as seed text. However, the revision violates Mac Low's principle for creating titles, and repeats the words "follow necessity" from the previous line, a repetition that feels awkward and might be suspect. I believe this may have been an accidental change on Mac Low's part, and that change has been replicated in the publication of the poem in *Thing of Beauty*. However, I've elected to respect both Mac Low's final version of the poem and Tardos's own decision on the textual authority of that final version. Previously published in *Thing of Beauty*, 379.

Stein 12

Previously published in *Thing of Beauty*, 380.

Stein 13

Previously published in *Thing of Beauty*, 381.

Stein 15

Previously published in *Thing of Beauty*, 382.

Stein 18

Previously published in *Thing of Beauty*, 383–89.

Stein 21

This poem is exemplary in its demonstration of Mac Low's attention to the details of visual prosody. In responding to an invitation to contribute his work to an upcoming issue of *The World,* Mac Low wrote to Ed Friedman sharing five of his Stein poems (only two of which were published). In reference to Stein 21, Mac Low wrote the following: "This one's tricky because the *font sizes change* within the ragged-right indented-paragraph / strophes and because there are precise numbers of empty lines between the strophes. If you accept this one, I'll mark up a copy to show *the numbers of empty lines* between the strophes—unless you are going to print the poem directly from the floppy disk I'll send, in which case, no sweat. (Also, *the numbers of spaced periods in each set of points of suspension* is precise and never to be broken at the right margin, which may easily happen if the piece is typeset by someone else, but won't if it's printed from my floppy. If necessary, I will reduce the width of the strophes to fit your pages better." (Italics in original unpublished letter.) Previously published in *The World* (St. Mark's Poetry Project), issues 56–57 (2000): 91–94.

Stein 27

In the final version of this poem, saved 16 February 2000 at 2:55 p.m., Mac Low deletes two earlier dates from his record of composition that concludes the text (23 February and 19 December 1999). Those dates were included on versions created less than an hour earlier. On the assumption that this was a mistake of transposition, I've reinstated those dates on the final copy. Previously published in *The World,* issues 56–57 (2000): 95–97.

Stein 31

This is one of the most complicated Stein poems, both in terms of Mac Low's production and in terms of preserving the formatting that results from his determinations and choices. In this case, the copytext is derived from a penultimate version saved to his hard drive on 24 February 2000. The final version, saved on 24 April 2000, eschews the use of the narrowed margins described in his extensive makingways note, unaltered in that final version. Both versions were saved in his folder "stein series all," suggesting alternative possibilities, both of which are authorized by the poet. The note concludes with a description of the complex process entailed in reducing the margins to a 3.5-inch textual field, and his structuring of line breaks according to "liminally determined criteria." As a result, I've elected to use the penultimate version in order to reflect the details of the makingways note and respect the considerable labor that Mac Low put into formatting the poem.

Stein 32

This provides an interesting counterpoint to Stein 31. In this instance, Mac Low again saved two versions to his "stein series all" folder—one with long lines and one with constrained margins. In this case, however, the makingways note does not specify the constrained margins, and the version used here as copytext was saved to his computer files some four months following the earlier alternative. This reflects the same choice made by Anne Tardos in editing *Thing of Beauty*, including preserving the tildes that demarcate stanza breaks. Previously published in *Thing of Beauty*, 389–98.

Stein 33

Previously published in *The World*, issues 56–57 (2000): 98–100.

Stein 37

In the case of this poem and the following two (Stein 38 and Stein 39), the digital files available to me were corrupted and unusable. However, the print files available at UCSD were the most recently dated, and provided certain justification as copytexts.

Stein 41

On 17 April 2000, Mac Low retyped this poem as the result of a corrupted digital file. In retyping, he omitted strophe seven of eight, which I've replaced from an earlier version dated 3 December 1999. Mac Low's makingways note indicates the poem should have eight strophes.

Stein 43

Previously published in *Deluxe Rubber Chicken*, issue 7 (2001): n.p.

Stein 46

In some cases (Stein 50 and Stein 51 would be other examples), Mac Low saved a final version of the poem in which he extended the lines of the poem, originally restricted by a four-inch right margin, to their standard one-inch right margin limit. His reasoning for doing so (or not, as in the case of the intervening Steins 47–49) is unknown. Note, however, that in the dateline for Stein 55, Mac Low actually records and dates the restriction of the right margin, so this is quite deliberate on his part. When this kind of altering of format occurs, I chose the most recent version (usually the wide version) as copytext. Mac Low saved these versions on his hard drive as "Stein ## wide."

Stein 50

Previously published in *Conjunctions: American Poetry: States of the Art*, ed. Bradford Morrow, issue 35 (2000): 445–46.

Stein 53

Previously published in *Thing of Beauty*, 398–400.

Stein 59

Previously published in *Conjunctions*, issue 35 (2000): 439–41.

Stein 60

Previously published in *Talisman: A Journal of Contemporary Poetry and Poetics*, issues 21–22 (2001): 4–6.

Stein 62

In digital typescript, this poem provides evidence of Mac Low's meticulous attention to visual prosody. He concludes the version dated 30 April 2002 with a note to a prospective printer, in underline and bold: "Printer: When published, all the lines must be broken and indented exactly as they are in this printout. Please follow italicized instructions as to strophe breaks."

Stein 69

Previously published in *Thing of Beauty*, 400.

Stein 72

Previously published in *Thing of Beauty*, 401.

Stein 74

Previously published in *Jackson Mac Low: Between Writing and Performance*, ed. Tyrus Miller and Carrie Noland (Slought Foundation, 2023), 311–13.

Stein 75

In his makingways note, Mac Low observes that he had lost his record of the procedure used to produce this poem and the following one. In Stein 76, I've retained Mac Low's original note, revised by editor Anne Tardos in *Thing of Beauty*, in order to explain that gap.

Stein 76

Previously published in *Thing of Beauty*, 401–02.

Stein 77

Previously published in *Sulfur*, issues 45–46 (2000): 174–75.

Stein 78

Previously published in *Jackson Mac Low: Between Writing and Performance*, 314–15.

Stein 86

Previously published in *Thing of Beauty*, 403–05.

Stein 87

Here Mac Low begins altering what has been the conventional form of his makingways notes. In the last version of Stein 88, he adds a revision date when the only change has been specifically to the alteration of the makingways note. This suggests a very deliberate decision, and it has been respected throughout what follows, although his changes are at times inconsistent (e.g., Stein 90 reverts to the earlier format).

Stein 94

Previously published in *Thing of Beauty*, 406–08.

Stein 96

Previously published in *Conjunctions*, issue 35 (2000): 441–45.

Stein 100

It's worth noting here that the proper title of this poem is, as printed here, "A Feather Table Likeness of the Justice Chair." In online sources, it has become commonplace to cite the title without the word "table." All of Mac Low's versions of the poem include that word in the title. Previously published in *American Poet: The Journal of the Academy of American Poets* (1999–2000): 36–37.

Stein 103

Previously published in *Deluxe Rubber Chicken*, issue 7 (2001): n.p.

Stein 105

Previously published in *Thing of Beauty*, 408–09.

Stein 107

Previously published in *Jackson Mac Low: Between Writing and Performance*, 316–18.

Stein 108

Previously published in *Thing of Beauty*, 409–13.

Stein 109

Previously published in *Conjunctions*, issue 35 (2000): 449–50.

Stein 111

Copytext in this case was the last digital version saved on 31 May 2000; however, a hard copy version revised in manuscript dated 10 March 2003 is located in the UCSD Mac Low fond. I've incorporated those revisions into this final version. Importantly, that dated hard copy indicates the last revisions Mac Low made to the Stein poems. Previously published in *Conjunctions*, issue 35 (2000): 446–49.

Stein 120

On 1 November 2000, Mac Low filed a version into his folder "stein series all," implying perhaps that that digital copy is a final version. However, UCSD has a print copy, marked 10 November 2000, with revisions that were never incorporated into any digital version. I attempt here to faithfully represent those revisions, noting that they are in pencil, difficult to read, and challengingly interlined by Mac Low.

Stein 122

As above, the last digital file was saved 1 June 2001; a superseding hard copy with unincorporated manuscript revisions in the UCSD Mac Low fond served as copytext for this poem. Due to relatively minor emendations (deletion of words, added punctuation, change of word order), this is a variant of the previously published version in *Thing of Beauty*, 412–13.

Stein 124

Previously published in *Bombay Gin*, issue 28 (2002): 23–25.

Stein 128

Previously published in *Bombay Gin*, issue 28 (2002): 26–27.

Stein 139

Previously published in *Deluxe Rubber Chicken*, issue 7 (2001): n.p. Also published in *Best American Poetry 2002*, ed. Robert Creeley (New York: Scribner, 2002), 80–81.

Stein 152

Previously published in *Thing of Beauty*, 414.

Stein 159

Previously published in *Thing of Beauty*, 415–16.

Stein 160

Previously published in *Thing of Beauty*, 416–17.

Publisher contact:
The MIT Press
Massachusetts Institute of Technology
77 Massachusetts Avenue, Cambridge, MA 02139
mitpress.mit.edu

EU Authorised Representative:
Easy Access System Europe, Mustamäe tee 50,
10621 Tallinn, Estonia
gpsr.requests@easproject.com

Printed by Integrated Books International,
United States of America